ROUTLEDGE LIBRARY EDITIONS
CURR

Volume 7

CURRICULUM PROVISION IN THE SMALL PRIMARY SCHOOL

CURRICULUM PROVISION
IN THE SMALL
PRIMARY SCHOOL

Edited by
MAURICE GALTON AND
HELEN PATRICK

Routledge
Taylor & Francis Group

LONDON AND NEW YORK

First published in 1990 by Routledge

This edition first published in 2019
by Routledge
2 Park Square, Milton Park, Abingdon, Oxon OX14 4RN

and by Routledge
711 Third Avenue, New York, NY 10017

Routledge is an imprint of the Taylor & Francis Group, an informa business

© 1990 Maurice Galton and Helen Patrick

British Library Cataloguing in Publication Data
A catalogue record for this book is available from the British Library

ISBN: 978-1-138-31956-1 (Set)
ISBN: 978-0-429-45387-8 (Set) (ebk)
ISBN: 978-1-138-31843-4 (Volume 7) (hbk)
ISBN: 978-1-138-32157-1 (Volume 7) (pbk)
ISBN: 978-0-429-45460-8 (Volume 7) (ebk)

Publisher's Note
The publisher has gone to great lengths to ensure the quality of this reprint but points out that some imperfections in the original copies may be apparent.

Disclaimer
The publisher has made every effort to trace copyright holders and would welcome correspondence from those they have been unable to trace.

Curriculum provision in the small primary school

Small primary schools have been a source of considerable debate in recent years, much of it emotive and one sided. This balanced and authoritative account, based on a detailed survey carried out by some members of the respected ORACLE team at Leicester University, should lay many myths to rest. It shows that small primary schools differ surprisingly little from their larger counterparts in the content of their curriculum and in the manner of its teaching, and that contrary to common belief there is no evidence that their pupils perform less well in language, mathematics and reading. While this may suggest that small is, after all, beautiful, the study also suggests that small schools do not yet maximise their potential, particularly in respect to small class sizes and the close relationships which are possible in such an environment. The implementation of the National Curriculum will provide a particular challenge for small schools. This timely study shows how they can meet that challenge, and examines in particular the possibilities of clustering and federation, by which they can pool resources while retaining the advantages of the small, community-based unit.

The editors

Maurice Galton is Professor of Education and Director of the School of Education at the University of Leicester where he has taught since 1970. He co-directed the ORACLE project which observed children and teachers in their primary schools, and directed the PRISMS project – the study of the curriculum of small schools on which this book is based.

Helen Patrick is Research Officer in the Council for Examination Development, University of Cambridge Local Examinations Syndicate. Before that she taught in a comprehensive school and worked in the School of Education at the University of Leicester where she was involved in a number of major research projects.

Curriculum provision in the small primary school

Edited by
Maurice Galton and Helen Patrick

London and New York

First published 1990
by Routledge
11 New Fetter Lane, London EC4P 4EE

Simultaneously published in the USA and Canada by Routledge
a division of Routledge, Chapman and Hall, Inc.
29 West 35th Street, New York, NY 10001

© 1990 Maurice Galton and Helen Patrick

Typeset by LaserScript Limited, Mitcham, Surrey
Printed in Great Britain by
Billing & Sons Ltd, Worcester

British Library Cataloguing in Publication Data

Curriculum provision in the small primary school.
1. Great Britain. Primary schools. Curriculum
I. Galton, Maurice *1937*– II. Patrick, Helen 1951–
372.19'0941

ISBN 0-415-03628-3
       0-415-03629-1 (Pbk)

Library of Congress Cataloging-in-Publication Data

Curriculum provision in the small primary school / edited by Maurice Galton
and Helen Patrick.
       p.   cm.
Includes bibliographical references.
ISBN 0-415-03628-3. – ISBN 0-415-03629-1 (pbk.)
1. Education, Elementary – England – Curricula – Longitudinal studies.
2. Rural schools – England – Curricula – Longitudinal studies. 3. Urban
schools – England – Curricula – Longitudinal studies. I. Galton, Maurice J.
II. Patrick, Helen, 1951-
LB1564.G7C89   1990
372. 19'0942–dc20
                                                                89-39339
                                                                CIP

Contents

Contents

Contents

Figures

Tables

Introduction

This book attempts to describe and comment upon a study of various aspects of the curriculum in small English primary schools. By small we mean schools which typically have not more than 100 pupils covering the age range 5 - 11 and not more than four teachers including the head. The study, carried out over a three-year period from 1983 to 1986, involved nine local authorities and included examples of small schools in urban as well as rural areas. The full findings of the project, including technical details, are to be found in the report to the Department of Education and Science.*

This book is based upon the material presented in the report but it has been written up so that it is accessible to the non-technical reader by keeping the number of detailed tables and figures to a minimum. In the book we consider the curriculum, the behaviour of pupils and teachers, and we examine the background of those who work in small schools. In general, it may be said that the findings do not support many of the gloomy predictions which have been made about the quality of staff in such schools and the performance of the pupils. Nor do they fully sustain the reservations expressed in government reports of a decade ago concerning the ability of small schools to deliver an adequate curriculum (Department of Education and Science (DES) 1979a, 1981). Teachers in small schools are in many respects very similar to their colleagues in larger schools and it is not therefore surprising that their practice should also be similar. As demands on primary schools increase, in the light of the government's recent proposals on the National Curriculum, however, it is likely that practice in large schools will change considerably and this will pose new challenges to those responsible for administering and teaching in small schools. These issues are considered in the final chapter.

The PRISMS Project (Curriculum Provision In Small Schools) was directed by Gerald Bernbaum and Maurice Galton and we owe a debt to the former for his support and guidance during the lifetime of the project and for his contributions to the original drafts of the project report. We should also like to thank Roger Appleyard, Helen Patrick's co-researcher, who carried out the bulk of the statistical analysis. Linda Hargreaves was also attached to the project while the recipient of a linked student award from the ESRC (Economic and Social Research Council). She also makes a contribution to the book.

In addition, nine teachers were seconded to the project and carried out the bulk of the observations. These were Brian Aldridge, Ray Allman, Gary Deeks, Helen Dunning, Rosemary Grant, Cherry Harrison, Jacqueline Jay, David Lea, and Stephen Watkins.

We owe an immense debt of gratitude for their efforts, not only in helping to develop the observation system, but also in maintaining excellent relationships with the schools throughout the lifetime of the project. Some of these teachers have also contributed to the book in Chapter Six.

Various drafts of the manuscript have passed through the hands of several secretaries, but most importantly Miss Vivienne Paul, who typed the original report, and Miss Carole Fitzpatrick, who produced the final version, and we would like to thank them for their work. Lastly we should like to express gratitude to the local authorities which supported the project by providing seconded teachers and to the Department of Education and Science which financed the study.

Maurice Galton and Helen Patrick

* The report is available from the School of Education, University of Leicester.

Chapter one

The debate about small schools

Maurice Galton and Helen Patrick

1.1 The small school: its educational viability

Educational debate, particularly when it leads to policy decisions affecting the lives and interests of teachers, pupils, and parents, is often characterized by strong passions and tends to involve rhetoric and emotion rather than evidence. In the process, relevant research findings are often ignored, distorted, or used selectively. In this country the continuing debate about the survival or closure of small primary schools, particularly those in rural areas, could hardly be bettered as an example.

In Britain the viability of the small primary school has been a major issue ever since the 1944 Education Act established a selective system of secondary education to which children were allocated on the basis of the results of the 11+ examination. Prior to this, most villages, by the beginning of the twentieth century, had established elementary schools where children attended from the age of 5 until 14 years. Before 1944 it was accepted practice that only the ablest children left the village school to attend the nearest grammar school, but the establishment of the secondary modern and the technical school necessitated the complete separation of the primary and secondary phases of schooling.

As a result most village schools became 5 to 11 primary schools. Paralleled with this organizational change was the continuing decline of the rural population, consequent on the increase in industrialization with better opportunities for well-paid employment in towns and cities. By 1950, village populations had decreased by 50 per cent from the time when most of the village elementary schools had first been established. As a result of the 1944 Act, many village schools became one-teacher schools and, in time, were closed. By 1977 only 1.8 per cent of all primary schools in England and Wales had fewer than twenty-five pupils, although 21.3 per cent had one hundred pupils or fewer (DES, 1979b). In western industrialized societies the declining rate of population increase since the second half of the 1970s has meant that

3

small schools are no longer a feature solely of rural areas but can now be found in city centres.

The debate about the viability of the small primary school is complicated by the fact that throughout its long history there has been no agreed definition of what constitutes a small school. The Hadow Report (1931) on the primary school, for example, took a special interest in the needs of children up to the age of 11 in rural areas. The report cites three examples of good practice: one with a single teacher and twelve pupils, another with one teacher and twenty-one pupils, and a third with one teacher and thirty pupils. The implication, within the report, is that these three examples were typical of small rural schools as studied in the report. In 1961, however, the Ministry of Education in a document entitled 'Village Schools' took as their typical example a school of around fifty pupils, divided into two classes. Such schools, in addition to needing a library area capable of housing as many as 500 books and workshop areas for making and constructing large maps, charts, and friezes, required children to have a place of their own and some free space for physical movement so that pupils could climb ropes and ladders, practise with balls, skip and dance to music. It was also said to be advantageous if the whole class could do dramatic work requiring some form of portable staging. Although the document was in the form of a planning brief for new buildings, it nevertheless had clear implications for the viability of existing schools, most of which would not have met the specification (Ministry of Education 1961).

Throughout this period, with the demise of the one-teacher school, the debate shifted and schools with one infant and one junior class came increasingly under threat of closure, mainly on the grounds of the poor state of repair of the existing buildings and the cost of bringing them up to the Ministry's standard, compared with the cost of building a new larger school to serve a wider area.

Further revision in official orthodoxy regarding a suitable size for a small school arose from the recommendation of the Plowden Report that, 'Schools with an age range of 5 to 11 should usually have at least 3 classes, each covering two age ranges' (Plowden Report, 1967, para. 480). This suggests a figure of around one hundred pupils and three teachers for an all-through junior and infant school. The report notes that in 1947 there were nearly 9,000 schools with one hundred or fewer pupils on the roll but this figure had been reduced to just over two-thirds by 1965. Noting a faster decline of schools with fifty or fewer pupils on the roll, the report applauds this trend arguing that, 'It is the smallest schools which are the least defensible both financially and, except in special circumstances, on educational grounds' (Chapter 8, para. 260).

Part of the reason for this view would appear to be conclusions drawn by Her Majesty's Inspectors (HMI) from their categorization of schools, the evidence on which the committee based so many of its conclusions. Although only the average size of schools in a category can be calculated from the data provided, it is possible to infer that it was the larger-than-average schools which dominated the top third of the categories, and that the smaller ones were over-represented at the bottom end of the scale. For example, there were 109 schools in the first category which were 'in most respects ... of outstanding quality'. Since there were 29,000 pupils in these schools, the average size of the school was around 266 pupils. In category 9, 'a bad school where children suffer from laziness, indifference, gross incompetence or unkindness on the part of the staff', there were twenty-eight schools with 4,333 pupils, giving a mean size of 155, while in the next worst category, the mean size was 145. Given that the typical primary school of that time contained 184 pupils, it is clear that a high proportion of schools having less than one hundred pupils on the roll must have been classified in the bottom two categories by HMI. It would therefore appear that these HMI appraisals are the main basis of Plowden's contention that small schools are educationally suspect, even though, as Simon (1981a) argues, the basis of the HMI categorization is open to criticism.

The Plowden Report also formally embraced the move away from a subject-centred towards a child-centred curriculum. The report devoted a whole chapter to the development of topic work, particularly in science, with the emphasis on a curriculum which was sufficiently varied to ensure that the needs of the individual child were met. According to Plowden, no one teacher could possibly be equipped to meet all these demands and it was therefore necessary for staff to pool their expertise so that different people could provide curriculum leadership across the range of subjects taught in the primary school. The report acknowledged the immense task of developing an effective classroom organization which allowed for individualized instruction to meet individual needs, and noted the problems of the wide ability range within mixed-age classes. The report concluded, on both the above counts, that, 'Schools should be large enough to justify a staff with varied gifts and correct flexible organisation, which does not force classes with a wide age range and teachers who are not convinced of their value' (para. 453). Although this comment does not come in that part of the report which concentrates on aspects of small schools, the implications are nevertheless clear. Support for the above conclusion is to be found in the parallel report of the Gittins Committee for Welsh schools which came out in favour of an optimum size of between eight and twelve classes for a junior school, mainly on similar grounds to that advocated by Plowden: the lack of available expertise among the staff and the high costs of providing resources to compensate for this deficiency (Gittins Report 1967).

5

Since the Plowden Report, this emphasis on specialization has been reinforced by information collected through various surveys such as those carried out by Bennett (1976), Bassey (1978), and HMI itself (DES, 1978). All these studies reached similar conclusions concerning the relatively limited range of experiences which many primary teachers provided, particularly in areas of science and mathematics, seen as vital ingredients of the curriculum for a society increasingly dependent for its prosperity on rapid technological change and innovation. The first survey on science carried out with a national sample of 11-year-olds by the Assessment of Performance Unit (APU 1981a) showed that in the majority of schools only 5 per cent of allocated teaching time was given to activities having any form of scientific content. In a similar manner, the report of the Cockcroft Committee (1982) on the teaching of mathematics concluded that there was a pressing need for in-service training of specialist teachers who could act as mathematics co-ordinators in primary schools to improve the skills of their colleagues.

This move towards greater subject specialism, at least at the older end of the junior school, was further endorsed by the government White Paper, *Better Schools* (DES 1985a). The White Paper was critical of existing practice for curriculum planning and implementation in schools. Curriculum-led staffing was suggested as a strategy for improving the situation. The White Paper proposed that in each area of the 'core' curriculum a teacher with expertise should take over some of their colleagues' teaching in the upper junior school and should also engage in a consultancy role in support of other staff. The authors of *Better Schools* recognized that the provision of such specialist consultancies was subject to the constraints of finance and of staffing. The authors concluded, therefore, that except for practical reasons, the number of pupils 'should not in general fall below the level at which a complement of three teachers is justified, since it is inherently difficult for a very small school to be educationally satisfactory' (para. 275).

The logic of *Better Schools* has been reinforced in the publication of the National Curriculum proposals. Local authorities, when attempting to implement these new proposals in the 'core' subjects, English, mathematics, and science, may make the assumption that in small schools, where there is less than one teacher per year group, the necessary expertise to provide the required broad and balanced curriculum for all the children will be unavailable. Local authorities may therefore make more use of clustering arrangements in an attempt to overcome this problem.

On the other hand, these assumptions are not shared by an increasing number of families, well-educated and well-off, who have strongly supported the maintenance and provision of rural life in general and small schools in particular. The recent changes in the nature of modern industrial economies which have produced a relative decline in the older manufacturing bases have also resulted in unemployment and in the old centres, a neglect of physical infrastructure which has, it has been argued, given rise to a bleakness and hopelessness resulting in violence, vandalism, and a lack of respect for individuals. This in turn has led to an increasing nostalgia for the apparent virtues of rural community life supposedly embodied in the earlier unity between family, church, and work place. One result, in recent years, has been a reverse movement of population among the mobile, prosperous, well-educated, and articulate middle-class from city centres and suburbs to rural villages. It is this group of people who have proved such formidable advocates for the retention of small schools.

The decline in school population has therefore occurred at a time when, for a variety of reasons, many people value highly what small schools, particularly small rural schools, are believed to offer. Thus policies with respect to merging and closing small schools that seem logical and coherent to education administrators are increasingly resisted by local populations. Such groups often contain supporters who are expert in the range of techniques used in mass advertising so that local disputes between the authority and the defenders of small schools have been conducted with an eye to the newspaper headline rather than the spirit of genuine enquiry.

It was in an attempt to restore some objectivity to the debate that the PRISMS study (curriculum PRovision In SMall Schools) was conceived. Sponsored by the Department of Education and Science, with the support of nine local authorities, the research attempted to provide at least a partial picture of life in the small primary schools of England. Throughout this book every attempt has been made to avoid the political aspects of the current debate. What follows is a discussion of various aspects of the educational provision found within a representative sample of small primary schools from both urban and rural settings. Given the history of the curriculum debate, schools with either fewer than one hundred pupils or with four or fewer full-time teachers covering the primary range from 5 to 11 years were deemed to be small.

The succeeding chapters cover the curriculum and the behaviour of the teachers and the pupils, together with a limited evaluation of the performance of the pupils, not only in the areas of so-called 'basics', but also for a range of curriculum activities commonly referred to as 'study skills'. Where possible, use has been made of data relating to other studies which have taken place in larger schools. The limitations of such comparisons, however, must be borne in mind when reading this book, since the extent to which observed differences between large and

7

smaller schools simply reflect different research strategies and a change in emphasis in both teaching and curriculum objectives over the period when the different studies were conducted, must remain uncertain. It should also be remembered that the history of research into teaching and school effectiveness suggests that the complexity involved is rarely conducive to the production of simplistic answers as to which kinds of school or teaching are most effective. It is to be hoped, therefore, that interested readers will remember these limitations when seeking to interpret specific findings.

In the last analysis, decisions concerning the effectiveness of small schools need to acknowledge a wider context than that addressed within this book. Nevertheless, the issues addressed here are of importance, and it is our hope that the contribution which the book makes will enable the debate to rise above the strident and vociferous claims of the advocates or opponents of small schools. Only if that happens will it be possible to consider the educational implications of many of the findings, findings which can be viewed not only in the context of the small schools, but in the broader context of primary schools and classroom research.

1.2 The case against the small school

The case against small schools can broadly be divided into three main areas of criticism. The first of these broad areas makes the assertion that, because of their size and the limited number of teachers, such schools are unable to provide the necessary range, balance, and depth of curriculum as compared to the larger schools. Critics suggest that, as a result, the standards of performance of children in small schools are likely to be less than those in larger ones, and this situation is likely to be exacerbated by the teaching difficulties involved, particularly those resulting from the wide age range and hence the ability differences within a particular class. They further argue that schools with a small staff find it difficult to offer opportunities to teachers for in-service, and that this in turn means that the staff are unlikely to gain promotion to larger schools, so that schools stagnate and there is little opportunity for the infusion of new ideas.

The second group of objections against small schools concerns the cost of their maintenance and improvement. It is argued that it is uneconomic to provide, say, a purpose-built hall for activities such as PE, drama, and dance for fifty pupils to use perhaps a third of the available time in school each week when a larger school would make use of the same facilities almost continuously. The small numbers of pupils almost invariably lead to lower teacher-pupil ratios since part-time help is required to relieve the headteachers so that they can carry out administrative tasks and to cover certain specialized areas of the curriculum such as music. Even where additional part-time help is available, it is likely that increased resources in the form of books, worksheets, and other materials will be required to cope with the lack of expertise among the teachers. Given the improvement in communication and transport facilities in the post-war period, critics argue that it is now considerably cheaper to bus children from outlying villages to larger schools in suburban areas.

The third and final set of criticisms sees the small school as socially limiting, in that it provides a narrow mix of children and fewer opportunities for pupils to engage in 'out of school' activities. Many of these arguments and counter-arguments rest largely on opinion so that, for example, it is claimed that any likely detrimental effects of social isolation are more than compensated for by the warm 'family atmosphere' and strong 'community links' exhibited by most small schools, particularly those situated in rural areas.

There are, however, a number of research studies which provide some evidence relating to these three sets of criticisms and these will now be considered.

1.3 Academic standards in small schools

Throughout the debate about small schools, one area of particular contention has been the standards achievable by children attending such schools. The debate concerning pupil achievement has been one where it has been particularly difficult to disengage prejudice from fact. In some of the earlier studies connected with this issue, insufficient care was taken to control, statistically, for initial differences between children from small and large schools, while in the later studies it has not proved possible to devise efficient research designs which could control for the numerous independent variables which might also account for any observed differences in attainment. This weakness has been difficult to remedy, with the result that Nash (1978) concludes that, on balance, 'There is no overall evidence either way' to decide whether children in small schools are under-achieving.

Earlier studies tended to concentrate on urban and rural differences. A review by Barr (1959) concluded that in many of the pre-Second World War studies, there was a confusion about what was being measured. It must be remembered that, at the time, achievement tests were not so sophisticated as now and largely measured factual recall, whereas problem solving and other higher-order skills were assessed through 'intelligence' tests. Earlier American studies, such as those by Terman and Merrill, were paralleled by similar ones in Britain, using measures devised by Burt. These studies all suggested that children from

9

among the rural population achieved, on average, lower intelligence quotient (IQ) scores than those from the urban areas. Where both intelligence and attainment were measured, no attempt was made to control for differences in initial ability between the two populations. Barr, for example, cites a study carried out at the Bristol Institute of Education where the average IQ of the rural population was 2.91 standard score units below that of the urban pupils. In attainment tests in English and arithmetic, the differences were only 1.65 and 2.13 standard score units and Barr argues that such a result could indicate that teachers in small rural schools were more effective, given that they started with pupils of lower ability. The data from the study, however, do not allow one to judge whether Barr's conclusion is the correct one.

Barr also quotes another study by Jan Morris in the early 1950s which measured the attainment of reading in the primary school. Small schools, defined as schools with three or fewer teachers, performed less well in reading than the sample of larger schools, mostly drawn from urban areas. However, the differences disappeared when the reading scores were adjusted to take account of differences in initial intelligence scores (Morris 1959). Barr argues that variation in the quality of teaching may have contributed to the differences in reading scores. He quotes, in support of this view, Morris's finding that a proportion of the staff in village schools were hostile to 'modern practice', citing as an example the fact that most teachers viewed the 'play' approach as a complete waste of time. Further, over 15 per cent of the ninety-eight teachers in the study were headteachers with infant-age classes and some of these had never undergone any training in infant methods. Barr speculated that, as a consequence, there could have been considerable variation in the amount of time given over to hearing children read in the different classrooms and this, in turn, affected pupil attainment.

Further evidence can be found in the Plowden Report (1967) where the results of a small-scale study of reading in Kent primary schools are presented. Reading scores for large and small schools (using the Plowden definition) were compared. A trend in favour of the larger schools was observed but the statistical significance of this relationship disappeared when factors such as parental occupation, school starting age, and so on, were introduced. Barker Lunn (1970), in the National Foundation for Educational Research (NFER) study of streaming in the primary school, also collected achievement data, which can be used to make certain inferences concerning the small versus large school controversy although it was not collected with this purpose in mind. Barker Lunn's study concerned junior classrooms and the smallest unit studied was a two-teacher school, either as a separate entity or as part of a four-teacher combined junior and infant school. Small urban schools were compared with larger urban ones. As with the Plowden Report, reading scores were higher in the larger schools, although the difference did not reach statistical significance. Against this, however, scores on arithmetic problem-solving were significantly higher in the smaller schools although this difference disappeared when the smaller schools were compared to a sub-sample of the larger ones where streaming took place. It is difficult, therefore, to separate the effects of size from the effects of streaming.

Some relevant information can also be extracted from a study by Jackson (1976) concerning school progress in rural areas. Although rural schools were compared with urban ones, no useful conclusion can be drawn concerning the question of size, since the number of pupils in the rural schools ranged from 29 to 200. The study concerned infant children, so teachers were asked to rate pupils on a number of reading skills and on their ability to understand stories, follow oral instructions, write, and copy. On only one of the reading abilities, the level of the child's reading, was there a difference in favour of urban schools. There was, however, a sustained difference in favour of the rural schools in mathematics. Here rural children were rated more favourably with respect to number work in the first two years although by the third year this difference had disappeared. When the children were tested, as opposed to rated, at the end of the third year, however, the rural children scored significantly better. The test results were not adjusted to take account of differences in intelligence quotient which were obtained by using a picture vocabulary test. Interestingly, in contrast to the pre-war pattern, rural children now had higher IQ scores, reflecting the trend for educated middle-class city dwellers to move to the rural areas during the late 1960s and early 1970s. Although, therefore, the trend here is broadly similar to that found by Plowden, it is probable that the difference in mathematics would have disappeared if adjustment for IQ had been made. These findings, therefore, cannot be cited as evidence that small schools are either superior or inferior to medium- and large-size ones. Trew (1977) draws a similar conclusion from a study of attainment in Northern Ireland schools. Trew found that any differences in achievement tended to disappear when socio-economic and other factors were controlled for.

Further evidence of the changing nature of the school population in rural and inner city areas can be seen from the results of the HMI survey on junior schools (DES 1978). Three out of five schools in the inner city were found to contain pupils with serious social problems, the result of deprivation in the home, whereas the figure was only 1 per cent in the case of rural schools. This represents a sharp transformation from the statistics collected during the first quarter of the twentieth century when the population of the rural schools consisted almost entirely of farm labourers' children (Richmond 1953). The data on attainment, using tests of reading and mathematics prepared specially by the NFER, again add little to our understanding of the effects of school size since, even in rural areas, only two-form entry schools were considered. On both attainment measures there were no significant differences between rural and suburban schools, although the rural pupils performed better than those from schools in inner city areas. HMI also examined the relationship between attainment and vertical grouping and found significant differences in favour of single-age classes. This, as we shall see, was an influential finding since it has often been cited by local authorities seeking, for economic reasons, to close small schools. However, later studies such as ORACLE, Observational Research and Classroom Learning Evaluation (Galton *et al.* 1980), while obtaining similar results, found that the differences in progress between vertically-grouped and single-age classes disappeared when account was taken of teaching style in the analysis. Poor performance, therefore, may not necessarily be a result of vertical grouping as such but of the use of inappropriate forms of classroom organization and teaching strategies with such groups.

Another study deserving a mention was a small-scale one by Edmonds and Bessai (1977, 1978) which took place in Canada and used a sample of schools from Prince Edward Island Province. No significant differences were found between small and large schools when the average school scores were compared to the grade average for the province as a whole.

Overall, therefore, in all of the above studies no discernible trend emerges. Differences in initial ability between the populations of small and large schools and factors such as the enforced use of vertical grouping, social deprivation, teaching style, and shifting patterns of population, combine to make it very difficult to interpret observed differences in achievement with any degree of precision.

1.4 The economic viability of small schools

The case for school closure on economic grounds was not part of the PRISMS study. Nevertheless, for the sake of completeness of this brief review, a summary of the main issues and the research evidence relevant to the debate will now be presented. As with the question of standards discussed in the previous section, the debate about the economics of small schools has yielded very few general conclusions, chiefly because those taking part in the debate cannot agree on which factors should be included in the 'economic equation' when drawing up a balance sheet for and against school closure.

The most widely used criteria are those of the Department of

Education and Science (DES) in which the unit costs per pupil for staffing and maintenance are offset against the costs of transport to alternative schools and the potential income to be derived by the use of the school premises for other purposes (DES 1977). Studies have shown that it is difficult to obtain objective information concerning these costings. The arguments are well documented in Forsythe (1983) who investigated the financial savings estimated by local authorities in fifteen cases of closure. In four cases there appeared to be no net saving and in three others the results were inconclusive even when the additional factors over and above the unit costs per pupil were included. One major difficulty is that some heads exercise considerable 'entrepreneurial skills' so that their schools gain a disproportionate share of available resources. As a result there exist considerable variations in costs between schools. This was clearly demonstrated in a small-scale study by Boulter and Crispin (1979) who found that some schools of comparable size were three times better resourced than others.

Groups with an interest in preserving the rural community have also criticized the DES criteria, arguing that the costs of rural schools should be seen as one part of the total spending and resourcing of rural and urban populations. The report of the 1978 Standing Conference on Rural Community Councils estimated that rural communities received nearly 10 per cent less grant aid than the urban conurbations. However, forms of funding vary, and while schools are a direct charge on the local authority a large part of the additional urban aid is derived from special funding such as the Manpower Services Commission, now the Training Agency and Equal Opportunities programmes. Such factors are difficult to quantify and, when included in the economic equation, decisions concerning the economic viability of small schools become extremely problematic. For this reason, many local authorities in areas where there are strong political pressure groups in support of retaining small schools have favoured, instead, schemes where, through self-help and the sharing of specialist teachers, some of the more obvious costs in terms of salaries and resources can be offset.

A number of researchers have examined some specific proposals for sharing teachers. Slocombe (1980) collected data from a sample of schools, and concluded that merging two adjacent schools into one offered a reasonable compromise. Some local education authorities (LEAs), such as Northampton, have followed Thomas's (1972) suggestion for co-operation between clusters of schools in sharing specialist teachers for art, science, and music. Boulter and Crispin (1979) evaluated Northamptonshire's Rural Schools Enrichment Project but found considerable variation in the use made of the scheme by different schools. Such schemes clearly have potential but headteachers appear to need specialist training and some degree of monitoring is required to ensure a fairer distribution of resources. This, however, adds to the costs. Alternatively, better information about curriculum provision in each school would enable limited resources to be distributed more effectively.

By far the most detailed summary of these economic arguments is provided by Bell and Sigsworth (1987). Starting from the DES circular 5/77 (DES 1977), they have examined the various local authority estimates of the economic costs of small schools based upon three main criteria: the unit teaching costs, the unit premises costs, and the unit non-teaching costs (other than premises) per child respectively. Their review of these data includes the study carried out at Aston University in the late 1970s (Comber *et al.* 1981). The Aston research showed that calculations based upon these three economic costs per pupil produced a threshold figure below which costs rapidly escalated. In one local authority, for example, a sample of ten schools with less than thirty pupils returned costs which were on average between 18 and 19 per cent higher than the typical figures for schools in the county. In another authority for similar schools the costs were, on average, 60 per cent above those for the typical primary school in the authority. Bell and Sigsworth (1987), in summarizing these and various other studies, showed that, in general, schools with rolls of less than seventy began to show sizeable disproportions in cost per pupil. They cite one particular study, carried out in the Border region of Scotland, which suggested that there were very sharp escalating costs in schools with fewer than twenty-five pupils and smaller disproportions up to a size of a hundred, after which there was no further marked trend.

In seeking further evidence on this question, Bell and Sigsworth carried out a small illustrative case study of a rural area with 5,000 inhabitants and seven schools, the largest of which had a roll of 109 in 1985 and the smallest 32. Three options were considered. Option A adopted the rationale of the White Paper, *Better Schools* (DES 1985a), and looked at the feasibility of creating one large school to serve the total of 349 pupils currently attending the seven separate primary schools. The second option retained all seven schools but remodelled them to meet the new school premises regulations. This option, it was assumed, would be the one favoured by parents. The third option reduced the number of schools to five, thereby creating schools having an average of 60 pupils and three teachers. Option A had the greatest net capital cost (£520,000) as opposed to £217,100 for the second option.

Bell and Sigsworth (1987), however, caution their readers against drawing too simplistic a conclusion from this analysis. They point out that, although both the second and third options were cheaper because they did not require extensive capital investment, they might not be more cost effective. The first option of creating a new school could provide many more attractive features such as large hall space and a gymnasium. On the question of recurrent costs a crucial feature was that of transport which was three times as great for the first option as for the second one. Many of these additional costs would not, however, be borne by local authority but by parents and were, therefore, generally hidden in calculations of this kind when carried out by local authorities.

On balance, the third option of retaining the five schools having the lowest capital costs but extra recurrrent costs of £20,000 per year when compared to the single school option, appeared to be the most satisfactory solution. However, when 'cash flow discounting', the usual technique employed by local authorities to deal with capital costs, was allowed for, over a period of twenty years the net cost of the single school option was £2,426,000, while for the five school option it was £2,250,000. If the additional recurrent costs for the third option were included then the difference between the options A and C was less than 7 per cent and this is generally accepted as being within the allowable margin of error for such calculations. Increasingly, therefore, a decision of this kind involves a judgement about the value placed upon the superior educational facilities which could be incorporated into a new building. Bell and Sigsworth (1987) concluded that 'unless there is some agreement on the value attached to different forms of educational provision, the economic analysis can only take us so far in answer to a question as to which set of proposals is the most cost effective'. Neither do such calculations take into account the indirect benefits to the local community. For example, it is often argued that the presence of a village school encourages people to move into the area and that other savings can be made by using the school premises, of an evening, for community activities.

1.5 The social effects of small schools closure

The arguments concerning the social effects of closing small schools, particularly those in rural areas, tend to be even more complex than those for educational standards and economic feasibility. Regional variations tend to exert an important influence in any discussion so that, for example, the Gittins Report (1967) paid much greater attention to the social factors than did the Plowden Report (1967) because it was concerned to preserve the Welsh language. Gittins recommended a policy of school amalgamation which would maintain communal life. These new schools would be similar in conception to the Cambridge village colleges established by Henry Morris in the 1930s and would overcome the social disadvantages inherent in small village schools, many of which were said to be insular, isolated, and deprived of suitable resources with which to expand the pupils' horizons and cultivate wider interests.

Gittins's ideas have been challenged by Nash (1977, 1978) who conducted a Social Science Research Council, now the Economic and Social Research Council (SSRC), project in Welsh rural primary schools. Research evidence of grouping in larger schools suggests that pupils tend to make friends with children from their own background. Nash argues, therefore, that with fewer alternatives available, children from professional classes in small schools will mix with children whose parents belong to other socio-economic groups. Nash also points to the positive qualities of the small school: the strong feeling of belonging to the institution and the opportunities to practise a range of important 'life' skills, such as answering the telephone and showing visitors round the school on occasions when the headteacher is taking a class. Further support for this view comes from the Scottish studies of Forsythe (1983) where in the Highlands local people saw their primary schools as an 'important and integral part of the community', promoting social interaction and integration in areas where geographical features made this difficult. Forsythe found no evidence that the children experienced greater problems of adjustment when they transferred to larger secondary schools, contrary to the view expressed by Gittins.

These conclusions are similar to those obtained by researchers in America and Canada. Barker and Gump's (1972) comparison of big and small American schools found that in the latter, parental and community participation was three to twenty times greater and that more children achieved positions of responsibility. Edmonds and Bessai (1977) asked Canadian pupils to rate schools on five measures. These were *satisfaction*, the extent to which they enjoyed school, *friction*, the degree of satisfaction with friendships in school, *cohesiveness*, co-operation within and outside school, *motivation*, the desire to get good grades, and *difficulty*, the extent to which the work was found to be hard. Data were collected in forty-five classes and in all cases, except that of motivation, classes in smaller schools responded more favourably. The researchers also report similar results on all five social factors from a small-scale comparative study in schools within the Cheshire and Pennine areas (Edmonds and Bessai 1978). In the Canadian study teachers were also asked to rate schools on a number of important factors. They rated small schools as friendlier places where it was easier to maintain discipline and where there was a greater degree of co-operation between both pupils and teachers.

More recently, the social effects of primary school reorganization have been examined by Comber *et al.* (1981) in a study based at Aston University. The research team conducted a questionnaire survey of changes in the pattern of provision of primary education in a number of rural LEAs and also conducted a detailed study of the effects of reorganization on six groups of communities in the West Midlands. In two cases they were able to observe the process of re-organization as it took place. The researchers report that the social role of the school within the community depends largely on the particular circumstances surrounding the community which the school seeks to serve. In the Midlands area studied, it appeared that the greater the amalgamation of the rural community with the surrounding urban area, the less important was the social role of the school. The majority of teachers working in this situation did not actually live in the catchment area of the school and took little part in community life. Although many parents, in response to the researchers' questions, argued that school was an important meeting place for the community, nearly 60 per cent had not attended one meeting in the school during the previous twelve months. In one instance, where an area 'community' school had replaced a number of smaller village schools, the researchers reported very 'high' levels of community involvement. These findings, therefore, suggest a degree of caution is necessary when interpreting the responses of the various interested parties concerning the positive social effects of small schools.

Bell and Sigsworth (1987) also claim that the atmosphere of the small school enables children to make the transition from home to school more easily and rapidly. They quote a study by one of their students, Finch (1986), of five schools of between eighty-two and thirty-two pupils. Finch found very little difference in the pattern of friendships between the different sexes compared to typical junior schools in this age range. Unlike larger junior schools, there was a greater tendency for friendships to exist across year groups. From interviews, Finch reported that the teachers tended to distinguish between children according to what they could achieve rather than by their age. Among the children she found very little negative reaction to the social climate of the small school. Most pupils were relieved because in a big school 'there'll be too much row', whereas in a small school 'you meet up with people more quickly', and pupils were able to 'know everyone in the school' (Bell and Sigsworth 1987: 105–6).

In summary, therefore, the evidence, such as it is, seems to support the idea of greater social cohesiveness among children in small schools. In such schools size dictates that older children play and work with younger ones so that the sharp differentiation between age groups reported in some studies of larger schools (Blyth and Derricott 1977; Meyenn 1980) are not reproduced. Neither is there strong evidence that children from the small schools were significantly disadvantaged when they moved to a large secondary or middle school at the transfer stage (Shanks and Welsh 1983). On balance, therefore, the evidence would suggest that small schools exert a positive influence in the development of a child's self-concept. This, of course, is no guarantee that this self-image will be maintained after transfer.

1.6 Curriculum provision in small schools

In their case studies of small rural primary schools, Bell and Sigsworth (1987) rely mainly on teacher reports to provide descriptions of curriculum provision in the schools that they studied. They question the possible disadvantages arising from the lack of specialist teachers in small schools by observing that there is little evidence in larger schools that specialists exert much influence on the curriculum outside their own classroom. They claim, on the basis of their interviews with teachers, that the advantage of the small primary school arises from the 'family atmosphere' in which the teacher is able to cater for the needs of individual pupils to a far greater extent than has been demonstrated in larger schools by Bennett *et al.* (1984). Bell and Sigsworth (1987) quote their student Finch's (1986) study in which children said they had much more time with the teacher and experienced far fewer interruptions. One pupil compared the experience of the small school with a larger one containing several hundred children where 'we never got a chance to talk. You just had to do your work, have lunch, do the rest of your work and go home' (Bell and Sigsworth 1987: 157). The family atmosphere was said to produce better relationships between the children and therefore more effective collaborative working. Teachers in Bell and Sigsworth's (1987) study all claimed this to be an important advantage of the small school. They also claimed greater curriculum flexibility allowing more opportunity to 'integrate ideas and subjects' and to devote a greater amount of time to activities which 'keep the children's interest'.

The teachers in Bell and Sigsworth's (1987) study saw the need for mixed age classes as a positive advantage in that it provided an incentive to organize a much more differentiated curriculum in which children, of necessity, spent more time working independently of the teacher. Bell and Sigsworth quote one teacher of fifteen years' experience who said, 'I organize my children so that the only thing I have to do is teach'.

This teacher organized a weekly rota so that pupils were assigned to specific jobs such as tidying the room, checking the playground, collecting and distributing milk, ensuring the television was correctly tuned five minutes before the programme was due on, and so forth. Older pupils were allocated and trained for more demanding jobs such as collecting dinner money, distributing notes to parents, and answering the telephone. Using pupils in this way ensured that the teacher was rarely interrupted. Bell and Sigsworth report an afternoon visit to one small school in which the thirty pupils were divided into five groups with the ages ranging from 4½ to nearly 11. All the pupils were involved in a craft activity in which the class teachers were assisted by a number of parents. Bell and Sigsworth describe the older girls making lace dressing-table mats while the teacher was doing woodwork. Elsewhere a mother was running a cookery group while across the playground, the other teacher and the welfare assistant were supervising three separate modelling activities: finger painting, computer drawing, and some delicate overlaying design. After break, with coffee prepared and served by the pupils, the junior class did geography while the infants had a music lesson. Bell and Sigsworth (1987) conclude of this particular school:

> Even after one afternoon, you sense that the kind of unspoken understanding between the two teachers (and the parents) on the principles that inform the curriculum – the whole working of the school. Most visibly, there is the openness to the community; this is shown in the encouragement that is given to parents to participate in a variety of ways by the frankness with which the headteacher explains his hopes and his concerns in all his transactions with parents . . . in the dealings that all the adults have with the pupils you can sense a respect being shown for their world; the formal curriculum does not dominate the interests and knowledge they bring with them to school but endeavours to utilize it; the dinner lady is absorbed in the skipping game that the three girls are playing in the playground; the weak boundaries between age groups and gender that exist outside school are reflected within it and there is the obvious belief that for all who go to school the experience should be enjoyable. (Bell and Sigsworth 1987: 177).

Curriculum surveys and accounts, such as those by Bell and Sigsworth (1987), largely address themselves to questions about the school's or teachers' intentions regarding the curriculum. In Bell and Sigsworth's (1987) study, for example, much of the evidence consists of teacher impressions, whereas we know from a number of studies (Galton 1989) that there is a 'perception gap' between what we, as teachers, think is happening, and what actually takes place in the classroom. Studies in the United States which have carried out more systematic analysis of curriculum provision have distinguished between three different levels (Denham and Lieberman 1980). At the first level there is the *total instructional time* that is given over to a particular curriculum topic or area. This in many cases is determined through discussion and the provision of 'curriculum guidelines'. In some primary schools it is enforced by means of direct timetabling. Within this instructional time is the actual *allocated time* during which the teacher provides activities which are appropriate to the curriculum area, for example, a workcard with mathematics problems. However, since pupils do not always remain 'on task' throughout an activity, a third level, *engaged time*, needs to be defined. This denotes the extent to which a child works rather than is distracted or engaged in some alternative activity. Differences between *instructional* time and *allocated* time arise mainly through the transition between activities or between dinner and play breaks, and are strongly influenced by the school 'ethos' and by classroom organization. Differences between *allocated* time and *engaged* time are largely determined by the way that the teacher presents the topic, the effectiveness of his/her classroom control, and the extent to which the children's interest is engaged.

Studies, both here and in the United States, show that there are wide variations in time not only between different levels but also within levels using this curriculum model. Both Bennett *et al.* (1980) and Bassey (1978) report considerable variation in the number of hours per week allocated to various subject areas within the primary curriculum. Variations in mathematics from two and a half to seven hours per week, and in language from four to twelve hours per week, were reported by Bennett *et al*. Nearly 20 per cent of the week was spent in administrative and transition activities such as clearing up, waiting, and moving to a new location. Even within this time allocation, as the ORACLE study showed (Galton *et al*, 1980), the curriculum experienced by individual children varied considerably, largely because of the use of different teaching strategies.

Questions about the breadth and balance of the primary curriculum in the small school must therefore take into account the manner in which the curriculum is prescribed and implemented. The inclusion of primary science in the curriculum is partly justified on the grounds that it provides children with opportunities for 'enquiry', but is the case equally convincing in a school where the science lesson consists of teacher demonstration, heavily 'guided' discovery, and note taking? If sufficient information about the implementation of the curriculum at classroom level is to emerge, it is necessary to use some type of observation to make an assessment of allocated and engaged time. Usually in such studies an observation system with clearly defined categories is preferred, although these are often criticized because they are said to lack any explicit theoretical basis (Scarth and Hammersley 1986). However, those who favour the use of a systematic approach argue that one of its main values is that it can define categories which reflect the assumptions and beliefs of various parties to the educational debate about what constitutes appropriate practice (Galton and Simon 1980).

Devising an observation system to monitor the entire curriculum provision of a small primary school is a very complex task. The curriculum today, as it generally manifests itself in primary classrooms, is the product of considerable debate between the proponents of competing ideologies. Much of the debate has centred round two main curriculum questions. One is mainly philosophical and concerns *what* children ought to know and be able to do as a result of their period of primary education. The second question, mainly a psychological one, concerns *how* to organize and sequence learning in ways which support our understanding of child development. All exercises in curriculum planning, either implicitly or explicitly, attempt to provide answers to such questions. An observation system, in attempting to describe the curriculum as it operates in the classroom from day to day, will reflect something of the current state of this 'ideological debate' in the way in which categories defining curriculum content are selected and interpreted.

In describing the curriculum it is also necessary to identify the various processes and activities which take place when pupils and teachers engage in a particular subject area. Is science taught mainly through experimentation? Does number work largely consist of computation or the application of those computational principles to practical problem-solving? In which curriculum areas do teachers engage the pupils in 'higher order' challenging questioning? Questions concerning the relevance and balance of the curriculum can then be asked.

At its simplest, balance can be equated with coverage so that the researcher is interested in the number of opportunities that the pupil has to engage in certain activities, practise certain skills and so on. At a more complex level, however, judgements have to be made about the desirability of particular practices that have been observed. Some help can be obtained from recent research into teaching and learning where, for example, there is now evidence to suggest that, in mathematics lessons, homework review is an important determinant of pupil learning. The teacher, largely through questions requiring factual recall on the part of the pupils, recapitulates the homework based on the previous lesson. Other studies have emphasized the importance of feedback (Brophy and Good 1985). Decisions concerning the value of integrating different content areas within a topic or thematic approach must remain a matter of ideological debate. But the research described in this book can help place that debate in a more realistic framework based on what actually happens rather than what is claimed to take place.

1.7 The PRISMS project

Curriculum Provision in Small Schools, the PRISMS project, was funded by the DES over a three-year period beginning in the spring of

1983. Nine local authorities were involved and in each authority a stratified random selection of small schools was made. The only limitation on the selection of schools was that they were a reasonable travelling distance from the base used by the seconded teacher whose task it was to conduct the field work in the schools of their own local authority. The local authority was allowed to comment upon the selection of the schools and in a few cases suggested alterations to the list. These alterations were few in number and largely resulted from the specialist knowledge the advisers had of particular schools which enabled them to suggest that some were not suitable. The reasons for such rejections were generally administrative as, for example, where there was no permanent headteacher in post at that time. In all cases schools which were rejected were replaced from a further random selection.

For reasons explained earlier, the working definition of a small school used in the project was one with fewer than one hundred pupils or four full-time teachers. In the event, however, because of variation in staffing provision and changes in circumstances of schools after the school lists had been produced, the sample did include a small number of schools with five, six, and seven teachers and one school with over 120 pupils. In the end, however, thirty-one schools had fifty or fewer pupils, thirty-two had 51-100 pupils, and the remaining five had between 100 and 132 pupils. Nearly 60 per cent of the schools had three or more full-time equivalent teachers. Just under 40 per cent had two full-time equivalent teachers and two schools had just one full-time teacher. More than 70 per cent of the schools were all-through primary schools, just under 20 per cent were first schools, one was a junior school, and five were infant schools. These variations, of course, reflected the administrative policies in the nine local authorities.

In addition to the use of observation schedules, background information was obtained by means of questionnaire and interview. This enabled the project to collect teachers' opinions on a variety of issues concerned with both primary schooling in general and small schools in particular. Two questionnaires were used, one for teachers, including headteachers, and one for headteachers only. These were sent out in the spring of 1984 to all teachers in the PRISMS schools and to teachers in a random sample of 102 other primary schools in the nine local authorities. The headteachers' questionnaire asked about the teachers and pupils in the school, about the schools' external contacts, for example, with other schools, and about aspects of the heads' role. The teachers' questionnaire asked about teachers' experience and qualifications, their responsibilities in their present posts, their opportunities for professional development, and their views on school management.

Interviews were conducted in the summer of 1984 with forty-five heads and teachers from fourteen schools in the PRISMS sample. A semi-structured schedule was used. It included questions about vertical grouping, class organization, curriculum provision, the teachers' careers, and the school's relationship with the community and other schools and the LEA. Unlike many previous studies of small schools, therefore, it was possible to obtain the opinions of a large number of teachers working in small schools in order to explore how far the 'typical' teacher conformed to the traditional stereotypes which have been used to argue either for or against the effectiveness of small school provision.

Although not a main objective of the project, data on pupil performance were collected in two ways. First, standardized tests were administered by observers to the junior pupils at the beginning and the end of the two-term observation period. The tests were shortened versions of the Richmond Tests of mathematics and language that had been used in the ORACLE study (Galton *et al.* 1980). Second, a mini-project called the Prismaston File was specially designed for use on PRISMS. It had two levels of difficulty, aimed at upper and lower juniors, and the pupils worked on it in the summer term after the observations had been completed. The Prismaston File was designed to be used under ordinary classroom conditions. It relied on chronologically appropriate levels of reading ability on the part of pupils and required them to apply a variety of skills such as reference skills, map reading, measuring, and drawing.

In summary, the study involved sixty-eight schools from nine local authorities. In these schools 188 classes containing approximately 3,600 pupils were visited. Half of these pupils, all those aged 7 and over, were tested, and 1,200 pupils were observed on at least five occasions. 1,380 lessons were observed altogether giving 8,000 observation records on teachers and 24,000 observation records on pupils. Each teacher record contained fourteen observations and each pupil record had ten observations of behaviour and one of curriculum. The volume of data was considerable. The number of observations collected over the two terms was equivalent to the entire amount collected throughout the three-year period of the ORACLE study.

1.8 The small primary school: a pen portrait

From the previous discussion two somewhat contrasting views of small schools emerge.

Those who wish to see the closure of more small schools argue that they tend to be traditional in their methods and resistant to change. The teachers tend to remain in post because they find it difficult to gain promotion to larger schools. Most of these teachers do not live within the catchment area of the school and consequently take little part in out-of-school activities or in community life. Innovation is infrequent, attendance at in-service courses poor, and consequently the curriculum, also, has a traditional bias in favour of number computation, reading, and standard exercises from English workbooks. There is little science, music, or art other than painting. Opportunities for team games are limited and pupils rarely have the opportunity to meet children from other schools as a result. Many of these schools have inadequate buildings and are under-resourced. Such schools are costly to run in terms of teaching, ancillary services, and maintenance, if these costs are averaged between the number of pupils on the roll and compared to the costs of larger schools. Schools which are within commuting distance of the local town or city often contain a higher proportion of 'above average' pupils than would be found in the typical suburban primary school. Such pupils would achieve more in a larger school.

The children also develop limited social skills, partly because they have few opportunities to meet other children outside the local community and therefore lack experience and knowledge about a wide range of topics. Almost all of them find difficulty in making the transition to secondary school because of the lack of social development, and when they do transfer they find that, in comparison to children taught in the larger schools, their standards of attainment are lower. Consequently, failure is built into the system from the beginning.

Supporters of small schools reject this picture. Although it is acknowledged that there will often be defects in the building housing the small school, supporters argue that the disadvantages are largely overcome by the enthusiasm and inventiveness of the teachers, with the help of local parents. While accepting that on a simple economic criterion of cost per pupil a small school is more expensive than either those of medium or larger size, this form of costing is rejected because it does not take into account the disproportion in the total sums spent on other forms of community provision, besides education. The small school is greatly valued by the community and the buildings are used for other activities at times when the school is closed. Many of the schools contain young enthusiastic teachers who are well-schooled in the latest primary methods and continually update themselves by attendance at in-service courses, usually during their spare time and during the holidays. Where there is a lack of particular skills in a subject teachers pool expertise with colleagues in neighbouring schools, drawing on each other's strengths to overcome each other's weaknesses. Headteachers of such schools are imaginative and flexible in their approach both to the school organization and to the deployment of resources. Use is made of local parents who have expert knowledge in certain fields to supplement the teaching. Much-needed resources are either borrowed from the local authority or provided by parents through fund-raising projects or community activities. Through these and other measures the school manages to provide children with as broad, balanced, and exciting a curriculum as pupils receive in larger schools.

The children thrive in the kind of atmosphere which is created in a small school. When they first come, as 5-year-olds, there are fewer traumas because classes are small and the children already know each other from the local playgroup. Throughout their time in school they build up confidence and independence through being assigned numerous tasks of responsibility in helping to run the school, an absolute necessity if the headteacher is to devote as much time as possible to teaching. Pupils are able to form a wider circle of friendships because neighbouring schools maintain close links, combining together, for example, to form teams for various sports. Opportunities are seized, whenever possible, to take the chidren away on trips with other schools, so that they experience different environments. Small classes help advance achievement so that by the time the children transfer to the secondary stage they are among the top group of achievers. The confidence gained throughout their time in the small school means that they find little difficulty in adjusting to the new school.

These, then, are somewhat parodied versions of the cases made out by those debating the continuing existence of small schools. Each version, no doubt, contains some element of truth so that reality lies somewhere between these two extreme viewpoints. Neither side can base its case on evidence of what pupils and teachers do inside the classroom. The PRISMS research described in this book attempted, in a modest way, to provide such evidence, paying special attention to the curriculum and the manner in which the teachers and pupils engaged in curriculum activities. Before discussing some of these research findings in the following chapters, we will present the data obtained through questionnaires and interviews. The questionnaires were also sent to teachers in a sample of large schools within the same nine local authorities. This allowed comparisons to be made concerning such questions as educational background, in-service experience, and career development. Contrary to some of the views discussed earlier these data suggest that the teachers in small schools do not differ markedly from their colleagues in larger institutions.

Chapter two

Small schools and their teachers

Helen Patrick

In this chapter we present the teachers' perspectives on some of the issues raised in the previous chapter and later in the book. We wanted to know what the teachers were like who took posts in small schools and to find out what their views were on their work. To do this, we used questionnaires and interviews.

All the teachers, including the headteachers, in the sixty-eight PRISMS schools were invited to complete a questionnaire and 80 per cent of them (259 out of 325) did so. In addition, the headteachers completed a questionnaire specially designed for them. In order to see how these teachers fitted in to the primary teaching profession generally, we also sent questionnaires to teachers and headteachers in a random sample of schools of all sizes in the nine local education authorities. Only about 40 per cent of these teachers (380 out of 967) responded, but because they represented a range of schools in all the authorities, we felt we could use the material for the purpose of comparison. The more detailed material obtained in interview, however, comes only from teachers in the PRISMS schools, where we interviewed forty-five teachers from fourteen schools. In the pages which follow, the term 'teachers' includes headteachers unless they are specifically excluded.

2.1 Qualifications, experience, and professional development

It was suggested in Chapter One that writers on small schools have perpetuated a number of ideas about these schools and their teachers without always having much evidence to substantiate their claims. We wanted to find out how much truth, if any, there was in the stereotype that teachers in small schools differed from their colleagues elsewhere in a variety of ways, that they tended to be older, not very well-qualified, isolated from new developments, and to remain in post for longer than average. We therefore pursued these kinds of issues in the questionnaires and interviews.

First of all, in the questionnaires we asked teachers for some biographical details. We found that just over three-quarters of the teachers who completed questionnaires in both PRISMS and non-PRISMS schools were women. Just over 60 per cent of the PRISMS teachers and just over 50 per cent of the non-PRISMS teachers were aged 40 or over. These figures on sex and age are very similar to DES figures on the primary teaching population nationally and suggest that in these respects small school teachers differed little from their colleagues elsewhere. Heads of PRISMS schools tended to be younger than heads of other schools and were much more likely to be in their first headship, as might be expected given that the headship of a small school is regarded in some LEAs as a step on the way to a headship of a larger school.

Around 90 per cent of both PRISMS and non-PRISMS teachers held a teacher's certificate and small numbers held other kinds of professional qualifications. The two groups were also very similar with regard to the subjects they had studied. English and art were the most common subjects in which the teachers held qualifications. Nearly 30 per cent of all respondents had studied each of these as a main subject in their higher education. History and geography had each been studied by about 20 per cent, while around 11 per cent of teachers had studied education as their main subject, and a similar proportion had a qualification in a science subject. In no other subject did the proportion of teachers holding a higher qualification of any kind reach 10 per cent. The figure for mathematics was fewer than one in twelve.

Just over half of all the respondents had trained to teach juniors and just over 40 per cent had trained to teach infants. Small proportions of teachers in both groups were trained to teach nursery, middle school, or secondary pupils. Again there was little difference between PRISMS and non-PRISMS teachers.

The length of teaching experience, both full- and part-time, of both groups was also similar, with over 40 per cent having taught for fifteen years or more. The PRISMS teachers were slightly older on average than the non-PRISMS teachers and, therefore, had slightly longer teaching experience. The PRISMS teachers were much more likely to have taught in a greater number of schools than were the non-PRISMS teachers. Nearly 60 per cent of the PRISMS teachers had taught in four or more schools. The corresponding proportion for non-PRISMS teachers was just over 40 per cent. The PRISMS teachers, too, had taught in a greater range of schools of different sizes. Comparatively few teachers in larger schools had taught in small schools (100 or fewer pupils), but small school teachers were just as likely as their colleagues elsewhere to have taught in large schools (over 250 pupils). PRISMS teachers also had experience of teaching a wider range of pupils of

27

different ages. Seventy per cent of PRISMS teachers, compared with 57 per cent of other teachers, had taught both infant and junior pupils. Virtually all the PRISMS teachers, though nearly 90 per cent of other teachers too, had experience of teaching vertically grouped classes.

This brief comparison of the qualifications and experience of PRISMS and non-PRISMS teachers suggests that the two groups had remarkably similar backgrounds, with the PRISMS teachers having the edge in some areas of experience. We believe that these data show that teachers in small schools are not, in some way, a peculiar breed, and this argument will be further supported by the evidence presented below on professional development.

It was suggested by some of the PRISMS teachers we interviewed that there was a danger that teachers in small schools could become professionally isolated. One deputy head, for example, felt there was little scope for him in a small school and missed the companionship of the larger group of colleagues with whom he had worked in his previous school. In addition, among those who completed questionnaires, the PRISMS teachers were significantly more likely than the other teachers to agree with the statement, 'My job gives me little opportunity to make personal contact with other teachers'. We found comparatively little evidence to support such a perspective, however, perhaps because, as the teachers themselves said, they were aware of the danger.

In an attempt to measure the degree of professional isolation of small school teachers, we asked a number of questions in the questionnaire about various aspects of this issue. Given the size of their schools, it was undoubtedly the case that PRISMS teachers had fewer colleagues within their own schools with whom they could exchange ideas. There was also evidence that they had fewer opportunities to meet new colleagues within their school. It was not that turnover among teachers in small schools was much different from what it was among teachers generally. Where the difference arose was in the total number of teachers. Because small schools had fewer teachers, there were longer gaps between the arrivals of new teachers. Thus, nearly a quarter of the heads of PRISMS schools reported that it was over three years since a new teacher had been appointed to the school. The corresponding figure for non-PRISMS schools was just under 10 per cent. To take a turnover rate of one in ten as an example, in a ten-teacher school this would give a new teacher every year, but in a three-teacher school it would barely give a new teacher every three years.

In a range of other ways, however, PRISMS teachers did not appear to suffer excessively from isolation or stagnation. Because some of our small schools were geographically isolated, we asked about the travelling distance to the nearest teachers' centre. It was certainly more difficult for the PRISMS respondents to visit teachers' centres because their nearest one was significantly farther from both home and school than was the case for non-PRISMS teachers. In fact, however, the PRISMS teachers were more likely than their colleagues to have visited a teachers' centre within the last term, though we suspect that this figure may have been artificially inflated by visits for our PRISMS meetings.

We also asked about attendance at in-service courses. According to their questionnaire responses, PRISMS teachers were just as likely as were non-PRISMS teachers to have attended one or more in-service courses during the current school year. Just over 80 per cent of both groups had done so, and over a quarter of these teachers had attended courses lasting more than five days, while 20 per cent had attended courses lasting for more than ten evenings. The most popular courses were on language (including reading), computing, mathematics, science, PE, art, music, curriculum studies, management, special needs, religious education, environmental studies, and infant work. Both groups of teachers had attended courses covering similar subjects, though there were some differences. PRISMS teachers were less likely to have attended courses on PE and environmental studies and more likely to have attended courses on computing and religious education. Among the headteachers, those in PRISMS schools were significantly less likely to have recently attended a course on management, though only slightly less likely to have ever attended courses for heads or prospective heads.

These figures suggested that teachers in small schools were just as likely to attend courses as if they worked in larger schools. We wondered, however, if it was any more difficult for them to do so, and we therefore asked if they had been unable to attend some courses they had wished to attend, and if so, why. About four in ten teachers from both groups had found some difficulty in attending courses and both groups gave similar explanations for the difficulty. The most common was lack of supply cover to release them from school. About 12 per cent of teachers in each group gave this reason. On the face of it, then, teachers in small schools were no more likely to face difficulties in attending courses than were their colleagues in larger schools and only small numbers of teachers from either group wanted to see more courses on particular subjects being made available locally.

These findings were confirmed by the PRISMS teachers who were interviewed. The great majority of these teachers thought that the opportunities for professional development in their area were reasonable and most said they were able to go on courses in which they were interested. It was difficult to get supply cover, particularly for short courses, and often teachers could attend only if the head was willing to give up 'office' time to take care of classes. Most teachers said their heads were very good about such arrangements, though staff felt inhibited about applying for courses. Obtaining supply cover for teachers attending longer courses seemed to present fewer problems, but competition for places on such courses was strong. About a quarter of the teachers interviewed specifically mentioned that they attended courses out of school hours. Although this meant that supply cover was not needed, it was not without problems. Some of the schools were situated at a considerable distance from the centres at which courses were held. Not only did this mean a long drive after a day's teaching but, in some cases, if the courses started too early, teachers could not get to them in time. Only a few teachers expressed reservations about attending courses. Some said that the same courses were offered year after year, while others felt it could be unsettling for the children if their regular teacher was away too often.

Within their own schools PRISMS teachers were just as likely as their colleagues elsewhere to report that they had opportunities to observe each other at work, and more likely to report that they could observe the headteacher at work. They were slightly more likely to say that they had opportunities to meet teachers from other schools, and most heads in both groups had opportunities to meet other heads. About a quarter of the teachers we interviewed referred to the desirability of meeting other teachers and visiting other schools. Such occasions were thought to be particularly valuable if they could be arranged within schools hours, so that teachers could see each other's schools at work, but of course such arrangements needed teaching cover. Three of the schools where interviews were conducted belonged to local small school groups in which the teachers believed they could offer each other valuable support.

According to the teachers' reports, small schools were just as likely as larger schools to be visited by local authority advisers or inspectors. Approximately two-thirds had received a visit within the last term, and nearly half the teachers had been visited in their classrooms. This suggests that advisers' visits were relatively frequent, though the teachers who talked about the advisory service in interview believed that the advisers were often too busy to give much help – 'perhaps they leave you alone if they think you are doing all right'.

These findings suggest that teachers in small schools are not unduly isolated or lacking in opportunities to encounter new ideas. Although it is certainly the case that they have fewer colleagues immediately at hand in school, they are by no means cut off from teachers in the neighbourhood, and they make as much use of the opportunities available to them for professional development as do their colleagues in other schools. On the basis of our evidence there is little justification for the traditional stereotype of the teacher in the small school.

2.2 School size, class size, and vertical grouping

In both the questionnaires and the interviews we asked the teachers a range of questions about school size, class size, and vertical grouping, all features which distinguish small schools from their larger counterparts. We thought that such features would affect the nature of the teacher's job and we were interested in whether the PRISMS teachers had been particularly attracted to working in small schools. In both the questionnaires and the interviews, therefore, we asked the teachers why they had taken their present post. On the questionnaire returns, there was little difference between PRISMS and non-PRISMS teachers. The most common reasons which teachers gave were promotion, convenience, gaining wider experience, and the availability of the post - 'it was the first job that came up locally'. Less than 10 per cent of the PRISMS teachers claimed to have taken their present post because it was in a small school. Nine of the forty-five teachers who were interviewed gave this reason, but six of these were heads who had also been interested in promotion.

It seemed, therefore, that teachers in small schools had taken their posts for reasons similar to those operating for teachers in larger schools. Relatively few of them had been specially attracted by the idea of working in a small school. Once in post, however, the teachers found that working in a small school differed in a variety of ways from working in a larger school. Because many PRISMS teachers had worked in a range of schools, they were able to comment in interview on how their present posts in small schools compared with posts which they had previously held in larger schools.

Most PRISMS teachers believed that teaching in a small school differed in a range of ways from working in a larger school. One difference, in the view of many of the teachers who were interviewed, was that they had more duties and responsibilities than they would have in a larger school because there were simply fewer adults in the school with whom to share the work. Thus, for example, there were fewer teachers but just as many lunch duties. In addition, support staff such as the secretary and the caretaker were usually only part-time.

By and large, the questionnaire data supported these perceptions. During the five days prior to completing the questionnaire, PRISMS teachers were much more likely than their colleagues elsewhere to have done lunch duty, playground duty, and bus duty, and slightly more likely to have helped with school maintenance work. Overall, PRISMS teachers had a significantly heavier load of non-teaching duties. They were just as likely as their colleagues elsewhere to have a designated responsibility for a subject or subjects within the school and only slightly less likely to have an administrative or organizational respons-

31

ibility. Only 60 per cent of PRISMS schools, compared with 88 per cent of non-PRISMS schools, had ancillary help, though PRISMS schools were more likely to have peripatetic teachers. Both groups were almost equally likely to have voluntary help in their classrooms and to have similar numbers of volunteers. PRISMS schools had less secretarial and caretaking help than larger schools.

Of course, most of these differences were accounted for by the smaller numbers of pupils in the small schools, but, as some of the teachers pointed out in interviews, the amount of work that might be done by a caretaker or a secretary did not necessarily decrease in proportion to the number of pupils. There were long periods of time in some small schools when neither the secretary nor the caretaker was present. At such times urgent maintenance and routine matters such as answering the telephone and receiving visitors had to be coped with by the teachers. As a result, as the questionnaire results showed, PRISMS teachers were much more likely than non-PRISMS teachers to have their teaching interrupted by such demands, and the effects of these interruptions are examined in some detail in Chapter Six.

There was therefore some evidence to support the PRISMS teachers' perceptions that they carried a heavier load of duties and responsibilities of various kinds than did their colleagues in larger schools. Despite such demands, however, PRISMS teachers had no compensation in the form of non-teaching time. Indeed, they were slightly more likely than their colleagues in larger schools to have less than an hour of non-teaching time per week. Also, they were significantly less likely than teachers in other schools to receive the usual rewards and promotion for their work. Just over 40 per cent of PRISMS teachers were on a Scale 1, compared with just over 30 per cent of teachers in other schools, and the PRISMS Scale 1 teachers were much more likely than other Scale 1 teachers to have designated responsibilities for particular subject areas in the curriculum. Only 13 per cent of PRISMS teachers were on a Scale 2 or 3 compared with 38 per cent of non-PRISMS teachers, though of course a higher proportion of PRISMS teachers were headteachers, nearly a third, compared with only a fifth in other schools.

The opportunities for PRISMS teachers to gain promotion within their schools were limited because most of the schools were too small to support promoted posts other than the headship. In interview some of the teachers commented that opportunities for promotion generally were restricted, as were opportunities for 'sideways' movement to gain wider experience. This was seen as a problem not just in small schools, but in primary schools generally. The teachers felt there were simply very few posts vacant at all.

The lack of opportunities, however, was not a major source of dissatisfaction for the PRISMS teachers we interviewed, except in the case of two teachers who had been at their schools for twelve and fifteen years respectively and who, despite their efforts, had failed to find other posts. In addition, a small number of teachers expressed serious dissatisfaction with their posts because they were on temporary contracts. Only six of the forty-five teachers pointed out that they had to take on the kinds of responsibilities which in a larger school would have been rewarded by promotion, but even for most of these teachers their involvement in the school was a source of satisfaction rather than complaint. On the whole, the great majority of the teachers claimed to be satisfied with their jobs, even though the interviews were conducted during a period of industrial action in schools.

The teachers gave a variety of reasons for their comparatively high level of job satisfaction. Most enjoyed having a range of responsibilities and they liked the atmosphere in small schools – 'more like a family atmosphere' – where everybody knew everybody else, teachers and pupils alike. Some teachers thought contacts with parents and the local community were particularly strong, that discipline problems were less severe, and that fewer rules and regulations were required. Small schools were therefore pleasant places in which to work.

We also asked the teachers whether they thought their pupils benefited from being in a small school. Most teachers thought they did, though they were aware that there could be disadvantages. Pupils in small schools had only a few adults to relate to, and a small peer group with whom to compete and to make friends. On the other hand, the pupils grew up in a warm atmosphere, with security, a relatively high level of informality, and the opportunity for all the pupils to participate in school events and to take their share of the responsibilities. Some teachers said there were pros and cons in being in a small school, but the great majority of those who were interviewed came down in favour of small schools.

One of the most tangible benefits which teachers saw in small schools was that the classes were significantly smaller than was the case in larger schools. Over three-quarters of the teachers in the PRISMS schools had classes of twenty-five or fewer pupils, while in the other schools in their authorities generally fewer than half the teachers had such small classes. Not surprisingly, the teachers who were interviewed told us they were more than satisfied with the size of their class, though some of them who had classes of around thirty children thought they were too large. The benefits of small classes – 'well, you've just got more time for individuals, haven't you?' – were balanced, however, by the wide age spread in most classes. Although many schools, whatever their size, have to put children from more than one year group into the same class, in the PRISMS schools the practice was virtually universal and nearly half the classes had three or more year groups.

We asked the teachers how they felt about vertical grouping and how they coped with it. The main advantages which the teachers saw in vertical grouping arose from the inescapable relationships between children of different ages. Almost without exception the teachers said that in a mixed age, mixed ability class, the older pupils and the more able pupils could help the younger and less able pupils. Although a few teachers felt this could go too far – 'I don't really think a teacher should exploit that'; 'I don't overuse it' – it was seen to have a range of benefits. Younger children, particularly in the reception class, had a ready source of help, which might reduce their anxiety at entering a new situation. They could see what was achieved by the older pupils and had an example to look up to – 'The younger ones see how the older ones or the brighter ones cope and it encourages them to do the same, to want to be the same, so I think that's beneficial'. Some teachers believed that having younger children in the class meant that the older chidren learned to take responsibility, to be helpful and tolerant, as well as encouraging them to work to retain the advantages they had from being older:

> I think perhaps that the older ones feel they've got to outdo the younger ones, in a way. They've got to be always slightly better because of their age . . . I think they've got the younger ones snapping at their heels, which sometimes is useful – a spur, I suppose, to work . . .

Some teachers said that having a very diverse class made life more interesting, that it was more natural, for example, more like a family group, and that it made the teacher more aware of the individuality of each child – 'I think it makes me more aware all the time that I need to stretch the more able and also spend time with the less able'.

Most teachers, however, also thought there were disadvantages in vertical grouping. The very diversity of the class made the teacher's life more difficult: 'It takes more planning'; 'I've got to consider a greater spectrum of things to do – upper limits and lower limits are greater. I'm almost bound to split them up into groups and therefore, of course, that's quite a bit of work'. As well as making life more difficult for the teacher, vertical grouping was believed to have detrimental effects on pupils. Some teachers suggested that being in a mixed age class could put too much pressure on the younger children and that sometimes the younger children became too dependent on the older children. A few teachers, particularly infant teachers, felt they could not devote as much attention as they would have liked to their younger pupils, while others felt there was a danger of the older pupils being held back or becoming bored. In some schools special efforts were made to combat these problems. One headteacher, for example, said:

We try to treat our leavers as a separate group and when I had one day's administration time I would take them out during the afternoon of that day quite a bit during their last year, treat them as a separate group, try to develop their opinions on things and get them to work as a more mature group, away from the younger children. But that hasn't been possible this year.

Most teachers accepted vertical grouping as part of the job and an inevitable concomitant of life in a small school. One teacher commented, 'It's like a lot of things in education, it's swings and roundabouts'. Another said:

you soon adapt to this and you realize that different groups of children have got different needs and you provide for them in the classroom and you soon realize it's quite possible to do this and not really all that much extra effort because you're thinking about the needs of individual children anyway and it's just an extension of that really, of your concern for each child and to provide what they want.

It seemed likely that having children of different ages together would affect how teachers organized their classes and this was one of the questions we investigated with the teachers in the interviews. The strategies which they reported suggested that most of them, like the teacher just quoted, thought that teaching a vertically-grouped class differed in degree but not in kind from teaching a single-age class. Their descriptions of how and why they organized their classes as they did were much as might be expected from any group of primary teachers, though they were aware of the special problems which vertically-grouped classes presented.

In talking to the teachers, we followed up the three main types of classroom organization which we were using in the observation schedule – whole class teaching, the use of groups, and individualization. The teachers' descriptions of their classroom organization suggested that they made more use of class teaching than we might have expected given the diverse nature of most of their classes. The teachers thought that some areas of the curriculum lent themselves to class lessons, an issue which will be explored further below and in Chapter Four. There was also the feeling that it was good for a class to be treated as a whole class from time to time. Some teachers suggested that class lessons in which something new was being introduced to the younger children could take the form of revision for the older children, while younger pupils might pick up more than the teacher expected from a class lesson aimed primarily at older pupils. But the teachers did feel constrained by the age and ability range in their classes. Most of the teachers who said that they did very little class teaching had at least three year groups in their classes, and many teachers were cautious about class teaching, as the following quotation from a headteacher illustrates:

> in class lessons you tend to aim at the middle, which means that you are not stimulating the brighter pupils and you've lost the less able ones – so despite the fact that class teaching is a time saver in many ways, it isn't a practical solution a lot of the time.

An alternative strategy was the use of groups. Most of the teachers said that they made some use of groups in their teaching. These took a variety of different forms, based on ability, age, sex, friendship, and so on, though the teachers reported that they allocated children to groups most commonly on the basis of age or ability or some combination of the two. In some classes the groups were maintained for all or most of the time, in other classes the nature of the groups varied according to what was going on. The teachers had different views on what constituted a group. Some groups existed only as administrative units in the teacher's mind or in her record book. Other groups were given names or numbers so that the teacher could gather them together easily. A group might refer simply to a seating arrangement, or might mean that a number of children were doing the same or similar work or that they were collaborating in some way.

No simple pattern emerged from the teachers' descriptions of how they used groups, but most of them seemed to be administrative or organizational groups rather than collaborative groups. For basic work in mathematics and language the teachers tended to group the children according to age or ability, though within these groups they usually worked individually. Some teachers liked to have each group doing different activities so that not all the children would require the teacher's attention at the same time – 'I think you've got to have one group in a class who will need my help while the others are perhaps getting on with something reinforcing'. This seemed to be a fairly common strategy, but the teacher just quoted expressed concern that activities which the children could do without any teacher help were perhaps not always very valuable. Another infant teacher, however, thought it was easier to keep an eye on the children's progress if both her age groups were working on the same curriculum area at the same time.

We asked the teachers specifically about their use of collaborative groups. Up to a quarter of those we interviewed said they very rarely, if ever, organized activities in such a way that the children had to co-operate with each other. Their reasons were that collaborative groups encouraged copying and that some of the pupils would be at a disadvantage. Only one teacher said that she often had the children working collaboratively, but the remaining three-quarters said that collaboration was a regular feature of their organization. These teachers felt that pupils could learn a lot from each other and should learn to enjoy working together. Much collaborative work was done in mixed age and mixed ability groups because in areas such as topic work teachers felt children of different ages and abilities could learn from each other. One teacher gave the following example of mixed age collaboration:

We went down to the wood one afternoon this week and I picked five group leaders from the second year who'd been before and wouldn't get lost, and they each had some second years, first years and top infants.

Although there was considerable use of class teaching and of groups, most teachers clearly believed that individual work was appropriate for most of the time, even though they felt it made their job harder. Thus, one teacher said:

I fully realize that individual work is perhaps wasteful of time in the sense that I have to spend a lot more time with a child, . . . a one-age class is better from that point of view, particularly when you get up to twenty-seven (pupils) – you're getting towards the upper limits of its viability.

Teachers who had relatively small classes certainly appreciated that it was easier for them to do individual work, though some teachers felt that certain kinds of individual work could have disadvantages. For example, a head who taught 8- to 11-year-olds said:

I try to ensure that they are working at a level that they can cope with. Quite a lot of work they do is book based . . . I'm not sure that book-based work is considered to be the most entertaining or interesting . . . Although we do some practical work, it's not always easy to organize it with a mixed ability and mixed age class . . . it's the age that's the problem – what they're capable of.

The PRISMS teachers were well aware of the advantages and disadvantages of working in a small school. In attempting to cater for the needs of individual children, they had the benefit of small classes, but they faced the additional complications associated with vertically grouped classes. Much of what they said about classroom organization implied that they saw themselves as a valuable resource and they used a range of strategies for distributing their attention as effectively as possible among their pupils.

Interestingly, in the teachers' descriptions of how they organized their classrooms, there did not seem to be much that could be defined as unique to small schools, or different from what might be observed in many larger primary schools. We found it difficult to distinguish the PRISMS teachers from those participating in the Inner London Education Authority (ILEA) study (Mortimore *et al.* 1988) which was taking place at around the same time. Most of the teachers had experience of larger schools and seemed to be carrying that experience over into their work in small schools without major modifications. When we asked them what was special about working in a small school, their answers almost invariably referred to the atmosphere in the school and to their greater involvement in the work of the school as a whole, rather than to anything unique about how they organized their classrooms. Again, we were forced to conclude that teachers in small schools were distinguished principally by the fact that they worked in small schools, rather than by anything unusual about their teaching strategies or their views on the relative merits of class teaching, grouping, or individualization.

2.3 The curriculum in small schools

Describing the curriculum in small schools was a central aim of the PRISMS project. Although most of the material about the curriculum was collected by means of classroom observation, we also asked the teachers a range of questions on the subject in our questionnaires and interviews.

In the interviews, we asked the PRISMS teachers first about the basic skills which they thought their pupils needed. Not surprisingly, most teachers answered in terms of the three Rs, or reading, writing, language, and mathematics. In addition, nearly half the teachers regarded the development of social attitudes as basic, for example, one head said she aimed to 'try to create a happy, confident social being, that has a sense of social responsibility to the school, the family, all the family, the world in general'. Smaller numbers of teachers mentioned practical skills and providing opportunities for pupils to engage in creative or expressive work of various kinds, in music, PE, art, movement, and drama.

Interestingly, given the increasing emphasis which was being given to science education and the relatively high levels of science work which we observed, none of the teachers said that they regarded science as a part of a child's basic education. Around 40 per cent of them, however, listed science as an area of the curriculum which they liked their pupils to experience. This was closely followed by work in history, geography, and environmental studies. About a quarter of the teachers mentioned religious education and small numbers specified that their children should have opportunities for work in art and craft, social skills, reference skills, physical education, moral education, drama, and health education. Although different teachers had different priorities for their pupils, overall every major area of the primary school curriculum was included in their answers to our questions about the curriculum. Responses to our questions on curriculum guidelines, both LEA and school guidelines, suggested that for most of the time most teachers were relatively unrestricted in what they taught and were able to pursue their own curriculum aims.

We also asked the teachers whom we interviewed about how they ensured progression in the curriculum. For most of the teachers this was a matter of particular concern, though a few seemed to take it for granted that children would naturally make progress. There were two common reactions to questions on the issue of progression. The first was that progression had to be assessed in terms of the individual child. The second was that it was up to the teacher to build on the skills and interests of her pupils. Teachers reported using various strategies for keeping track of pupil progress – published schemes, tests, and examples of pupils' work collected over time. It was suggested that projects in which the whole school participated helped make staff aware of progression, as did the development of curriculum guidelines for the whole school. Also, although having the same pupils in the class over a period of two years or more might tax the teacher's repertoire, it could enable her to take a long term view of pupil development.

Some of the teachers expressed concern about the whole issue of progression. They felt it was difficult to provide work which matched a child's ability, particularly for teachers whose experience was limited. It was also difficult to define what progression was. One respondent suggested teachers should avoid the temptation to use 'tick lists' which showed what pupils had covered because this was not the same as recording what they had grasped or understood. Most teachers were clear that the assessment and recording of progression were easier in some areas of the curriculum than others. There was general agreement that progression was built into mathematics and that mathematics schemes provided a structure which clearly showed such development. In other areas of the curriculum this was not so obvious. In language work, for example, some teachers thought it was not clear that certain aspects of punctuation needed to be done before or after others. The seven teachers who raised the issue of progression in science disagreed about whether it was possible to build in progression. In expressive subjects such as art and music, the teachers tended to agree that children's skills could be developed, but that progression in terms of creative or imaginative development was difficult to define and measure. In topic or project work, it was suggested that progression could be measured to some extent in terms of reading and writing skills.

We looked earlier at how teachers organized their classes. Here we consider how that organization related to the curriculum content. What the teachers told us supported the findings of the observation, namely, that they saw a close relationship between teaching methods and curriculum content.

For some areas of the curriculum, the teachers reported, the main, and often the only, form of organization was whole class teaching. These areas included music, watching television, creative writing, music and movement, PE, drama, 'news', and other kinds of discussion and oral work. These were areas of the curriculum where pupils of different ages and abilities could make different kinds of contributions, or where teachers would expect different outcomes from different children attempting the same task. They also included activities which were noisy and needed space. In some small schools the only practical solution was to have the whole class doing them at the same time. Even in these areas, however, class teaching was not universal and individual teachers varied their practice, as we describe in Chapter Four.

The teachers felt that activities of a practical nature were often suitable for organized collaborative work. As a result, the areas where teachers encouraged their children to collaborate were topic or project work, including science-based work, practical mathematics and mathematics games, art and craft, drama, PE, and play. A few teachers said they liked children to form discussion groups as part of their language work, to read to each other, or to work together at the computer.

The most common form of organization, as we saw above, was individual work. In most teachers' classrooms almost all the work in 'the basics', reading, language work, and mathematics, was done individually. Individualization was commonly achieved by using published schemes, particularly in mathematics, though many teachers also made use of reading and language schemes. Schemes, it was thought, helped ensure progression and gave teachers a basis from which to work. Almost all the teachers to whom we talked, however, had reservations about using schemes. They talked of the danger of becoming 'scheme-bound' and almost all said that they supplemented schemes with other material. Nearly half the teachers also made a point of saying that they used schemes selectively and did not expect their pupils to work through every example provided. The use of schemes in mathematics is considered in more detail in Chapter Six.

Among the teachers we interviewed, all of those who had full-time responsibility for a class laid aside some time specifically for pupils to work on the three Rs, and a few also timetabled time for PE, music, and art. The majority of teachers stressed that they made every effort to incorporate aspects of language and mathematics work into projects and topic work. They did not try to do so artificially, but used opportunities which arose. About a fifth of the teachers, however, said they did not do much by way of integration but tended to keep basic work separate.

Again, we found that the PRISMS teachers, in describing the curriculum in their classes and how they organized it, sounded little different from their colleagues in other schools. The views they expressed on what should be included in the curriculum and their accounts of how they organized the work were much like those reported in the ILEA study (Mortimore *et al*. 1988) and in previous studies of the primary school curriculum (see Alexander 1984). We wanted to pursue these issues further, however. A common criticism of small schools is that they do not have the resources, in terms of either equipment or teachers, to provide as broad a curriculum as can be provided in larger schools. Forsythe (1983), for example, states, with no supporting evidence, that, 'Small schools are unlikely to offer as broad a curriculum as larger schools'. We therefore put these claims to the teachers we interviewed in the PRISMS schools.

First of all we asked the teachers if they thought their teaching was restricted in any way by the physical resources in their schools. About half the teachers thought it was, though in some cases the teachers did not see the restrictions as severe. The teachers argued they could get most things they wanted by borrowing them, appealing to the PTA, organizing fund-raising events, or using their capitation. Some teachers pointed out that when a small school did have a facility such as a computer or a swimming pool it had to be shared by far fewer pupils than would be the case in many larger schools.

In their responses to the questionnaire items on the need for physical resources, there was no clear evidence that PRISMS teachers perceived a greater need for more resources than did non-PRISMS teachers, perhaps because, as some teachers suggested, teachers in schools of all sizes could always think of something else it would be useful to have. In interview, however, teachers in five of the fourteen schools said they experienced fairly severe problems. Their main difficulties were lack of equipment, particularly for PE, and lack of space. One of these schools had over a hundred pupils and was one of the biggest in our study. The problem there, according to the head, was years of neglect on the part of his predecessor, rather than the size of the school as such. The four other schools, however, were two-teacher schools where space, in particular, was at a premium. The teachers saw little hope of solving the problem because of the cost of any kind of building. Nevertheless, the teachers tried to make the best use of what they had, and used the local village or church hall if necessary.

We then moved on to the more general issue of breadth of curriculum. We asked the PRISMS teachers whether they thought the curriculum in their schools covered the same kind of range as might be found in larger schools. Again, it should be remembered that most of the teachers could answer this question in the context of their experience of working in larger schools. Only four of the forty-five teachers interviewed thought that the curriculum range in their schools was definitely limited, and three of these teachers worked in the school just described where there appeared to have been years of neglect. The remaining teachers divided into two approximately equal groups in their reactions to this question.

The first group consisted of teachers who were uncertain about how their curriculum compared with what was done in larger schools, but they felt that there were probably a few areas in which their provision was limited. PE, including sports and movement, and music were the two areas most commonly mentioned. In the case of PE, teachers were constrained by lack of equipment and lack of space. Musical provision depended less on resources and more on teachers' abilities. If a school did not have a musician on the staff, the teachers turned to radio programmes and peripatetic teachers to remedy the deficiency, but were not always convinced that their provision was sufficient. Some teachers believed there were simply too few teachers in their schools to cover everything adequately. It was not that they missed out any of the major areas, but rather that they feared that some areas were not covered as well as they might be. Thus one teacher said:

> Well, again, you can only hope that you are doing your best. With three members of staff, obviously you're pretty pushed sometimes ... We try and cover everything. Maybe we don't do it as well because we haven't got the expertise, if you like. I mean, maybe someone doing drama in another school might be much better at it than I am, though I do it and I like to think, you know ... Games, PE is pretty well covered. We have teams, they mix with other schools. I don't think they miss out there at all. Music, well, possibly. One of the other teachers plays the guitar. Maybe we don't make full use of the piano. It's not one of my strengths. We still have a go. We use percussion instruments. I suppose, again, a music specialist would get much more out of them.

The other main group of teachers were those who believed that what they provided was comparable with what could be provided in a bigger school. Most of them emphasized, however, that such provision was only possible because of the extra effort which the teachers made to ensure that their children did not miss out on anything. They often described themselves as opportunists, seizing every chance to extend their curricular range. As we have already seen, they went on courses, developed specialisms, invited parents and other volunteers in to help, and drew on LEA resources such as teachers' centres and advisers. In addition, questionnaire responses showed that teachers in PRISMS schools were much more likely than their colleagues elsewhere to use members of the local community and to link up with other schools to help to provide skills and expertise in the curriculum. The following quotation from a headteacher illustrates the ways in which PRISMS teachers enriched the curriculum in their schools:

> Some of my colleagues around will tell you, 'Oh, well, we're a small school, so we don't do that . . . . I always say 'Well, we're a small school, so we should do that.' We should offer the children as wide a range of things as possible . . . it's no excuse, being a smaller school . . . For example, environmental studies – I would never do at my last school. I would have a specialist in things like that. We prepare concerts and things here ... I would never front a concert at my last school, but I do now. For example, it's a cricketing village . . . and so I have one of the parents this week helping me coaching, and we've got the -------shire cricket club coming helping with coaching . . . We get peripatetic help with music. We all (the schools) had the option, but not all of us took it up, but we rang in almost straight away . . . You almost overcompensate for your school. You take every opportunity that comes. If there's an environmental studies thing, like this CAP project, then you join it, because it all brings something to the school that you haven't got.

It was clear from what the teachers told us that they were well aware that small schools were vulnerable to the criticism that they could not provide a broad curriculum. Although some of the teachers were doubtful about how far they were succeeding in providing a curriculum comparable to what might be available in larger schools, most seemed to have clear ideas on what was required and had developed strategies for providing it as far as they could.

2.4 Management and the role of the head

It is only in recent years that management has been recognized as an issue in schools. There is comparatively little published literature on the management of primary schools, and even less on the management of small primary schools. Yet certain kinds of management issues are of particular significance in small schools.

One major difference between headteachers in small schools and their colleagues in larger schools is that the former are usually teaching heads, that is, they have the main responsibility for one of the classes in the school. According to their questionnaire reports, the PRISMS heads spent their time within school hours in many respects differently from the way in which their non-PRISMS colleagues spent their time. First of all, most of the PRISMS heads had a class to teach and consequently had much less non-teaching time than did non-PRISMS heads. Also, heads in PRISMS schools were much less likely than other heads to report that, during lesson time, they engaged in staff development or curriculum development or took over classes to release teachers to go on courses or to visit other schools. When it came to more immediate demands on their time – seeing parents and other visitors, and doing routine administrative work – there were no significant differences between the two groups of heads. But this meant that PRISMS heads were much more likely to interrupt their teaching to undertake such work.

We thought this would lead to role conflict for the heads of small schools, but in the questionnaire items which we used to test this idea, we found no differences of any size between our two groups of heads. It could be, of course, that the small school heads did not want to admit that any conflict existed. Those whom we interviewed were less inhibited and raised issues such as dealing with interruptions and finding time to fulfil their responsibilities for staff development, though only two out of the fourteen said they thought their teaching suffered because of their administrative preoccupations. This issue was followed up by one of the observers who worked on the study and he reports on it in Chapter Six.

Another major feature of the head's role in small schools was its all-embracing nature. Heads felt that the reputation of the headteacher could be more important in a small school than in a larger school because there were so few other teachers to whom parents could relate. Despite pressure of time, heads had to face up to issues of staff development in a more positive way than might be necessary in a larger school. An unsatisfactory teacher was difficult to 'hide' on a small staff. Two of the PRISMS heads we spoke to had found it necessary to persuade colleagues to attend prolonged in-service courses and had been very satisfied with the results, though a third head, after struggling for five years with a colleague in his previous school, had eventually given up and moved schools himself. Most heads, however, had nothing but praise for the hard work and commitment of their staff.

A related issue of significance in small schools was delegation. We have already suggested that most PRISMS teachers were comprehensively involved in the life of their schools, and several of the heads who were interviewed recorded their appreciation of their colleagues' willingness to be involved. Heads said they felt inhibited about delegating responsibilities, not only because there were so few people to share the load, but also because there were usually no scale posts in the school. Some heads felt there should be at least one scale post, other than the head's, in every school, so that there was someone to deputize and some recognition of the responsibilities which, in larger schools, would merit a responsibility payment. Two deputies, however, commented that their posts were largely redundant because their heads retained their hold on the major areas of the work of the school.

We asked a number of questions in the questionnaire about aspects of management. The responses suggested that in a variety of ways small schools were managed differently from larger schools. It seemed that in small schools there was more consultation between heads and teachers on issues such as the allocation of pupils to classes, the allocation of resources, and assessment and evaluation. Even though fewer staff meetings were held on average in the PRISMS schools than in the other schools, the PRISMS teachers did not express any more dissatisfaction than their colleagues with the number of meetings. Many PRISMS teachers wrote in the margins of their questionnaires that they did not need many staff meetings because they saw each other all the time, and similar comments were made in interviews, though a few teachers made a point of saying that they believed formal staff meetings were just as necessary in small schools as they were in large schools. When meetings were held in PRISMS schools, however, according to the teachers' reports, a greater range of issues was discussed than was the case in larger schools, again suggesting more consultation in smaller schools.

In some respects the style of management in small schools seemed to be more informal, with more consultation on a greater range of issues. Even so, the heads themselves saw their responsibilities as basically the same as they would be in a larger school. In the responses to an item in the questionnaire on the role of the headteacher, there were no significant differences between the PRISMS heads and the non-PRISMS heads. The heads to whom we spoke in interview also felt that, apart from their teaching commitments, their role was very similar to what it would have been had they worked in larger schools. This quotation illustrates the kinds of comments which they made:

> We have the same expectations and pressure in spite of the size. You lack people to delegate things to. I have a lot of things to do. I have one hour off teaching while my .1 [half-day relief] is here. I use it for administration, for example, opening the post. There are no scale posts. The teachers work hard. They teach as well as you would expect and do extra bits, extra-curricular activities. I used to do that, and couldn't understand why the head only came occasionally. Now I understand, because I try to go out with the other teachers, but can't much. I would prefer to go out with the children, bird watching or whatever, rather than sitting musing over requisitions . . . I do feel the amount of pressures are increasing, literally annually, and I don't think I'm alone in that . . . We're

getting snowed under with things that are not vital to the immediate task as teaching heads.

2.5 Links with the community and other schools

One important value of small schools is often said to lie in the role they play in the local community. Forsythe (1983), however, points out that much that has been said and written on this issue is based on emotion rather than evidence, and that the evidence which has been gathered often does not support the view that the school is 'the heart of the community'.

Because of lack of time, it was not always possible in the interviews to ask the teachers about community involvement, but where we were able to do so we found that the sentiments of the teachers were very much in sympathy with the view that their school had a special role in the community. They described in detail the extent of parental involvement in their schools, most of which had a PTA. Most of the schools also had other links with the local community. Community groups used school facilities and the schools in turn went out into the community, for example, by putting on concerts in a local old people's home. Nine of the fourteen schools where we did the interviews were church schools and had direct links with the local church.

But although the questionnaire responses supported the claim that PRISMS schools had numerous local links, they did not on the whole provide much support for the view that the role of small schools in their local communities was significantly different from the role of larger schools.

We found that PRISMS teachers were no more likely than non-PRISMS teachers to be involved in local or community activities within or near their school's catchment area, and, indeed, were significantly more likely than other teachers to live more than five miles away from their school. PRISMS and non-PRISMS schools were almost equally likely to have a PTA or other parents' organization and the PRISMS school buildings were actually slightly less likely to be used by the local community than were non-PRISMS school buildings and facilities. Although the PRISMS schools were much more likely to make use of local churches and halls than other schools were, often this arose as much out of necessity as out of a desire or policy to integrate with local activities. Only in their much heavier use of members of the local community to provide skills and expertise in the curriculum, did the PRISMS schools differ from their neighbours.

With respect to their links with other schools the PRISMS schools were also different from other schools. Eight out of ten PRISMS schools, compared with six out of ten other schools, were involved in co-operative schemes of various kinds. The teachers saw links with other schools as valuable not only for their own professional stimulation, but also because they had financial spin-offs and could supply experiences and activities for the children which could not be provided by one school acting alone.

Our study, therefore, found that small schools, in terms of tangible links at any rate, did not display a substantially stronger degree of community involvement than larger schools did. Where small schools did seem to be more outgoing, however, was in their links with other schools.

2.6 Conclusion

To finish this chapter, we would like to reiterate some of the conclusions which, we believe, arise from the findings presented above.

It is our view that teachers in small schools, on the whole, are as well qualified and have as great a range of teaching experience and opportunities for professional development as can be found among primary teachers generally. Because they work in small schools the context within which they work is different from what it would be in a larger school. Their classes are likely to be smaller and to be vertically grouped. They are more likely to have a wider range of responsibilities, but less likely to be in a promoted post. They perceive that the atmosphere in which they work is more relaxed and informal than they have known in other schools, and they have a particular concern about how rich a curriculum they can provide for their pupils. They are well aware of the advantages and the disadvantages of small schools for teachers and pupils alike and most are happy in their work. Their descriptions of their classroom practices suggest that, despite the different context within which they work, they approach their job in much the same way as they would if they worked in larger schools. Given their backgrounds and experience, this is what we might expect. We are well aware, however, of what has been described as the 'perception gap' between what teachers claim they do and what actually takes place in the classroom (Elliott 1976). Most of the rest of the book, therefore, is devoted to describing life in small schools as we observed it in our study.

Chapter three

The curriculum in small schools

Maurice Galton

3.1 Describing the curriculum

The main purpose of the PRISMS project was to describe the curriculum of small schools. Much of this chapter, therefore, provides information about the work of pupils and teachers in this type of primary school. The information presented suggests that the curriculum provision which small schools make is similar, in many respects, to that described in earlier studies of larger suburban schools (Bennett 1976; Bennett *et al.* 1980; Galton *et al.* 1980; Barker Lunn 1984). Much of the argument, within the book, addresses itself to the consequences of this finding.

In the first chapter it was pointed out that curriculum decisions about what should be taught in schools are closely bound up with educational ideologies. Richards identifies several competing ideologies underpinning the primary curriculum (Richards 1982). There is a 'conservative' view which sees the main purpose of the primary curriculum as equipping children with an understanding of the knowledge developed by earlier generations so that present students, in turn, may contribute to further advances. Dearden (1976) lists the main characteristics by which this approach can be identified. It assumes a limited number of 'forms of knowledge' through which man is able to express his experience. The curriculum is divided into subjects based on this framework. It is rationally planned in that the aims of the curriculum can be stated in terms of knowledge to be learnt, the extent to which pupils succeed in acquiring this knowledge can be assessed, and the quality of the curriculum provision can be improved as a result of this evaluation.

This rational 'conservative' approach may be contrasted with what Richards terms a 'romantic' view, originating in the child development movement of the nineteenth century. The curriculum is planned so that it follows the sequence of man's natural order of development. Early curriculum developers argued that a close study of children would lead to a scientific theory of development and that the experiences provided by the curriculum could be based on these theories. Much twentieth-century primary practice, associated with these ideas, has made use of the developmental theories of Jean Piaget which emphasize the need for a curriculum consisting of activities determined by the child's interest, attitudes, and subjective experience. Unlike the 'conservative' view, the stress is placed not on knowledge but on those skills which concern the development of 'the whole child ... emotionally, physically, socially, morally' and according to Dearden, 'always last nowadays, intel- lectually' (Dearden 1976). Such views were strongly endorsed by the 1967 Plowden Report.

A third basis for curriculum planning derives from the work of Malcolm Skilbeck and Denis Lawton (Skilbeck 1976; Lawton 1983). They adopt as their approach 'reconstructionism' which sees education as a means of improving society. Like the romantics, they place the emphasis on the processes rather than on the products of educational provision, for example, the development of thinking skills in young children, thus developing the capacity to respond to a rapidly changing society. Lawton also addresses himself to the issue of what content should be chosen as a basis for developing these thinking skills. His answer is that content should be chosen so that it reflects the diverse cultural interests of our whole society and would include, for example, the study of trade unionism as well as the study of Shakespeare. Many of the curriculum proposals developed by the Schools Council during the late 1960s and early 1970s reflected Lawton's views.

In the public arena, however, the struggle for the primary curriculum has largely been conducted as a debate between the conservative and the romantic views. Kelly, for example, characterizes the 'great' curriculum debate of the 1970s in this way (Kelly 1982). Recent government curriculum publications are seen by Richards (1982) as an attempt to strike a balance between these different views, as well as implying that: *'the raison d'être* of the primary school as an educational institution is the fostering of children's intellectual development through their engagement with a carefully devised, adequately justified, and widely-defined curriculum'. Kelly sees the same documents as part of 'an accelerating movement towards increased external control over the curriculum with a major concern for content of the curriculum ... together with an emphasis on that which is economically or vocationally useful' (Downey and Kelly 1986). Writers such as Kelly criticize empirical research designed to examine practice in the primary school because the researchers do not make explicit their assumptions about the curriculum activity they monitor. The results of such studies are, therefore, in Kelly's view, open to misinterpretation and can be used by what he sees as the 'forces of reaction' to undermine good primary practice (Kelly 1986).

Writers such as Kliebard (1986), however, have rejected this polarization of the curriculum debate. They argue that several ideologies are reflected within current practice. There now exists a 'curriculum hybrid' whereby curriculum prescriptions arising from the ascendant ideology of a particular period in time have been grafted on to existing practice. Thus the narrow curriculum of the late nineteenth century, based on the theories of 'faculty psychology', was modified because of the influence of the 'social efficiency educators' in the period immediately following the First World War. Their efforts resulted in the updating of mathematics and the introduction of French in place of Latin into the curriculum. In much the same way changing views of child development, particularly the greater emphasis placed on personal development, have resulted in changed approaches to the curriculum, including greater stress on social skills as well as cognitive ones.

Observation schedules reflect similar changes. Most systems, as was indeed the case with the ORACLE schedules on which the PRISMS system is partly based, were developed from still earlier instruments. The ORACLE Pupil and Teacher Records owed much, in their design, to Medley's PROSE (Personal Record of School Experience) (Medley *et al.* 1973), and the Science Teaching Observation Schedule (Eggleston *et al.* 1975). The latter can be seen to have been derived in part from the earlier work of Flanders (1960). Thus the observation scheme used in the present study followed a similar 'hybridization' process as the one which has taken place in curriculum planning in primary schools. The major categories take account of the range of subject areas defined in such documents as *The School Curriculum* (DES 1981), as well as providing a measure of the opportunities offered for pupils to exercise a range of skills appropriate to the child's stage of cognitive and personal development. The main limitation of the present scheme is that no account can be taken of the sequencing of activities for an individual pupil over the course of a day, a week, a term, or a year. This limitation is a consequence of the need to cover a large number of pupils in a wide range of small schools. Thus no single pupil could receive more than a few hours' observation during the study. Taking this limitation into account, an attempt has been made to provide a 'snapshot' describing the curriculum on which a pupil was engaged at a particular time, with further 'snapshots' at intervals throughout the year.

The basic view of the curriculum which is used in this study is that, at any time, each pupil is engaged on a 'task'. This task may be a piece of individual work or it may consist of listening to the teacher or may take several other forms. The task for a pupil at a particular point during the day may or may not be connected with his tasks at other times. Within this basic view of the curriculum as being embodied in a series of tasks, it is possible to enquire about the nature of those tasks in terms of the subject areas covered, the skills exercised, the resources used, and many other features of possible importance to the pupils' education.

The observation schedule was designed by the research team in collaboration with the project observers who were all experienced primary teachers. The final schedule, which was completed after several earlier versions had been piloted, contained 109 curriculum categories, and the observers were instructed to use as many as necessary on any occasion to describe the task on which the pupil was engaged.

The full list of categories used is given in Appendix I together with a brief description of their meaning. The observers used much fuller written instructions to decide, in each case, whether or not a particular category applied to a task. The application of any category was indicated by a tick in the appropriate box of the observation schedule. Any combination of ticks could, in theory, be used. Where tables are presented in the following sections it should be noted that when percentage frequencies are added together for all the curriculum categories the totals do not come to 100. This is because, as indicated earlier, the observers could tick more than one category to describe the particular task or activity. Overall, for both infants and juniors, the total percentage frequencies added up to approximately 600. This implies, therefore, that on average six categories were used to describe each specific curriculum activity. Unlike the ORACLE study where observation was carried out over several years, it was not possible to undertake a full replication study, which Croll (1986) argues is the best way to ensure that satisfactory generalizations from relatively small samples of observation data can be made. Because of the large number of observations carried out during the two school terms, however, it was possible to divide the sample into two halves (A and B). Sample A was used to conduct the main analysis which was then compared with sample B. Cases where there were marked discrepancies between the results from the two samples were then rejected.

3.2 The typical curriculum in the small school

Taking the total number of observations in each of the broad categories of the curriculum to represent the proportion of time that pupils spent on each subject area, there were few differences compared to other studies of the primary school classroom, such as those of ORACLE (Galton *et al.* 1980), the ILEA Junior Schools Study (Mortimore *et al.* 1988), and the study of infant classes in some London schools (Tizard *et al.* 1988).

We shall look first at our findings on the different subject areas in the primary curriculum. Over 20 per cent of the pupils' time was spent on work which included aspects of mathematics, but number work was more frequent than practical maths or work with mathematical concepts. Pupils spent nearly 40 per cent of their time on tasks which included a large element of language work, though almost no foreign language or English as a second language work was observed.

Approximately 10 per cent of pupils' time was spent on activities involving aspects of science and about 15 per cent on activities involving art work. Other subject areas which were recorded, mostly on 5 per cent or fewer of observations, included history, geography, drama, music, movement, religious studies, and social and moral education. Only a small amount of environmental studies work, about 5 per cent of the observations, was seen, partly because the observation was carried out in the autumn and spring terms only. We have returns from teachers which provide evidence of this kind of work taking place in the summer term. Small amounts of physical activity such as PE were recorded but, since most observations were made inside classrooms and physical activities mainly took place elsewhere, a more accurate figure is provided from the analysis of the 'day sheets', on which the observers recorded the curriculum and pattern of organization followed by each class for the whole of each day on which the class was observed. These show that 6.4 per cent of time was spent on PE and 3 per cent on dance, drama, and movement.

These overall percentages do not take account of the differences between infant and junior classrooms which we now give separately for individual curriculum categories.

3.3   The mathematics curriculum

Table 3.1 shows the percentage frequencies, for infant and junior classes separately, for the categories relating to number work. This table is in two parts: the top shows the maximum number of digits that were in use in any line of a pupil's calculation, while the bottom shows the kind of sum being attempted. The figures given in the row marked 'Total' show the total percentage of observations on which any of the number work categories were recorded. If several of these categories applied to a particular observation this would still only count one to the total.

There are few surprises in this table. The large fraction of infant number work which involved counting is noteworthy and it can be seen that a great deal of counting persisted into the junior classes, although these would be more complicated exercises. Compared to the infants the junior figures show an increase in multiplication and division problems, in exercises involving carrying between columns, and in problems using larger numbers of digits. Addition and subtraction problems were at about the same level for infants and juniors, but those for the juniors tended to be harder.

Tables 3.2 and 3.3 show the frequencies for the practical mathematics and the mathematical concept categories. The small amount of

Table 3.1 Curriculum categories for number work

No.	Category	Meaning	% of observations Infants	Juniors
01	DIGITS	(the problem has at most one digit in any term)	7.4	2.0
02	DIGITS	(the problem has two digits in some terms)	7.3	7.8
03	DIGITS		0.3	5.4
04	DIGITS		0.00*	1.8
05 To 09 DIGITS			0.04	0.6
10	COUNT	(the problem involves counting)	12.6	7.9
11	PLACEV	(the problem involves place values)	4.1	9.5
12	ADD	(addition must be performed)	5.3	6.6
13	SUBTR	(subtraction must be performed)	3.2	4.6
14	MULT	(multiplication must be performed)	1.0	5.1
15	DIVIDE	(the problem involves division, fractions, or decimals)	0.3	5.5
16	CARRY	(the problem involves carrying between columns)	1.6	6.6
17	TABLES	(there is explicit use of tables or number-bonds)	0.4	1.9
	TOTAL**	(any number work)	14.7	17.8

Notes * Item observed on less than 0.005% of observations.
** Note that the TOTALS in Tables 3.1 to 3.5 are not the same as the sum of the individual categories because more than one category may be coded for a particular observation.

time spent on both practical mathematics and mathematical concepts should be noted. Not all of the 'practical mathematics' observations actually involved practical work. Some merely involved calculations using the various units of measurement, for example, sums involving units of length would be coded under this heading, but a 'true' practical mathematics activity, involving the actual measurement of length, would be indicated by the use of the category APARAT (apparatus) together with the practical mathematics category. In infant classes 4.4 per cent of mathematics observations included the use of apparatus in practical mathematics, while for junior classes the corresponding figure was 5 per cent. In the totals that are given for the 'practical mathematics' categories, SYMMET and SHAPE are only included where these do not appear in conjunction with a coding of ART. The relationships between pairs of categories will be treated in later sections.

Compared with the other practical categories, the frequencies for WEIGH, AREA, VOLUME, TEMP were low. Compared to SETS in the mathematical concepts table (3.3) SCALE, LOGIC, and NTWORK were also low, showing the rarity of these kinds of activities. Thus although considerable time was spent on mathematics, more than was first suggested as reasonable for the National Curriculum, much of this time involved basic numerical computation rather than problem-solving and practical activity.

Table 3.2 Curriculum categories for practical mathematics

No.	Category	Meaning	% of observations Infants	Juniors
18	LENGTH	(either sums about lengths, or measuring length)	1.9	2.7
19	WEIGH	(either weighing or sums about weight)	0.6	0.8
20	TIME	(either measuring time or sums about time)	1.4	1.7
21	AREA	(either measurement or sums about area)	0.1	0.7
22	VOLUME	(either measuring or sums about volume)	0.5	0.5
23	ANGLES	(angles are involved in the problem)	0.1	1.0
24	SYMMET	(the problem uses symmetry, e.g., art)	0.4	0.6
25	SHAPE	(shapes must be recognized or measured)	3.9	3.7
26	MONEY	(recognizing, counting, using, or sums about money)	0.8	2.6
100	TEMP	(temperature)	0.04	0.03
	TOTAL	(any practical mathematics)	8.2	10.4

Table 3.3 Curriculum categories for mathematical concepts

No.	Category	Meaning	% of observations Infants	Juniors
27	SETS	(classification into sets, or unions and intersections)	3.1	1.4
28	SCALE	(ratios of fractions, e.g., on maps)	0.00	0.6
29	LOGIC	(logical puzzles, writing computer programs)	0.04	0.5
30	MATRIX	(using two-dimensional tables of data)	0.1	1.2
31	GRAPHS	(graphs, bar-charts, pie-charts, etc.)	1.1	2.0
32	NTWORK	(networks, e.g., flow-charts, road maps)	0.02	0.2
	TOTAL	(any mathematical concepts)	4.5	5.0

3.4 The language curriculum

Table 3.4 gives details of aspects of pupils' work with language, here defined solely in terms of the components of language work (sentence, poem, story, etc.) rather than the activity (e.g. reading, writing). These other aspects of language will be treated in different sections.

The large amount of work with extended passages of text for juniors is particularly noteworthy. Even infants did a fair amount of work involving extended passages. However, work concentrating on the smaller units of language is not neglected.

It can be seen from Table 3.4 that a considerable proportion of the pupils' time at both junior and infant level concerned language work to do with sentence construction and completion or filling in missing words as in cloze procedure. Typical of such tasks in the infant classroom would be writing out a sentence from a worksheet and filling in a missing word as in 'There are (five) dogs in the picture'. The observed frequencies were similar for both infants and juniors.

Table 3.4 Curriculum categories for language work

No.	Category	Meaning	% of observations Infants	Juniors
101	LETTER	(work concentrates on letters, e.g. handwriting)	5.4	2.7
102	PARTWD	(work uses partwords, e.g. phonics with letter-pairs)	3.0	1.7
103	WHOLWD	(Work concentrates on whole words, e.g. CLOZE)	13.4	11.7
104	SYMBOL	(work uses symbols other than numbers, e.g. map-work)	1.4	2.0
105	SENTNC	(work concentrates on sentences, e.g. creative writing by infants, or cloze sentences – this is WHOLWD also)	11.0	10.4
106	PASSAG	(work with extended passage, e.g. creative writing, reading aloud by juniors, following long instructions)	12.1	23.2
107	POEM	(involves metre or rhyme, e.g. song, story in verse)	2.9	3.6
108	STORY	(the teacher reads or tells a story)	7.0	4.4
109	FOREGN	(foreign language, including ESL)	–	–
	TOTAL	(any work involving any of the above categories except SYMBOL)	35.4	38.8

The trends in the remaining categories were as expected. There was more STORY telling in infant classrooms than in junior (7 per cent and 4.4 per cent respectively) and also more work involving LETTER and the use of PARTWorDs. Within that part of the curriculum specifically concerned with the components of language work, the provisional conclusion can be drawn that pupils in small schools experienced a range of activities.

3.5 Other subject areas within the curriculum

Apart from mathematics and language work, many other areas of content are of importance in the primary school curriculum. Table 3.5 lists the main categories here, and shows how often work within each of these was observed. The rows for science (SCIENC), social subjects (SOCIAL), and expressive arts (FINART) show the total observations in any of these areas. In the analysis these were the three main subject divisions within which the individual categories were differentiated.

Table 3.5 Curriculum categories for topic (Subject headings, often, but not always, part of topic work)

No.	Category	Meaning	% of observations Infants	Juniors
89	HIST	(work with historical elements)	2.1	7.1
90	GEOG	(work with geographical elements)	0.7	3.6
91	BIOLGY	(work with elements of biological study)	3.0	3.5
92	PHYSCS	(work with elements of physical science)	0.4	4.6
93	ENVIRS	(work having aspects of environmental studies)	3.9	4.6
94	ART	(art and craft, including cooking, woodwork)	14.6	15.3
95	DRAMA	(dramatic work: plays, puppet plays)	3.2	2.4
96	MUSIC	(playing, listening, singing, or moving to music)	7.0	5.3
97	RELIG	(religious studies of any kind)	2.6	4.6
98	MOVEMT	(movement: gymnastics, dance)	5.7	3.3
99	SCLMRL	(social and moral education; must go into general concepts)	8.4	4.3
TOTAL TOPIC		(any work involving any of the above categories)	39.8	43.1
SUBTOTALS WITHIN TOPIC:				
	SCIENCE	(BIOLOGY, PHYSCS, OR ENVIRS)	6.2	11.4
	SOCIAL	(HIST, GEOG, RELIG, OR SCLMRL)	13.2	18.0
	FINART	(ART, DRAMA, MUSIC, OR MOVEMT)	16.5	25.1

By far the largest subject frequency for both infants and juniors was art and craft. This had about the same frequency for both groups (14.6 per cent and 15.3 per cent respectively). The percentage of observations for each of the other artistic categories (DRAMA, MUSIC, MOVEMT), however, declined from the infant to the junior classes. This reduction was more than compensated by the increase in frequency of the 'academic' subject areas of science, history, and geography in junior classes. The observation that juniors were engaged in activities in some science-related area for more than 11 per cent of the time in small schools is in contrast to the findings of the APU survey of science in junior schools, which indicated that in most schools only 5 per cent of lessons involved any science work (APU 1983). The increase is presumably a result of the priority which has subsequently been given to primary school science in many local authorities. The form this science teaching takes, and the other items in the curriculum associated with it, will be discussed in a later section.

If frequencies for each of the subjects listed are totalled and divided by the total given at the bottom of Table 3.5, the ratio is about 1.3:1 for both infants and juniors, showing that in about 30 per cent of the observations two or more of the separate subjects were used to describe the same task. The most common occurrences of overlap were much as expected: environmental studies was correlated with geography and biology; drama, music and movement were correlated with each other; music was correlated with RE, for example, in hymn or carol singing. There were no other significant correlations, suggesting that there was little integration between these subjects *within* the tasks in which pupils were engaged. The 'snapshot' nature of our observation, however, gives no indication of the extent of subject integration *between* tasks, but data from the 'day sheets' show that for 8.4 per cent of the time pupils were working within a class theme, for example 'Christmas', again suggesting a relatively low level of integration.

3.6 Media of information and expression

An important concept in the PRISMS study of the curriculum was the identification of the media which pupils used to take in information, instructions, and ideas, and the media which they used to perform their set tasks. A large part of the primary school curriculum seems to be aimed at giving children practice in using different kinds of media for these two purposes. Nine different ways of taking in information and expressing results were coded by observers. Mathematics tasks involving writing only numbers were not included in the analysis.

By far the most commonly used medium for both infant and juniors was LISTEN. This is perhaps an unexpected finding given the emphasis in the prevailing ideology of primary school practice on pupil autonomy. The LISTENing medium was used for 30 per cent of the time. Five of the other media, READing, OBSERVing, WRITing, VOCAL presentation (talking or singing), and DRAWing (painting or crayoning), were used for between 15 per cent and 23 per cent of the time. Expressing oneself through MATERiaLs (the use of clay, Lego, etc.) was used slightly less frequently (13 per cent) and ACTing OUT by means of movement or dance even less frequently, for only 8 per cent of all observation. HARDWaRe, the operation of equipment such as computers and tape recorders was rarely used. In general, reading and writing were the dominant activities in both the infant and junior classes although there were some interesting relationships between the use of particular media with other curriculum categories. These will be discussed when the findings relating to the remaining main categories on the observation schedule have been presented.

3.7 Criteria of performance

When teachers set tasks in the classroom they define the performance expected of the pupils according to certain criteria. Such criteria were recorded by the PRISMS observers under six categories. The three main categories used were CREATE, where pupils were required to produce for themselves, COPY, where pupils had to reproduce as accurately as possible in the same medium (for example, transcribing a passage from a text into a handwritten account), and LEARNing where pupils were expected to memorize material such as spelling.

Frequently pupils were required to produce an imaginative response to an idea. They might, for example, be asked to respond to a picture or a piece of written work such as a poem. The category CREATE was used here and, for both infants and juniors, approximately 16 per cent of the time was spent on work of this kind.

COPYing, however, was another frequent activity. Usually this involved writing where children were engaged either in handwriting practice or making fair copies of a piece of work which had been constructed in draft form. Sometimes also questions or written instructions were copied down or a passage would be recorded prior to filling in missing words. Drawings were also often copied from books. COPYing was more frequent in infant than junior classes, possibly because these kinds of exercises took the infant pupils longer. LEARNing or memorizing activities were comparatively rare (2.7 per cent infants and 2.2 per cent juniors).

An important distinction was made between tasks which required pupils to COPY, that is, to use the same medium, and tasks in which they were expected to transform information from one medium to another. In COPYing pupils were expected to reproduce the material in the same medium as accurately as possible. In many cases, however, pupils were expected to produce something which, although similar to the original, had to be translated into another medium. This process was termed MAPping. Thus a pupil reading aloud would be producing something which was clearly different from the original text but the spoken words would still be expected to 'match' the written ones and the teacher would evaluate the result by means of this criterion. It was this concept of a match between different media which was incorporated into the category of MAPping. MAPping was about as common as COPYing (19 per cent infants, 18 per cent juniors).

The most frequent kinds of MAPping were from LISTENing to VOCAL expression. This included all cases where pupils were required to repeat what they had heard but not verbatim. The next most common form of MAPping was from READ to VOCAL expression and from READ to WRITing. The former was an exercise in reading aloud and the latter was more than simply copying, involving some task such as making a summary of information. Matching from LISTENing to WRITing and LISTENing to DRAWing were very rare compared to other instances of LISTEN MAPpings.

In summary, there were certain important pairs of media which teachers could have used to provide opportunities for pupils to practise MAPping exercises. It appears from the PRISMS evidence that there were particular preferred MAPpings which children were encouraged to use while others, although logically possible, were somewhat neglected.

The remaining categories in this section concerned TESTing, where juniors spent approximately 1.5 per cent of their time being assessed either formally or by individual diagnostic tests. Only 0.2 per cent of this category was observed in infant classes. The final criterion category was PLAY. Generally PLAY was not associated with any other criteria such as CREATE which would also have been recorded had children been set a specific imaginative task. PLAY was fairly common in infant classes (7.7 per cent) but little used at junior level.

Games which can be defined according to the players' success either against an opponent or against a problem situation were analysed separately from other forms of PLAY. Such activities, for example, playing Scrabble or netball, were comparatively rare. PHYSiCaL activities such as PE and football accounted for only 2.5 per cent of all observations in infant classes and 2.3 per cent in junior ones. EDUCatioNaL games or puzzles took up 1.9 and 1.3 per cent respectively of class time in infants and juniors. It should be remembered, however, that observations were carried out only in the classroom or in adjacent areas of the school such as the hall. Many small schools did not possess additional accommodation of this kind so that some games took place further afield, including activities such as swimming. From the 'day sheets', the estimated amount of physical activities of infants and junior classes combined was 6.4 per cent. This may still underestimate the total extent of such physical activity because in schools without a hall more PE takes place in the open during the summer term when observations were not made.

3.8 Actions with curricular material

Observers also recorded the actions that pupils took to convert the information which they obtained to the presentation required. These action categories were numerous and only the most common will be described here.

By far the most common action was SELECTion. Both infant and junior classes spent about 15 per cent of the time selecting items from some defined set. Such activities included selection of letters to complete words or selecting answers from a number of listed choices. The categories ANSWERing (5.1 per cent infant, 8.2 per cent junior) and DISCUSsing (6.5 per cent infants, 7.8 per cent junior) were the next most frequently observed activities. ANSWERing did not include mathematics questions since most of this kind of work involved pupils in answering sets of questions from workcards. If this type of action was included then pupils spent about 30 per cent of their time formulating answers. It was noticeable, however, that when ANSWERing and DISCUSsing, pupils were generally responding to the teacher's questions rather than initiating their own.

There were other activities which pupils had to undertake in order to complete their tasks. These involved establishing different kinds of relationships as part of the task. For example, MATCHing where pupils had to compare two objects in order to identify differences, or ORDERing where pupils had to put a number of objects into order of size or importance. MATCHing was more common in infant classes than juniors (7.0 per cent compared to 2.7 per cent). More complex thinking tasks such as ORDERing, COMPARison, and PREDICtion occurred far less frequently, but were more common in junior than in infant classes.

Some tasks required several steps such as PLANning, ASSESSing progress, and REPORTing results, though these were comparatively rare. There were also stages where children had to wait, for example, for their turn on the apparatus or were required to tidy up or fetch materials as part of the task. Overall WAITing took up less than 5 per cent of time in both infant and junior classrooms, receiving INSTRuctions around 5 per cent in both, and ROUTINe activities nearly 9 per cent of time in infant classes and under 8 per cent in junior classes.

3.9 Resources and equipment

A recurring theme in the educational provision of small schools concerns the access which pupils have to various kinds of resources and equipment. The categories used to record this information by the observers can be found in Appendix I.

Three kinds of resources stand out as being far more frequently used than any other. For more than a quarter of the pupils' time they were engaged on tasks for which the teacher (TCHR) was a resource. This category was coded whenever information from the teacher was necessary in order for the task to be completed, as in oral work, story, class music sessions and so on. When the teacher's contribution was limited to giving instructions about the form that the task would take or marking work then this category was not used. Every occurrence of the category therefore indicates that the completion of the task required the direct involvement of the teacher.

Published workcards (SCHEME) were used as a resource for more than a fifth of the time in both infant and junior classrooms. Apparatus was in use for about 15 per cent of the time in junior classrooms and for

21 per cent of the time in infant classes. Apparatus included things like Unifix cubes for counting exercises, tools for craft work, toys for play, and so on.

The use of information from other PUPILs was similar in both infant and junior classrooms (between 7 and 8 per cent in each). This category indicated the extent to which pupils were required to share and co-operate. The use of books for reference increased, as might be expected, in junior classrooms, as did the use of the blackboard. The use of the ENVIRoNment as a resource was relatively low compared to other categories. The category referred to making use of what was available in the classroom or the surrounding environment as, for example, when children paced out the perimeter of the school building. It should not therefore be equated with studying the school and its surroundings as part of environmental study.

The use of computers in the junior classroom was not high. It should be remembered, however, that the field work took place during the first year in which most primary schools had received their computer and very little use was made during the autumn term because the teachers themselves were learning how to use the machines. If we assume that the 1.9 per cent use for juniors was mainly concentrated in the spring term then the average annual use would be of the order of 3.5 per cent. In the primary school computers are used by small groups of children or by individual pupils. If we assume, for the purpose of calculation, that the figure of 3.5 per cent consisted entirely of individual usage, then a single machine would have been operating for 90 per cent of the time.

It appears also that infant classes in particular, and to a certain extent junior classes, made use of recorded broadcasts, both radio and television, as the major focus of tasks. In general, tape recordings appear to have been normally used as a substitute for the RADio in order to gain access to programmes which had been broadcast at inconvenient times.

The above descriptions of the curriculum are complex. They involve more than simply a categorization of the subject content. When describing a task observers were able to select from over a hundred categories. Within this complexity, however, certain patterns did emerge.

Some categories were comparatively rarely observed, such as the use of the immediate environment. However, given the large number of activities on which pupils were engaged, it is only to be expected that the frequencies of some of the categories on the observation schedule would be very low. On the other hand, some categories such as listening and using the teacher as a resource pervaded many of the curriculum activities, suggesting that the curriculum of small schools in the PRISMS project involved considerable amounts of teacher-directed instruction.

In the past this strategy has often been associated with single subject teaching (Bennett 1976). The question of how far a similar relationship existed in PRISMS will now be examined.

3.10   Curriculum integration and the small school

Central to the rhetoric of the primary school curriculum in recent years has been the belief that concepts and skills can be generalized and practised across different areas of content. It is widely held that children in primary schools should learn a range of skills and perhaps attitudes to those skills which would serve them well in later life. Such arguments underpin the case for a broad integrated primary school curriculum.

As part of the PRISMS research we gave particular attention to the way in which certain areas of curriculum content were associated with certain skills and activities. In order to make this analysis manageable it was necessary to collapse some of the individual curriculum categories. For example, categories from COUNT to TABLES in Appendix I were designated NUMBER. SCIENCe included BIOLoGY, PHYSiCal Science, and ENVIRonmental Studies. FINe ART encompassed art, drama, music, and movement. The full list of the collapsed curriculum categories is given in Appendix II.

In small schools integration occurred far less frequently than one might expect in the light of recommended practice. For example, in infant classes 15 per cent of all observations involved number work of which 17 per cent involved some element of practical mathematics, but only 0.5 per cent of number activities were associated with science work. At junior level nearly a third of all number activities involved practical mathematics but only 3 per cent involved science. Science activities in the small primary school therefore provided relatively few opportunities for pupils to measure distances, time, and weight. Although at both junior and infant level numerical calculation was positively correlated with a range of skills that might be expected to relate to work of this kind (practical mathematics, mathematical concepts, and matching), there were other important areas such as creative activities and oral work where mathematics was negatively correlated. On the other hand, individualized working, making substantial use of published work schemes, was the main way in which mathematics was taught.

Language could have been expected to offer many opportunities for teachers to impart a variety of skills and methods of learning. Language was indeed positively correlated with a range of skills such as writing, copying, selecting appropriate answers, and reading from various sources. Poetry offered pupils the opportunity to practise vocal and learning (memorizing) skills. On the other hand, language work was negatively correlated with certain practices which might be expected to have been related to it, for example, some aspects of language work were negatively associated with art work and drawing. There were positive correlations in the science work with such skills as assessing, observing, analysing, and discussing. Art work was particularly associated with drawing, the use of three-dimensional materials, and creative work, but negatively correlated with literary activity and with music. Musical aspects of the curriculum went with listening, movement, drama, and pupils expressing themselves vocally. It was also associated with religious education which, as already stated, was in part a function of the amount of hymn singing in many of the small schools in the sample. For social and moral aspects of the curriculum the teacher acted as a major resource. SoCiaL and MoRaL education was negatively correlated with the use of published materials, unlike the small amount of work in history which even at this early stage of the pupils' schooling was mainly associated with the use of textbooks. Geography often involved working on matrices, charts, and problems of scale, and was generally correlated with ENVIRonmental Studies.

Media categories were associated, as might be expected, with certain curriculum areas. For example, READ and WRITE were generally associated with language work, as expected. But language work was also associated with OBSERVation which in turn was highly correlated with LISTENing. This suggests that much observation concerned teacher demonstration rather than pupil activity. Indeed, LISTENing was highly correlated with the teacher as a resource. OBSERVation in junior classes was, however, also positively correlated with drawing and the use of three-dimensional materials, suggesting a more structured approach such as, for example, sketching a model rather than, as would be more common in the infant classes, drawing a picture and colouring it in.

In both infant and junior classes much writing and about a third of reading and drawing were associated with COPYing activities. Use of materials was associated with SELECTion, for example choosing a library book or picking out particular coloured bricks from a box. Only the obvious media such as WRITing, DRAWing, ACTing OUT, and using MATERiaLs had a large creative component. MAPping, the transforming of material from one medium to another, was one of the few cases of an activity which was associated with most of the other media. Most LISTENing and VOCAL activity or ACTing OUT made use of the teacher as a resource.

The various actions and criteria relating to the pupil's task were also described earlier. The way in which the criteria were distributed across various categories was of interest. Creative work was largely associated with FINe ART (ART, MUSIC, MOVEMenT, and DRAMA) and with writing. Not surprisingly, most work involving explanation of meanings of words and concepts was associated with language work and most matching exercises were associated with some aspect of mathematics.

These data suggest that 'creative' exercises were seen by teachers in terms of 'free expression' rather than an opportunity to integrate different media and different resources to achieve a particular form. Creative activity in the sample of small primary schools observed was a less complex activity, in terms of the number of skills, resources, and activities being exercised, than was the case with MAPping activities, which by their nature were more structured.

The use of resources also showed close associations with specific subject areas of the curriculum. For example, teacher-prepared materials were mostly used in language work and schemes were particularly associated with number work and with language. The teacher as a resource occurred in most subject areas though less often in mathematics. EQUIPment was most frequently associated with FINe ART, while collaborative work (using other pupils as a resource) was used infre- quently although it did occur across most subject areas and in particular social studies and games. It was also associated with listening, oral work, and role play and with middle and higher order skills.

In general, therefore, what is being said is that the PRISMS study affords little evidence that integration occurred as part of a distinct planning process where teachers were concerned to provide opportunities for pupils to practise skills across a range of curriculum areas. Where associations occurred between various curriculum categories these appeared to be the result of a particular choice of task rather than of a policy of rational curriculum planning. One further way of demonstrating this was to carry out a cluster analysis of the various curriculum records coded by the observers to see if any general patterns emerged. The assumption of such a cluster analysis was that each curriculum record in a particular cluster would have more characteristics and categories in common with other members of its own cluster than with the curriculum records in other clusters. Such patterns would therefore indicate particular forms of 'integrated' activity.

The analysis, however, showed that this assumption was incorrect. Although there were common elements between clusters, for example in 15 per cent of the sixteen mathematics clusters, workcards or schemes were involved in 100 per cent of the cases, there were also considerable variations. The same was true of other clusters such as oral and written language.

It is, of course, possible that the reason for so many different cluster arrangements was that different teachers held different 'theories' about the nature of the integrated curriculum, but the alternative hypothesis that the large number of clusters was the result of the unique demands made by a specific task rather than as a result of a particular planned sequence of tasks within an integrated framework, would appear more tenable. Certain activities such as number work and language were associated with certain skills and resources but the opportunities to make use of these elements in other areas of the curriculum were limited. If, therefore, the breadth of the primary curriculum is to be defined in terms of the range of curriculum activities taking place, there is ample evidence from this chapter that small schools meet this criterion. There is less evidence, however, that teachers in small schools endeavoured to develop in their pupils the ability to transfer particular skills from one area of the curriculum to another.

It would, however, be a mistake to assume that in this respect teachers in small schools differed from primary teachers in general. This conclusion receives further support in the next chapter where the organization of the curriculum is considered. It will be shown that a further explanation for the association of discrete sets of skills within specific curriculum areas arose from the practice of PRISMS teachers during a teaching session (usually lasting around one hour) of concentrating on two curriculum areas for most of the time, either leaving some pupils to work independently on another activity or requiring all pupils in the class to work in the same two curriculum areas. Similar patterns of organization were recorded by Mortimore *et al.* (1988).

PRISMS teachers therefore seem to have operated similar practices to teachers in larger schools, at least in the Inner London Education Authority (ILEA). Mortimore's study involved only junior pupils. What is interesting about the PRISMS findings, however, is that the patterns in infant and junior classrooms were not dissimilar. The integrated day was not, therefore, more common in the infants than it was in the juniors.

3.11 The curriculum in the small school: class size and vertical grouping

As part of the PRISMS study seventy-three of the curriculum categories were correlated with class size, school size, and with the extent of vertical grouping in these classes. For this analysis some of the less frequently used curriculum categories were combined. For class and school size few aspects of the observed curriculum appeared to be associated in any way. In each case the number of significant correlations obtained was not greater than would have been expected to have occurred by chance, given the large number of curriculum categories involved.

In the case of vertical grouping there were a few more significant associations with the curriculum categories than might have arisen through chance, but no clear-cut pattern emerged. However, there were more interesting relationships between the curriculum, the age of the pupils, and the age range within the class.

First we shall examine in greater detail the relationship between the age of pupils and the curriculum followed. For example, most time was spent on mathematics around the ages of 8 and 9 when about a fifth of the curriculum experiences of pupils involved number work. As might be expected, older pupils were more likely to undertake work involving a greater number of digits. Multiplication and division work peaked at the age of 9 and tables at the age of 8. The older pupils (9+, 10+, and 11+) spent between 40 and 50 per cent of their time on activities involving sizeable elements of language work. Not surprisingly, work involving individual letters and parts of words were more common with younger pupils, and work involving longer passages took place more frequently in the top junior classes. In other subject areas older pupils tended to study history and geography more often but did less drama and less social and moral education. In primary science the trend was not linear, since 8-year-old pupils spent most time on this activity.

The range of skills experienced by pupils also varied with age. Most writing was done by 7- and 8-year-olds while the youngest pupils spent more time on art, drawing, and role play. Older pupils tended to engage in a range of higher order activities such as planning, questioning, predicting, and assessing, all of which required some analytical ability. The use of the teacher as a resource did not vary across the age range in these small primary schools. Older pupils made more use of textbooks and reference books but as pupils grew older less use was made of equipment.

These results are much as expected. With vertically grouped classes, however, this orderly progression in the curriculum raises interesting and important questions about the 'match' of the work to the child's age and ability. For example, in mixed-age classes where the range exceeded twelve months, did the teacher's choice of curriculum activity favour the younger or the older pupils, or were activities chosen so that they differentiated between pupils of different ages? Our analysis provided clear evidence that the experience of, for example, a 9-year-old pupil in a class with an average age of 9 was different from that of a 9-year-old pupil in a class with an average age of either 8 or 10. The amount of time which such pupils spent on different aspects of the curriculum was significantly influenced, not only by the age of the pupils, but also by the mean age of the class to which the pupil belonged. If a 9-year-old pupil was in a class with a mean age of 10, then this child would have a curriculum experience which was 'older' than that of a 9-year-old pupil in a class with a mean age of 8.

It would appear, therefore, that teachers in small schools, with vertically grouped classes, tended to teach to the 'majority' group in the age range. It could clearly be of benefit for a younger child to be placed within a class having a majority of older pupils. Part of the explanation for this finding can be found in the practice of some schools of promoting a number of more able younger children into a class of a higher age group in order to even up numbers. Nevertheless, there must also be an element of 'self-fulfilling prophecy' associated with such a strategy.

3.12 Comparison of the curriculum in PRISMS with other studies

The findings presented in the previous chapter regarding the background of teachers in the PRISMS study suggested that they expressed opinions and had educational histories which were little different from teachers working in larger schools. Given this finding it might be expected that the curriculum provision in small schools would also be similar to that offered in larger schools and this appears to be so. The evidence for this assertion is drawn from two main sources. The first of these is the ORACLE study, although the main field work took place seven years prior to the PRISMS observations. More recently, however, two large-scale studies, one of which used the ORACLE observation system, have been completed in the London area. The first of these, at junior level, was conducted by Peter Mortimore and his colleagues of the ILEA Research and Statistics Branch (Mortimore *et al.* 1988). The second was conducted by Barbara Tizard (Tizard *et al.* 1988) and concerned younger children of infant age. To make comparisons it is necessary to normalize the PRISMS data in order to reduce the percentages to 100. In the ORACLE study only one curriculum category was recorded at each time interval, while in the PRISMS study a combination of categories could be used. The normalized figures are shown in brackets in the following tables. From the data it can be seen that provision in different subject areas was approximately similar when allowances are made for the different ways of recording. It can be seen, for example, in Table 3.6, that the amount of practical mathematics in the two studies was very close indeed, but that ORACLE pupils did more work with mathematical concepts while PRISMS pupils did more work in number (in this table practical maths involves the use of apparatus, as it was defined in the ORACLE study; calculations involving units of weight, etc. but no apparatus have been added to number work). PRISMS pupils did considerably more reading and oral work than ORACLE pupils, and they did much less writing. This is probably because reading and oral work in PRISMS were recorded throughout the entire curriculum, while in ORACLE they were recorded

Maurice Galton

only in connection with language work. Art and craft was more common in the PRISMS classrooms, while general studies was less common in infant classrooms, but these differences are nowhere near as large as those for reading, writing, and oral work.

Table 3.6 Comparison of curriculum in PRISMS and ORACLE classes (% of observations)

Activity	PRISMS categories	PRISMS	(Infants)	PRISMS	(Juniors)	ORACLE
Number	NUMBER	18.5	(17.5)	23.2	(18.4)	14.0
Practical maths	PRMATH	4.4	(4.2)	5.0	(4.0)	4.3
Abstract maths	MCNCPT	4.5	(4.3)	5.0	(4.0)	10.2
Reading	READ AND LANG	14.6	(13.8)	17.6	(14.0)	4.4
Writing	(WRITE WITH CREATE) AND LANG	11.5	(10.9)	13.8	(11.0)	21.2
Spoken English	(LISTEN OR VOCAL) AND LANG	13.5	(12.8)	13.6	(10.8)	2.0
Creative writing	CREATE AND WRITE	5.0	(4.7)	6.7	(5.3)	8.5
Art and craft	ARTCR	14.6	(13.8)	15.3	(12.2)	10.9
General studies	SCIENCE OR HUMAN	19.1	(18.1)	25.7	(20.4)	24.4
Total		105.7	(100)	125.9	(100)	99.9

Key:
1. The use of AND indicates both categories must be present to be counted.
2. The use of WITH indicates the first but not the second category must always be present to be counted.
3. The use of OR indicates only one of the categories must be present to be counted.
4. The figures in parentheses have been normalized to a total of 100%

Table 3.7 shows the comparison for the main subject areas only. Thus the three mathematics categories have been put together, as have the four language categories. For the ORACLE results this is a matter of simple addition, but for the PRISMS data the overlaps between the various categories have had to be allowed for, or else they would be counted twice and so inflate the total for the compound category. Thus the totals for the first two categories in Table 3.7 are smaller than the sums of the corresponding rows in Table 3.6 in the PRISMS columns.

This combination of categories shows that, in these broad terms, the curricula in the two sets of schools correspond quite closely, although, as shown in Table 3.6, the detailed composition, particularly of the language curriculum, is different. However, the combination, with overlaps within categories being excluded, shows that there was slightly less mathematics work done in the PRISMS schools than in the

ORACLE ones, with a corresponding increase in the amount of art and craft work in the PRISMS schools. The amount of language work and general studies was quite similar in the two sets of junior classrooms.

Table 3.7 The pupils' curriculum (ORACLE and PRISMS) excluding play and music

Activity	PRISMS	(Infants)	PRISMS	(Juniors)	ORACLE
			% of observations		
Maths	21.5	(23.7)	24.8	(23.7)	28.5
Language	35.4	(39.1)	38.8	(37.1)	36.1
Art and craft	14.6	(16.1)	15.3	(14.6)	10.9
General	19.1	(21.1)	25.7	(24.6)	24.4
Total	90.6	(100.0)	104.6	(100.0)	100.0

In the Mortimore *et al.* (1988) study very little detail concerning the curriculum balance was given. The study, like ORACLE, was more concerned to examine the interactions between teachers and pupils and to look for relationships between these processes and pupil performance.

Table 3.8 Comparisons of curriculum in PRISMS and the ILEA junior classes

Activity	PRISMS (Juniors)	ILEA (Juniors)
	% of observations	
Quiet reading	14.0	6.3
Language (excluding reading)	27.1	23.5
Maths	26.4	29.1
Project (mainly humanities and science)	20.4	13.8
Art and craft	12.2	6.8
Mixed activity (including maths and language)	–	20.5

Source (ILEA): *Junior School Project, Part B. Differences between Junior Schools*, ILEA Research and Statistics Branch, 1986.

Table 3.8 is an attempt to construct a table of curriculum provision making use of data available from an interim report of the ILEA junior study. The curriculum categories do not correspond completely to those of either ORACLE or of PRISMS. For example, the ILEA data have a 'mixed' category of which little is said except that it included some mathematics and language. The presence of these two subjects, therefore, helps to distinguish the category from that of the project which Mortimore *et al.* (1988) state consisted mainly of history, geography, and science. These three subjects, although they might be focused around a common theme, would rarely be taught simultaneously. Presumably, therefore, the 'mixed' category denotes cross curriculum integrated activity where at least two subjects were being taught simultaneously. Elsewhere Mortimore reports that a large proportion of this kind of work involved art and craft (Mortimore *et al.* 1988).

The discrepancy between the percentage of art and craft in the ILEA study and in PRISMS could well be a function, therefore, of the different classifications employed in the two studies. The same could be true for language but not for mathematics, since even without the inclusion of some additional mathematics from the 'mixed' category, the ILEA teachers spent more time on mathematics than did teachers in the PRISMS study. The PRISMS reading category included more activities than quiet reading and should be expected to take up a greater proportion of time. What is most revealing from these figures, however, is the greater amount of time devoted by the PRISMS teachers to science and humanities. This is the one area where a lack of specialist teaching in the small schools might have been expected to result in fewer activities of this kind.

When one turns to the descriptions of how the ILEA teachers organized the curriculum, the similarities with PRISMS become more marked. Ninety-five per cent of the teachers in Mortimore *et al.*'s (1988) study taught language as a separate subject for most of the time. Nearly all the teachers followed a scheme. Forty-three per cent of the teachers, for example, used the *Sound Sense Series,* while a further 25 per cent used *Science Research Associates* (SRA) cards. Mortimore and his colleagues (1988) reported that most teachers in mixed-age classes did not vary the language work for pupils of different ages. In mathematics most teachers again used a single scheme. The *Fletcher* series was the most popular (40 per cent) followed by *Maths Adventure* (31 per cent), while the *Scottish Primary Maths* scheme was used by a further 20 per cent of teachers. Only 28 per cent of the teachers stressed the importance of practical work in mathematics. In project work there was little differentiation. This work was mostly undertaken as a whole class activity even when the classes were vertically grouped (Mortimore *et al.* 1988).

Turning to the infant age range, it is more difficult to make comparisons between the present study and the research carried out by Barbara Tizard and her colleagues in inner London schools. The Tizard study used a different observational technique from that developed for ORACLE and later adapted for PRISMS. The backgrounds of the children were also very different. The Tizard study was designed to focus specifically on questions of ethnicity. In twelve out of the thirty-three classes sampled, the proportion of children of Afro-Caribbean origin was greater than 30 per cent. Tizard also reported that in most of the schools there was a number of children from other ethnic groups, most frequently from India and Pakistan. The majority of these schools were also in materially very disadvantaged areas (Tizard *et al.* 1988).

Only in the one or two inner city schools in the PRISMS project could conditions be said to be similar. One would predict, therefore, that in Tizard's study the proportions of time devoted to all language activities would be much greater than in PRISMS. This is shown to be so in Table 3.9 where a comparison between the curriculum of the two samples of infant schools is provided. The additional amount of time spent on reading could also be accounted for by the different backgrounds of the children in the two samples. Further comparisons are difficult, however, because in the Tizard study there was no category for science and humanities activities. Presumably some of this activity was recorded, along with art and craft, as construction or according to the language demands made. Even so, and allowing for the particular difficulties of the London inner city schools, the curriculum of the PRISMS infant sample appears to be as wide and covers all the main subject areas. The lack of specialist subject teachers in the small schools does not appear to prevent teachers from providing this wide coverage.

Table 3.9 Comparison of curriculum in PRISMS infants and London top infant classes (Tizard *et al.* 1988).

Activity	% of observations	
	PRISMS (Infants)	LONDON (Top Infants)
Reading	12.9	18.0
Writing	14.5	11.4
Oral language	11.9	29.5
Maths	24.2	17.5
Art and craft and construction	12.9	20.6
General studies (science and humanities)	15.9	–
Free play	6.8	3.0

Like the Mortimore study, the descriptions provided by Tizard *et al.* (1988) of the way in which the curriculum was organized show striking similarities with the descriptions obtained from the PRISMS study. Ninety-five per cent of teachers drew on some kind of published mathematics scheme, and more than three-quarters of these teachers used *Nuffield Mathematics*, either on its own or in combination with another scheme. Teachers were asked, by means of a curriculum check list, to describe what elements of the curriculum they had taught in their classes during the year. These lists showed a progression of mathematics items from early concepts in number, to simple written numbers, to number operations and measurement and recognition and handling of money. In writing children progressed from tracing over adult writing to copying and finally to producing their own sentences without a fixed model. Tizard *et al.* (1988) observed the same tendency, seen in PRISMS, for teachers to limit the extent of curriculum differentiation within a single class. There was, however, wide variation in the range of curriculum activities taught in different classes. For example, they report that about one third of top infant classes had introduced children to long division but that in one top infant class, written addition work had not yet been introduced, while in another children were working on complex vertical format division sums with remainders.

In general, therefore, after making allowances for the disproportionate number of children with special language difficulties in the Tizard sample, there was a general similarity between the two sets of data with regard to the three Rs and, in particular, the organization of curriculum activities and the progression of activities were somewhat similar. It needs to be pointed out, however, that in these London schools, less than half the school day (46 per cent) was devoted to learning activities in the classroom. Forty-three per cent of the remaining time was taken up in non-work activities such as dinner time, school breaks, lining up, tidying up, register time, and so on (Tizard *et al.* 1988). Although there are no comparable data for PRISMS schools over the whole sample, the data collected by one of the PRISMS observers and reported in Chapter Six suggest that no more than a third of the school day was, on average, taken up by non-work activities of this kind.

In one local authority studied, details of out-of-school time were collected. Taking the most extreme case, one group of infants had only 5 hours and 55 minutes of time at school each day. In all the schools studied, the highest total non-contact time observed was 2 hours 15 minutes. If these figures are combined they yield a figure for the maximum 'out-of-class time' of 38 per cent, 5 per cent lower than the average figure for the London schools. In the PRISMS calculation settling-in time, at the beginning of the lesson, was omitted, but in the local authority studied, time spent in transit, settling down, and waiting was reported as generally very low. In the twenty-three small school classes studied loss of time in class occurred in only 61 per cent of recorded occasions. This is in keeping with the general finding from the PRISMS study that, compared to ORACLE, PRISMS children engaged in greater amounts of work activity. Thus the amount of the school day given over to various curriculum activities in Table 3.9 was probably greater (in terms of actual number of hours and minutes) than was the case in these London schools.

In summary, therefore, the pattern of curriculum organization and the subject content appeared to be similar in our small schools and in these larger ones, when allowance was made for the different populations of pupils and the different ways in which the data were collected. There was no evidence from the data available that PRISMS teachers in small schools neglected areas of the curriculum such as humanities and science because of a shortage of specialist teaching. Indeed, the evidence seems to suggest that they may have carried out more activity in these subject areas. What does emerge from our study, however, is an apparent lack of planning in the organization of this curriculum. Pupils did have opportunities to experience different curriculum areas in ways which conform to current thinking about 'best' primary practice but these experiences appeared to be the result of opportunism rather than design. Teachers seemed to choose tasks because they fitted in with a particular topic or theme rather than because they afforded opportunities to practise a particular range of skills in a cross-curricular context.

The PRISMS study, however, is the only one available which provides such detailed systematic data on the primary school curriculum. It should not be inferred that larger schools, with more specialist teachers, are any more effective when planning the integration of content and skills. Indeed, there is evidence from studies of teachers' decision-making processes that many primary teachers reject the planning model. Calderhead (1984), for example, concludes on the basis of his review of research that:

> Research on teachers' planning suggest that teachers engage in a process that contrasts sharply with the prescribed rational planning model ... In reality the process of planning seems to be more appropriately conceptualised as a problem-solving process. Teachers, faced with a variety of factors, such as pupils with certain knowledge, abilities and interests, the availability of particular textbooks and materials, the syllabus, the timetable, the expectations of headteachers and others, and their own knowledge of previous teaching encounters, have to solve the problem of how to structure the time and experiences of pupils in the classroom. Teachers, it seems, adopt a much more pragmatic approach than that prescribed for curriculum design. Rather than start with a conception of what is to be achieved and deduce which classroom activities would therefore be ideal, teachers start with a conception of their working context and from that decide what is possible.
>
> (Calderhead 1984: 74)

Given the findings in Chapter Two, it is not surprising that we should reach such conclusions about the primary curriculum in small schools.

In Chapter Two we saw that in background, views, and training, PRISMS teachers differed little from their colleagues in larger, urban schools. With this similarity in background, therefore, it is only to be expected that the content and the manner of delivery of the curriculum in small schools should be similar to that in larger ones. If this is true of the curriculum, then we might expect it to be true also of ways in which teachers and pupils relate to each other in the classroom. Those who argue the case for small schools maintain that the smallness makes it possible for children to develop independence in a secure and friendly atmosphere. We should expect to see signs of this development in the way in which pupils and teacher interact in the classroom. The PRISMS findings on these and other questions of classroom behaviour are reported in the next chapter.

Chapter four

Teachers and pupils in small schools

Linda Hargreaves

4.1 Observing pupils and teachers

This chapter is about classroom life in small schools. It is based on
detailed observations of how the teachers and children go about their
work.

How much of the time, for example, do teachers and children spend
talking to each other? Who talks most and who listens most? What do
they usually talk about ... is it whether '16 x 3 = 48', the whereabouts of
the last pair of scissors, how to be good, or, even, life outside the
classroom? This chapter describes how the children are organized; how
the teacher presents the work, whether by telling, questioning, demonstrating, or by means of workcards; how much time the children spend
concentrating, daydreaming, or just chatting; and whether the teacher
can find moments to stand back and observe the children at work or
listen to their discussions.

These aspects of the social life of the classroom are the essence of
classroom relationships, which are of particular importance in a small
school where the same teacher and a small class may be together for
three or four years. They are a major component in the infrastructure of
the curriculum.

Certain issues in primary education have exaggerated implications
for teachers in small schools. Classroom organization, for example, and
its effects on how time is allocated to different curriculum areas is one
of these. In a large school, with at least one teacher for each year group,
the number of teachers should ensure that the children are exposed to a
variety of teaching styles and complementary strengths and interests. In
a small school, however, the effects of any slight, unintentional bias
towards a particular curriculum area must be multiplied by the number
of years that the children will stay with the same teacher.

Teachers in small schools are, of course, aware of these problems, as
shown in the PRISMS interviews and questionnaires, and they make

great efforts to develop their expertise to ensure that the children's experience is not restricted.

Nevertheless, research such as the *Beginning Teacher Education Study* (Rosenshine 1980) and surveys by Bennett *et al.* (1980) and Bassey (1978), show considerable variation in the time given to particular subject areas. In Bennett's study, for example, the time allowed for mathematics ranged from two-and-a-half to seven hours a week.

The amount of time spent on a curriculum area can be interpreted in various ways. It is possible for pupils and teacher to spend different amounts of time on the same area; consider, for example, the difference between the time a child spends reading to the teacher, and the time the teacher spends listening to children read, and organizing things so as to minimize interruptions. It is understandable then, if the teacher's response to subsequent questions about time spent on reading reflects the teacher's time rather than the few minutes accorded to each child. Furthermore, if the teacher supervises one area more closely than others, this may purvey a strong implicit message to the children about the relative importance of different aspects of the curriculum.

For these reasons, amongst others, classroom observation is essential to present a more objective picture of life in the classroom. In this chapter we shall look at these issues in the light of the PRISMS observations.

Two further issues of fundamental concern to small primary schools are class size and vertical grouping, and although these are discussed again in Chapter Five, they are dealt with briefly, where appropriate, here.

In this chapter the general aspects of the teachers' and the pupils' day will be presented. We shall also look at the relationship between classroom behaviour and the content of the curriculum, and the way in which teachers distributed their time, particularly when working with individual pupils. General details concerning the method of observation were given in Chapter One. In the section of the observation instrument used to record behaviour, the observer would focus on one of the 'target' children and record the child's behaviour every five seconds. After making ten such recordings and noting the child's task, the observer would focus on the next target child, and so on until all nine target pupils (the complete class in one case!) had been observed. The teacher was observed at six regular intervals during each lesson. Both the teacher's and the pupils' behaviour was recorded in terms of a set of categories of talk, non-interactive behaviour, audience, and location. These are shown in Appendix III.

The full observation frequencies totalled 130 per cent because, where two or more things were going on at once, the observer coded all of them. For example, if a child was painting when a friend asked, 'How did you mix that colour?' and at the same time the teacher announced to the whole class that it would be a 'wet play', the observer would place ticks in the pupil-pupil and the pupil-teacher interaction categories, as well as the 'quiet task' category, if the pupil continued to paint.

The PRISMS observation schedule was a modified form of the ORACLE schedule. Comparisons between the two studies can be made, provided that certain factors are borne in mind. First, the ORACLE study took place seven years before the PRISMS. Second, certain curriculum areas such as music, dance, and PE were excluded from the ORACLE observations. Third, the observations were made at different time intervals. In the ORACLE case the time interval was twenty-five seconds, and in the PRISMS study the observer recorded behaviour after five seconds.

As in Chapter Three, the PRISMS observations will also be compared with the two recent studies of London junior and infant schools by Mortimore *et al.* (1988) and by Tizard *et al.* (1988) respectively. At junior level, Mortimore has confirmed that the pattern of teacher-pupil interaction was substantially the same as that observed some seven years earlier in the ORACLE study. Thus there exists a degree of continuity in behaviour in junior primary classrooms in which to locate the interactions of teachers and pupils within the smaller schools in the PRISMS study.

4.2 Small school classrooms: the pupils' experience

There are two striking features of the PRISMS classroom behaviour observations. One is the similarity between the infant and junior observations, and the second is the high level of task work observed in the PRISMS classes. The infant/junior differences are so few that they can be dealt with briefly before a more general description of classroom behaviour is given.

4.21 *Infants and juniors in the classroom*

One might expect to need separate chapters to describe infant and junior classes. Infant teachers have often trained specifically to teach early-years children (3- to 8-year-olds), and, for children, the transfer from infant to junior school at 7 can be a serious matter where it occurs. Nevertheless, the picture which emerges from the PRISMS infant and junior observations is one of surprising similarity. As might be expected, the greatest observed difference is in how much the children move about. Even so, this difference is relatively small at only 3.4 per cent. Infants were observed 'out-of-base' in 15 per cent of all the observations, compared with the juniors' 11.6 per cent, although observations were made throughout the infant age range, and included some 4-year-olds. Observations of 'out-of-base' did not necessarily mean 'not sitting down', however, and the child's base could refer to the area assigned for that activity. Thus the base could be the house corner, or the painting area with the children bustling around 'in base'. Some of the PRISMS infants, however, were in rooms too small to permit much movement, whilst others, often in city schools with declining rolls, enjoyed the luxury of large open-plan areas for their activities.

Some of the out-of-base observations may arise because the infants spent more time waiting for the teacher than the juniors. Once her attention had been won, however, the infants got more individual teacher contact (6.3 per cent of all observations) than the juniors (3.9 per cent).

The remaining difference concerns time spent in quiet task work. Here, the infants were observed slightly less often (46.2 per cent of all observations) in quiet task work, whereas half of all the junior observations were in this category. Again, one might have expected a larger difference, as infants might be likely to need more support from friends and teachers in order to work at their tasks.

In all other respects the infant-junior differences were a matter of 1 per cent or less, but one area needs a word of explanation. Infants are generally less skilled than juniors at certain mundane matters such as undressing for PE or mixing paints. These would usually have been coded as routine tasks for juniors, unless, for example, the teacher was making a particular point, about, say, how to apply glue to a model, or how to use a ruler. At infant level, more of these routine procedures would constitute learning situations for infants, and as such would be coded as 'task' rather than 'routine'. Infant teachers have to allow specific time periods for these activities to take place. Thus, fastening shoes, routine for a junior, could become task work, in our coding system, for young children.

4.22 Small school classrooms: hard work and tranquility

The striking feature of both the infant and junior records is the high level of task work. When all the observations are put into just three major categories, 71 per cent of observations were task-focused, and this increased to 86 per cent if routine task-supporting jobs, such as sharpening pencils or ruling lines, were included. Only 13 per cent of the observations were coded as off-task or distracted behaviour such as chatting or daydreaming. In the ORACLE study, the equivalent proportions were 64 per cent task work, 17 per cent routine jobs, and 19 per cent distraction. The PRISMS children, then, worked harder. The children were talking to each other in only 13 per cent of all observations at both infant and junior levels, and over half (55 per cent) of this conversation was specifically about their work. Less than a fifth concerned routine aspects such as 'Can I borrow your ruler?' Just over a quarter was purely social talk.

In about half of all the observations, the PRISMS children were quietly engaged in their tasks. When the percentage of quiet routine is added to this, the PRISMS pupils spent just under three-fifths of their day in quiet orderly work, without talking to friends or to the teacher. As a proportion of all non-conversational behaviour, task and routine activities accounted for 85 per cent (70 per cent task and 15 per cent routine) of the observations. Even when not concentrating on their tasks, the children rarely talked.

The picture that emerges, then, of the 'typical' small school is of a relatively tranquil place in which to work. This pleasant image is endorsed by the minute amount of 'fooling around' observed. Despite the impression sometimes given by the media that disruptive behaviour is a feature of primary schools, very little was observed in the PRISMS schools. Less than 0.2 per cent of all the observations involved children fooling around, or acting so as to distract other children. This reassuring finding reflects both the earlier ORACLE study in which only 0.3 per cent of all observations were of disruptive behaviour or 'horseplay', and Tizard's recent study of thirty-three inner-city infant schools where only 4 per cent of all observations involved disruptive behaviour and less than 1 per cent involved aggression (Tizard *et al.* 1988). Tizard's study used a slightly different observation system which involved a broader definition of fooling around behaviour than that used in the PRISMS study. It will also be recalled from Chapter Three that the Tizard study took place in the London inner-city area where one might have expected to encounter more incidents of disruptive behaviour. In the Tizard study the teachers *judged* the amount of disruptive behaviour in school to be greater than the observations suggested. The PRISMS evidence, coupled with that of Tizard, indicates the need to treat alarmist reports of classroom behaviour with caution.

4.23 *Teacher-pupil contact*

From the teacher's point of view, as shown in the PRISMS interviews, one advantage of working in small schools with small classes is the possibility of being able to give children more individual attention. We shall see how this operates in terms of teacher time in a later section, but here we present the children's experience of the teacher's attention. About 30 per cent of all junior, and 36 per cent of all infant observation involved the teacher in some way and about a quarter of all observations involved teacher-pupil interaction. This is an area where infant-junior differences were found in the amount of time spent waiting for the teacher, as reported earlier, and in the balance between individual and whole class attention.

Table 4.1 enables us to compare the distribution of teacher-pupil interaction in three different studies. In both the PRISMS and the Tizard studies teacher-pupil talk accounted for about a quarter of all observations, but in the ORACLE study this proportion was only 16 per cent. Therefore, although the figures for PRISMS juniors and the ORACLE children look similar, the ORACLE figures actually represent a much smaller overall proportion. Teacher-pupil 'interaction' is a slight misnomer here, as the PRISMS children spent about 90 per cent of this time listening to the teacher, and both PRISMS and Tizard found that the small proportion of observations of teachers listening to pupils decreased as the children got older. As Table 4.1 shows, about two-thirds of these observations occurred when the teacher was interacting with the whole class, although the infants experienced relatively less 'whole class' attention (65 per cent), and the PRISMS juniors (71 per cent) less than the ORACLE classes (76 per cent). This is quite surprising since the PRISMS observations, unlike ORACLE, included curriculum areas such as music and PE in which more whole class instructions and encouragement might be expected.

Table 4.1 Teacher-pupil interaction from the pupil observations (in % of pupil-teacher interactions)

| | Infants | | Juniors | |
	PRISMS	Tizard	PRISMS	ORACLE
Individual	24	17	16	14
Group	11	19	13	10
Whole class	65	65	71	76

When compared with the ORACLE results, the PRISMS children seemed to get more individual attention. In ORACLE classes only 14 per cent was on a one-to-one basis, compared with PRISMS' 20 per cent for infants and juniors combined, giving the PRISMS children more chance of getting the teacher's attention.

It was the younger children, however, in both the PRISMS study and in Tizard's study who were less often just 'one-of-the-class', and who got more interaction as individuals or group members. Whilst the PRISMS infants got more individual attention than any other group, the amount of teacher-group interaction in the Tizard study was considerably higher.

Figure 4.1   Team and base arrangements in junior classes
(Proportions of base and team observations: only junior class
arrangements are depicted since the infant arrangements were
very similar)

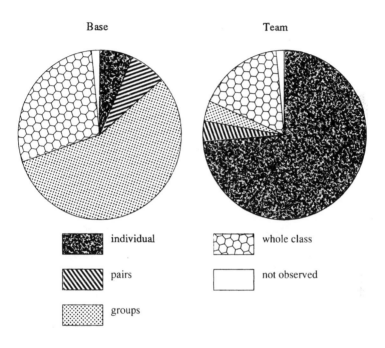

Grouping	Base junior %	Team junior %
Individual	7.4	81.2
Pairs	16.0	4.2
Groups	56.7	5.0
Class	18.7	8.0
Not observed	1.2	1.6

Linda Hargreaves

In all, the children in small schools were observed to work harder and talk less than their ORACLE counterparts, but, when they did so, the topic was more often about their work. PRISMS children received more individual attention from the teacher, especially at infant level, and less whole class instruction. Nevertheless, the relative proportion of teacher talk greatly exceeded Flanders' 'two-thirds rule' that two-thirds of classroom behaviour is talk, and that two-thirds of this emanates from the teacher. Even so, since the ORACLE observations were seen as favourable to primary schools, so the PRISMS observations are even more so.

4.24 *Seating and working arrangements*

The PRISMS observers recorded details of the pupils' seating or working 'base' and their 'team' when they were required to collaborate with other children. The mismatch between 'base' and 'team' is illustrated in the pie-charts in Figure 4.1.

In over half of the observations the children's base was with several children in a seating group. Mixed groups of girls and boys were the most common grouping observed (43 per cent infant observations and 38 per cent junior observations). Children were sitting on their own in about 7 per cent of all observations in both age groups, and the whole class was grouped together in 28 per cent of the infant observations and 19 per cent of the junior observations. In the ORACLE study no distinction was made between mixed groups and the whole class as base, but single-sex groups were more common in the ORACLE classes (30 per cent of observations) than in the small schools (19 per cent juniors; 13 per cent infants), presumably because there were more boys and more girls to make the groups.

When base and team are compared, as in Figure 4.1, the most striking aspect is the mismatch between individual seating and individual tasks. The children were seated in groups, often round large tables or desks pushed together, 'facilitating conversation, collaboration and co-operation', to quote Mortimore *et al.* (1988), who found that the teachers in the ILEA study also preferred to seat children in groups. Yet, in spite of these seating arrangements, the children were rarely given collaborative tasks. Only 5 per cent of all the observations involved team 'group', and collaboration between pairs was only 4 per cent.

When the amounts of concentration and distraction were compared with the seating arrangements, we found that distraction was highest when children were sitting in groups, but were required to work individually, which was 80 per cent of the time. On the other hand, task work was high during co-operative activities. Single-sex pairs and groups tended to do a little less work than mixed pairs and groups, especially if individual tasks were assigned. Most surprising is that children sitting alone, often perhaps deliberately separated from others to 'help them concentrate', showed lower than average task work (58 per cent infants and 63 per cent juniors). Perhaps these children found concentration difficult, or perhaps, as observed informally, they devoted themselves to trying to attract the attention of those from whom they had been separated!

Task work was highest when the whole class was grouped together, often listening to a story or gathered together to sing a song or watch television. In these situations, the level of task work rose to 86 per cent of observations compared with an average of 70 per cent overall.

It would appear from these results that when children were seated in groups but working individually, which was the most common pattern, distraction levels were at their highest. One way to increase task involvement, and yet retain the positive social aspects of grouped seating, would, it seems, be to increase the amount of collaborative work.

4.25 *Waiting for the teacher*

One of the observation categories recorded 'waiting for the teacher'. We found that the average proportion of time each child spent waiting for the teacher declined by half during the primary years. It stayed at about 7 per cent through the infant years and then dropped to 4 per cent at the 8-year-old stage.

When we looked at the curriculum areas associated with these behaviour categories, we found significantly higher than average levels of 'wait teacher' and 'out of base' associated with reading and writing activities at infant level, but not at the junior stage. Older infants beginning to write independently still frequently need to 'get a word', that is, to ask the teacher for the correct spelling of a word for their writing. Juniors, on the other hand, are likely to be more confident in their spelling, or to be capable of using a dictionary.

A final comment to make is that the amount of individual teacher-pupil attention, which was about the same as 'wait teacher' time, also decreased by half over the primary years, but had a steady decline. It is not surprising, perhaps, that the age when distraction was highest (15 per cent of observations at 7) coincided with the biggest gap between time spent waiting for the teacher's attention and time spent in possession of it. Another interpretation of the dip in task work, in favour of routine and distraction at this stage, is that the pupil style identified in the ORACLE project as 'easy riding', which may account for the apparently high levels of task work in the upper juniors, had not yet been mastered by the 7-year-olds. In other words, as top infant teachers introduced more basic, formal work through mathematics schemes and so on, the 7-year-olds had not learned to 'pace' themselves through the day to work slowly and steadily, filling the time and so avoiding any disturbing (exciting) challenges that the teacher might have up her sleeve.

4.26 *Classroom behaviour and vertical grouping*

In the PRISMS study of curriculum activities, it was found that children of, say, 7, in a class of children whose ages ranged from 7 to 9, tended to follow a curriculum similar to the 8-year-olds, as did the 9-year-olds in such a class. When we looked at the effects of vertical grouping on behaviour, this was not the case, however. The 7-year-olds' classroom behaviour matched that of other 7-year-olds, rather than tending towards a 'mean' within the class age range. This is perhaps surprising, particularly when one argument for vertical grouping is that the younger members of the class might be expected to admire and identify with their older classmates, and so modify their behaviour accordingly. It is interesting, too, that classroom behaviour which might be expected to develop through powerful psychological socialization processes such as indentification and peer group conformity, which may be difficult for the teacher to influence, failed to find a 'common denominator', whereas curriculum activities which were entirely within the teachers' control, did so.

One possible explanation for the strong relationship between behaviour and age, irrespective of the degree of vertical grouping, may be in our findings on classroom organization. These demonstrate clearly that in both infant and junior classes more individual work took place in vertically grouped classes where the age range was widest. In single-age classes, in contrast, whole class work was more common. As the ORACLE studies demonstrated, patterns of pupil behaviour were strongly associated with the particular forms of organization adopted by the teacher. Thus, a 7-year-old pupil working on an individual assignment, whether this was similar to the work being done by 8-year-olds or by the remainder of his own age group, would be likely to engage in practices such as intermittent working which the ORACLE studies demonstrated were associated with styles of teaching based on individualized instruction. Differences in the overall behaviour between children of different ages arise from our finding, also confirmed by Mortimore *et al.* (1988), that as children got older the extent to which they concentrated on their tasks increased. This explanation must, however, be somewhat speculative given the difficulty of disentangling the interactions between factors such as age, vertical grouping, class size, and organization.

4.3 The teachers in the small school

The observation of the teachers was briefly described at the beginning of this chapter, but to recap, the teachers were observed six times in each typical session, bounded by playtimes, lunch time, and 'home time'. Each round of observation consisted of fourteen observations at five second intervals.

4.31 *Observing the teachers' behaviour*

The major categories of the teacher observation schedule were:

1. The teacher's action, including exclusive subcategories of teacher talk such as questioning, making statements, giving feedback, listening, and non-conversational actions such as marking, showing, reading or telling stories, and 'housekeeping'.
2. The teacher's audience: this could be the whole class, an individual, a group, or an individual representing the group or the class. In addition, the observer recorded times when the individual in an interaction changed so that a measure of the length of interactions could be obtained.
3. The 'medium' of the work, where applicable. Thus if a child came to ask for help with written work, 'WRITE' would be ticked here; if the work was essentially practical involving the use of materials, e.g. craft work, or weighing and measuring in mathematics, 'MATERIAL' would be ticked. The other subcategories were READ, ORAL, and MOVEMenT. MATHematicS without apparatus was coded as WRITE.
4. The broad curriculum area of the interaction, such as language, science, mathematics, and humanities (used as a shorthand for general topic work involving historical, geographical, and some religious and social issues). Art, social/moral, music, and play completed the eight subcategories. If several of these were involved, as in some topic work, the observer could consult the teacher after the lesson as to the central curricular aim.

As in the case of the pupil observation record, the teacher behaviour categories form a less detailed version of the ORACLE schedule.

4.32 *Teacher behaviour: an overview*

In this section we shall look briefly at general aspects of the teachers' classroom behaviour, focusing particularly on classroom interaction. In Table 4.2 the results of the first section of the teacher schedule combined into six major types of behaviour are given.

Table 4.2 Overall pattern of teacher interaction compared with ORACLE (Figures are percentage of all observations in this section of the teacher schedule)

		PRISMS		ORACLE
	Teacher interaction	*Infant*	*Junior*	*Junior*
1.	Questioning (task + routine)	10.8	10.4	12.0
2.	Statements (content + feedback + routine)	34.8	37.6	44.7
3.	Non-conversational interaction (e.g. story, listen, show, mark)	49.9	45.3	38.4
4.	No interaction with class (other adults or pupils)	4.4	6.5	4.4
5.	Not coded (e.g. teacher out of room)	0.1	0.2	0.5

We shall look first at teacher talk. Teacher statements outnumbered questions by over three to one. About 10 per cent of teacher interaction consisted of questions, and two-thirds of these were about task content. The rest were routine questions. Both the recent ILEA study by Mortimore *et al.* (1988), which used the ORACLE teacher observation instrument, and the ORACLE study, found a preponderance of teacher statements. We can see from the table that slightly more questioning was observed in the ORACLE classes, where the proportion of task to routine was 85 per cent to 15 per cent. Some questions coded as routine in the PRISMS study, however, would have been called task supervision in ORACLE.

The teachers were making statements, or telling the children facts, methods, and/or information, much more frequently than they were observed asking questions. At infant level there were more statements concerned with routine matters (39 per cent of all statements), and task and feedback statements were equally divided (about 30 per cent each). In the junior classes, however, the proportion of task statements increased to 39 per cent, whilst routine statements and feedback reduced to 34 per cent and 27 per cent respectively. Thus, although the juniors got less feedback from the teacher, it is likely, considering earlier 'WAIT TEACHER' figures, that they demanded less, as they concentrated for longer periods on their tasks. Verbal feedback decreased over the three years observed in the ILEA study, confirming this downward trend. One point to be made is that teacher talk took up about three-quarters of the PRISMS classroom talk when listening was added to the teacher question and statement categories. The relative scarcity of questions and the small amount of pupils talking to teachers, coupled with the high proportion of teacher talk, lend little support to the idea that English primary education is an enquiry-based pupil-centred process.

4.33 *Teachers' non-conversational activity*

Table 4.3 shows that for just under half of the time the teachers were involved in non-conversational activity. This included listening, watching, reading or telling stories, showing or participating, marking, and 'housekeeping'.

There were some differences in the way infant and junior teachers spent this non-conversational time as shown in Table 4.3. As might be expected, the infant teachers spent more time on stories, on showing and joining in activities, whereas the junior teachers spent more time marking work. In other respects the two were similar: both spent about 15 per cent of the time listening to the children reading or talking. In about 5 per cent of all observations the teachers were watching, or monitoring pupils. 'Housekeeping' (tidying up, putting up pictures, sorting out books, etc.) took up about 8 per cent of the teachers' time. Some of these figures can be compared with the ORACLE figures, although the listening category is not directly comparable, as the ORACLE category referred only to children reading aloud.

Table 4.3 Teachers' non-conversational activity

| | PRISMS | | | | ORACLE |
	(% of all observations)		(% non-conversational activities)		(% non-conversational activities)
Teacher reads/tells story	3.6	2.2	7.2	4.9	2.3
Teacher listens	15.6	14.3	31.3	31.6	13.8
Teacher watches	5.2	5.6	10.4	12.4	5.0
Teacher shows	14.0	10.5	28.1	23.2	6.8
Teacher marks	2.6	4.8	5.2	10.6	26.3
Teacher house-keeps (e.g. tidies classroom)	8.9	7.9	17.8	17.4	45.8
Total	49.9	45.3	100.0	100.0	100.0

Some of the other differences are considerable, however. For example, the ORACLE teachers were observed marking pupils' work more than twice as often as the PRISMS teachers. Some of this difference must be due to the difference in class sizes and the inclusion of curricular areas such as music, dance, and PE in the PRISMS observations. The ILEA study by Mortimore *et al.* (1988) also comments that the teachers spent a considerable amount of time marking children's work and that this increased over the three junior years they observed. Verbal feedback decreased, on the other hand, as it did from infants to juniors in the present study.

Another feature of the PRISMS teachers was that they did only half as much housekeeping as the ORACLE teachers (8 per cent PRISMS; 17 per cent ORACLE), a feature which the ORACLE research describes as, 'the main cause of the lack of pupil-teacher interaction'. In that study, non-interaction time decreased as class size increased, and this is congruent with the PRISMS findings. In summary then, the PRISMS teachers appeared to be 'busier' and more involved with the children's activities than their ORACLE counterparts. They appeared more likely to be demonstrating or joining in with children's activities, they listened to, and watched them at work more often and spent less time marking work and housekeeping. Two factors are likely to contribute to these differences. First, smaller classes in the PRISMS schools probably account for the reduced time spent marking in class, and enabled the teachers to spend more time interacting with the children. The ORACLE teachers, we are told, with the pressure of large classes, seemed to need to avoid interaction with the children at times. Second, a wider range of curriculum activities was observed in the PRISMS project, although they accounted for only a small proportion of the total observations.

4.34 *Interruptions*

Headteachers in small schools usually have responsibility for a class, and are allowed perhaps an afternoon or two of extra help in which to meet some of the administrative duties of their posts. The heads' duties do not, of course, restrict themselves neatly to those afternoons but can need attention at any time of the day. One problem expressed by teaching heads is the number of unscheduled interruptions to their teaching time caused by visitors, such as parents, telephone calls, dealings with ancillary staff, lunch time staff, and so on.

In fact such interruptions accounted for 6.5 per cent of the observations of junior teachers (the heads tended to teach the older children) and 4.4 per cent of the infant teacher observations. For nearly 60 per cent of this time the junior teachers had to leave their classes, and for 35 per cent of it they were talking to other adults in the classroom. The remaining 5 per cent was spent with pupils from another class.

PRISMS junior teachers spent about twice as much time on these interruptions as the ORACLE teachers who were in schools with non-teaching heads. Thus, although these interruptions took up a relatively small part of observed time, they were more frequent in the small schools, in both age groups. This issue is followed up in Chapter Six.

4.4   Classroom organization in small schools

It was pointed out in the opening section of this chapter that recent studies of primary classrooms both here and in the United States have brought out close links between the teacher's organizational strategy and the pattern of teacher-pupil interaction. One measure of classroom organization is the teacher's audience.

4.41   *The teacher's audience*

The PRISMS teachers were involved with the children in their classes for over 80 per cent of the time they were observed. Table 4.4 shows how much of this time was spent interacting with individuals, with the class, and with groups. It also shows the comparable figures from the ORACLE and ILEA Junior School project (Mortimore *et al.* 1988).

Table 4.4 The teacher's audience (% of audience observations)

Teacher interacts with	PRISMS		ORACLE	ILEA	
	Infants	Juniors		J2	J3
Individuals	60.8	57.3	71.6	67	63
Groups	12.6	15.8	9.4	9	11
Class	26.6	26.9	19.0	23	24

Teachers spent the greater part of their observed time interacting with individuals and a relatively small part interacting with groups. The PRISMS teachers, however, as shown in the table, spent less time with individuals and more time with groups than either the ORACLE or the ILEA teachers. They also interacted with the whole class more frequently. This seems to conflict with the earlier statement that pupils received most of their teacher attention as a member of the class but, although the *teachers* spent most of their time with individuals, each *child* received only a small amount of individual time.

Nevertheless, the PRISMS pupils did get more individual attention than the ORACLE pupils and it would be feasible to suppose that class size might play a part in this. One might expect, however, that, with a smaller class, an even greater proportion of the teacher's efforts would be devoted to individual attention. As we shall see later, however, both PRISMS and ORACLE found higher levels of distraction were associated with individualized work. It seems likely, then, that in the PRISMS classes, teachers, by their more frequent use of class and group audiences than in either ORACLE or ILEA classes, were able to boost the level of on-task behaviour. In addition, the PRISMS figures were raised slightly by the observation of such activities as music and movement (omitted in ORACLE) which were largely taught as class activities with high levels of pupil involvement.

4.42   *Individual teacher-pupil contacts*

The PRISMS observers recorded the times when the teacher's attention moved from one child to another, either as an individual, or when one child was speaking as representative of the class or a group. Previous studies, such as ORACLE, suggest that teacher-pupil interaction occurs at a rapid pace with each interaction lasting only a few seconds (Galton *et al.* 1980). This is particularly true of individual contacts. It was, therefore, of interest to see whether the PRISMS teachers, in small classes, would maintain this rapid rate, or would adopt a slower rate, giving each child more time per interaction.

The PRISMS schedule was designed to show each time the teacher's audience changed from one child to another individually, or within a group. Since observations were made every five seconds, even a fast rate of interaction could be picked up.

Remembering that the teachers spent over 80 per cent of the time they were being observed interacting with the children, and nearly 70 per cent of this time was spent with individuals, we found that the infant teachers worked at a faster rate than the junior teachers. Whereas four out of ten individual contacts were with a new individual in the infant classes, only three out of ten showed a change of individual at junior level. If we link these figures to our ten five-second intervals, teacher-child conversations were lasting 10-15 seconds at infant level and 15-20 in the junior classes, on average.

The teachers' use of the technique of interacting with an individual to represent a group or the whole class, so that the rest of the children were the audience, was, in fact, rare, occurring in only 7 per cent of the observations. These interactions were sustained for longer, however, when they occurred. Thus, we see the teacher stepping up her rate of interaction to deal with individual work, and slowing when working with a group or the class.

4.43   *How do teachers 'target' their talk?*

As well as looking at the rate of teacher interactions, we were able to consider the kind of teacher talk used in different situations. Were questions addressed mainly to individuals or to the class, for example? Did the teacher spend more time 'teaching' in the didactic sense of giving information, and showing what to do, with the whole class, with individuals, or groups? Was feedback more likely to be given to individuals than the class as a whole?

Teachers' interactions with pupils were 59 per cent with individuals (38 per cent same individual; 21 per cent other individual), 14 per cent group, and 27 per cent with the class. These proportions varied, however, from these overall figures with different types of question or statement, and, as shown in section 4.5, in different curriculum areas.

We found, for example, that routine questions such as 'How are you getting on?' or 'Have you finished yet?' were aimed at 'other individuals' much more frequently than would be expected, but were relatively rarely directed at the class. In other words, they were used to initiate new interactions, and, no doubt, to 'bring back' wandering minds! Questions about the content of children's tasks differed little, however, from the overall proportions, although they were slightly more often directed at groups.

Facts, 'how to do it' statements, and demonstrations were generally addressed to the whole class, whilst feedback was usually given individually. Managerial tactics such as, 'Well done, everyone – you've really worked hard today,' were little used.

The teachers tended to watch groups from a distance more frequently than individuals or the class. Listening to a group of children talking was very rare. Similar results were found in a follow-up to the ORACLE project, where it was observed that teachers tended to take over when they joined a group, rather than listening to the discussion (Galton 1989).

4.44 *Praise and disapproval*

The PRISMS teachers were rarely judged to be either strongly positive or strongly negative in their responses to children. Only 2.3 per cent of all observations at infant level, and 1.7 per cent at junior level, showed strong emotional tone. Praise was three times as common as criticism in the infant classes, but both were meted out in equal proportion in the junior classes. Other observational studies have also found that teachers' comments are generally unemotional in tone. In the ORACLE study, emotional tone was rare, but praise for work was observed only half as much as critical control. Tizard *et al.* (1988) found that criticism was three times as common as praise in their inner-city infant schools.

The ILEA research (Mortimore *et al.* 1988) again found praise and criticism to be relatively rare, and found that such statements decreased in the older classes. It is worth noting that the ILEA teachers said that they praised children's work relatively frequently, but, in fact, the observations did not support these impressions.

4.45   *The teacher's location*

The teacher's desk can be an emotive subject, with some teachers firmly rejecting its use while others seem content to sit in authority behind it; or so popular staffroom stereotypes would have it.

In the PRISMS classes both infant and junior teachers spent over a third of their time moving about in the classroom. Junior teachers, however, were observed more often at their desks (38 per cent of teacher location observations) and spent only a quarter of their time at the pupils' bases. In the infant classes, this situation was reversed, with the teachers spending a third of their time at the pupils' bases and only just over a quarter at their own desks, or 'base'.

In fact, 20 per cent of the teachers were hardly ever at their desks, while, at the other extreme, 20 per cent spent well over half their time there.

4.5   Classroom behaviour and the curriculum

In the preceding sections we have looked at general aspects of the classroom behaviour of teachers and pupils in the small schools. Some of the comments already made indicate that different modes of behaviour were characteristic of both teachers and pupils in different curriculum settings. In the next few paragraphs we shall consider how classroom behaviour varied within the broad classification of curriculum content used in the teacher and pupil observations.

First of all we shall look at how the teacher's audience varied across the different subject areas.

4.51   *Organization within different curriculum areas*

When the teacher audience categories are broken down by broad curriculum area, some very clear patterns emerge, which are illustrated in Figure 4.2.

The top bar of Figure 4.2 shows how the teacher's audience was distributed when all observations are combined. The bars below show how the audience category varied in the different curriculum areas.

Mathematics, art and craft, and play were clearly monitored on an individual basis and were rarely the subject of whole class interactions. On the other hand, some curricular areas were very clearly class-based. Work on history, geography, and religion was often class-based, a finding echoed for 'project' work in the ILEA Junior School project, and, in music, 83 per cent of all teacher-pupil contacts were with the whole class and less than 5 per cent were with individuals. This suggests perhaps, that much of the music observed consisted of whole class singing, perhaps with piano accompaniment.

Figure 4.2 Relationships between curriculum and organization (% of total teacher audience)

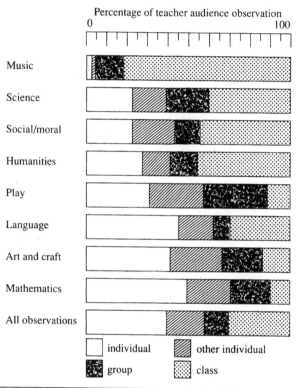

	Audience as % of total audience			
	Individual	*Other individual*	*Group*	*Class*
All observations	38	21	14	27
Mathematics	50	24	16	10
Art and craft	(41)	28	17	14
Language	43	(21)	9	(27)
Play	30	28	34	8
Humanities	26	13	(13)	48
Social/moral	20	(20)	(14)	46
Science	20	15	25	40
Music	3	1	(13)	83

(entries in brackets not significantly different from total audience figure)
Note: Table on which bar chart is based

93

Science revealed a slightly different pattern. Although there was a high proportion of class-based teaching, the attention to a group audience was also significantly high (25 per cent of the science audience, as opposed to 14 per cent of the total teacher audience). The only other area showing a high group audience was 'play'.

4.52 *Pupils' behaviour and the curriculum*

There were large variations in pupils' time on task within different curriculum areas, and although there were some quantitative differences between the observations of infants and juniors, the directions of the effects were the same.

In general, in 71 per cent of the total observations the pupils were on task (infants 70 per cent) and in 13 per cent of the observations they were distracted, for example, daydreaming or chatting. To compare time on task in the different curriculum areas, the proportions of observations involving each 'subject' area were calculated.

Particularly high levels of concentration on task (around 80 per cent) were found in science and 'humanities'/topic work. These were areas where the whole class was frequently observed listening to the teacher. These observations were supported by the highest levels of on-task behaviour (infants 82 per cent; juniors 84 per cent) which occurred when the teacher was coded as a major 'resource', when, for example, she was telling or showing things to the children.

In contrast, the lowest levels of concentration were found in mathematics, particularly in number work (around 65 per cent) at both age levels. Infants worked harder on mathematics involving practical apparatus, however, and juniors concentrated more on mathematical concept work such as sets, graphs, and matrices. Work on mathematics was also associated with more time spent waiting for the teacher and higher levels of distraction. Mathematics was found to be dominated by the use of published schemes on which children worked individually, and, indeed, the lowest figures of all for time on task and highest for distraction were obtained when published schemes were in use.

Language work produced intermediate levels of task-oriented and distracted behaviour, just above the overall frequencies in both cases. If we look more closely at the kinds of skills involved, writing and, in particular, copying were associated with low on-task figures, and reading produced only average levels. At the infant stage, only 59 per cent of observations of writing activities were on task and distraction was particularly high, 21 per cent compared with an overall value of 15 per cent.

In the creative arts, as a whole, time on task was relatively high, and distraction low, but when different aspects of the arts were considered we found different patterns. Activities involving acting out (which included music and movement tasks), vocal work, such as singing, and tasks involving three-dimensional materials were associated with higher than average levels of task-oriented behaviour. Drawing, on the other hand, was associated with low concentration and higher than average distraction. When we look at the curriculum in terms of skills it was clear that very high levels of concentration (80 - 90 per cent) tended to go with the active, and often collective, skills such as listening, speaking, singing, and acting-out.

In summary, the highest levels of task behaviour occurred when the teacher was the main focus of attention for the whole class, such as was often the case in history- or geography-based topic work and science. Low levels of task work and high levels of distraction were associated with subjects such as mathematics where individual work from published schemes was very common and where class teaching was rare.

4.53   *Teacher involvement in the curriculum*

Teacher involvement in different curriculum areas was determined from the pupil observations by considering together all 'teacher' categories, including 'wait teacher' and 'teacher present' (which meant that the teacher was close to the target pupil, but not interacting with him or her). The pupil observation sheets were put into three groups according to whether 'teacher' categories were ticked in over half, under half, or none of the observations in each round.

Overall, infant teachers were more involved with the children's activities than were the junior teachers. Forty-nine per cent of the junior observations showed no teacher involvement, compared with 39 per cent of the infant observations, while 36 per cent of the infant observations were in the high teacher involvement group, compared to 30 per cent of the junior observations. The activities where observations of teacher involvement were high included, not surprisingly, times when the children were listening, observing, involved in vocal work, such as a class discussion, poetry or singing, music, religious and moral education, infant level topic work and, of course, when the teacher was giving instructions or was the main source of information, as, for example, when reading a story.

In number work, and when using published schemes, teacher intervention was minimal. This may seem odd as teachers spent a large proportion of their time teaching maths. The paradox is that in individually-organized subjects, as mathematics was found to be, any particular child got very little teacher contact.

Art activities and creative work also received little teacher intervention. There could be two reasons for this. First, there might be a deliberate policy of non-intervention so as not to influence or inhibit the child's self-expression. Second, art tasks could be used as 'fillers' so that teachers could work more closely with other children. Whatever the teacher's intention, distraction was higher than usual in this area. Perhaps children perceive 'working independently' as work which is not important to the teacher.

In science the teachers were as likely to be highly involved as to leave children to get on by themselves. Science lessons often consisted of individual or group tasks, interspersed with plenary sessions.

If we look back to the pupils' involvement with their tasks, it would seem that high levels of teacher involvement tended to go with high task behaviour. For instance, high teacher involvement tended to be associated with the areas of high task-oriented behaviour such as topic and humanities work, while in number work and drawing tasks where the individual received little teacher supervision, task work was lower than the norm and distraction was high.

To summarize this section, then, whilst mathematics, language, art, and play seemed to have been supervised largely on an individual basis, with the children working without teacher help for most of the time, other areas, such as humanities, science, and social/moral education, seem to have been taught on a class basis, regardless of age and ability differences.

4.54   *How are different subject areas taught?*

In Figure 4.3, the profiles of teachers' conversational and non-conversational behaviour in different curriculum areas are shown.

Science teaching stood out as having high levels of task questioning, content statements, and teachers listening to the children. Feedback and marking were very low, however. A dominant feature of maths teaching seemed to be marking (11 per cent of maths observations compared with a 5 per cent average). Marking was almost never observed in the other curriculum areas apart from language (5 per cent). The language peak for teachers' listening resulted from the inclusion of reading and class discussions in this area. In music, on the other hand, where some listening and feedback on children's performance might be expected, the observed values were surprisingly low. The large amount of showing and participating (60 per cent) makes it clear that the teachers preferred to join in, perhaps accompanying the children.

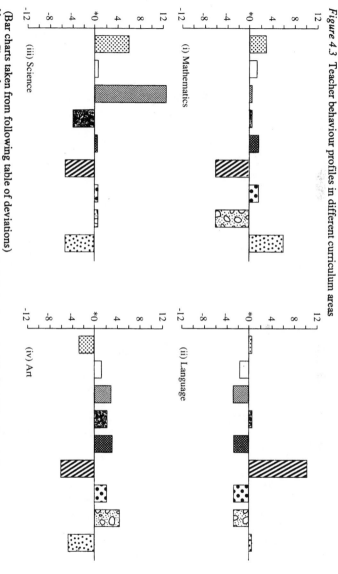

Figure 4.3 Teacher behaviour profiles in different curriculum areas

(Bar charts taken from following table of deviations)

Note: Charts show percentage deviation from mean: deviations shown significant at 1% or beyond.
  * '0' represents mean for each teacher behaviour across all curriculum areas.

Figure 4.3 cont.

	Task questions	Routine questions	Task statements	Feedback statements	Routine statements	Listen	Watch	Show/ participation	Mark
Mathematics	+3	+1	0	0	+1	−6	+1	−6	+6
Language	0	−1	−3	0	−2	+9	−2	−2	0
Science	+6	0	+9	−3	0	−4	0	0	−4
Art	−3	+1	+3	+2	+3	−6	+2	+4	−5

Note: Only those figures differing from the means for the whole curriculum at the 1% level of significance have been inlcuded

4.55 *How teachers' time is distributed across the curriculum*

The PRISMS teachers spent about 20 per cent of their time on routine matters, giving general instructions, notices, and supervising clearing up, and so on, as well as on routine comments to maintain order and keep things going. The rest of the time was spent on curriculum topics.

Both infant and junior teachers spent the largest proportion of their curriculum time supervising language-related activities, with infant teachers spending almost a third of their time on this, whereas the junior teachers spent just over a quarter of their time on these activities. Mathematics took up the next largest proportion of teacher time, taking up about a fifth of the observations, although infant teachers spent slightly less time on mathematics. The arts came next; teachers in both phases spent about 11 per cent of their time on the visual arts and 4 per cent on music.

A discrepancy between the two phases appears in science; junior teachers devoted 6 per cent of their time to this, compared with the infant teachers' 1.5 per cent. Play, by definition, occupied the smallest amount of the teachers' time: 2.3 per cent at infant level and 0.2 per cent at junior level.

When the PRISMS figures were converted to make them into proportions of total subject area observations, it was clear that ORACLE teachers spent more time on language and mathematics than the PRISMS teachers. This was at the expense of spending time on art activities and topic work, in which PRISMS teachers were more involved.

4.56   Teacher-pupil 'supervision ratios'

It was pointed out earlier that although the pupils might spend a certain amount of time in one curriculum area, the teacher's time in that area might not be the same. For example, a pupil might spend, say, thirty minutes on mathematics and then move on to some topic work. The teachers, on the other hand, could be supervising mathematics for a much longer time, especially if the pupils were able to plan their own time, as when an integrated day form of organization was in use. In vertically-grouped classes, this form of organization might be expected to be common, enabling the teacher to cope with the wide range of ages and ability levels.

One indicator of the match between teacher and pupil time in any one area is the 'teacher-pupil supervision ratio'. These ratios are shown in Table 4.5 where comparisons with equivalent ORACLE results are also given.

Table 4.5   Comparison of teacher and pupil curriculum for PRISMS (juniors) and ORACLE schools (excluding play and music) (% of observations standardized to 100 per cent over all the subjects shown)

Subject areas	PRISMS (Juniors)			ORACLE		
	Teachers	Pupils	T/P ratio	Teachers	Pupils	T/P ratio
Maths	27.9	23.7	1.17	33.1	28.5	1.16
Language	34.4	37.1	0.93	37.8	36.1	1.05
Art and craft	14.8	14.6	1.01	10.3	10.9	0.94
General topic	23.0	24.6	0.94	18.8	24.4	0.77

In the table, the figures in the 'ratio' columns are the 'supervision ratios': that is, the ratio of teachers' time divided by pupils' time for each subject area. In mathematics, the ratios in both studies were about equal and were greater than one. This indicates that the teachers spent more time supervising mathematics than pupils spent working on mathematics. On the other hand, the PRISMS pupils spent more time than their teachers on language and topic work, whereas ORACLE pupils spent more time than their teachers on art and craft, and topic work. The ORACLE supervision ratios suggest that these pupils were left to 'get on with' topic work more often than the PRISMS pupils, although similar amounts of time were spent by the *pupils* on this work in both studies.

Furthermore, we have suggested earlier that topic work (humanities and science) was frequently associated with whole class teaching, which would lead us to expect a ratio of 1.0:1. It seems likely that the PRISMS pupils were 'taught' as a class, and then left to work with relatively little teacher intervention leading to the 0.94 supervision value. In the ORACLE study pupils were required to work independently on topic work for longer periods.

Art work in the PRISMS study provides a similar paradox; the ratio was almost 1.0:1, indicating a match between pupil and teacher time, and yet the observations in Figure 4.3 showed a very high individual teacher audience in art, leading us to expect a ratio less than 1.0:1, as found in the ORACLE figures (0.94 per cent). One possible explanation for these differences was the difference in class size between the two groups. The PRISMS average class size was twenty pupils, compared with ORACLE's thirty. This could mean that, although the pupils did work individually and independently, the PRISMS classes were often small enough for the teacher to have individual contact with each child during their art time. The ORACLE teachers, on the other hand, with larger classes, were perhaps forced to spend more time in the explicitly assessed areas such as mathematics and language, 'getting round' to everyone in the class. As a result, the teachers spent less time involved in areas that were not typically formally assessed, such as art and topic work.

In the PRISMS study we were also able to consider teacher-pupil supervision ratios in the use of different media, and here we found that in the medium 'material', which referred to the use of three-dimensional craft materials and models, the supervision ratio was about 0.9:1. In other words the pupils spent more time than their teachers using artistic and constructional skills, which were not necessarily pure 'art' but might have been coded as maths, topic, or play in the conventional curriculum classification. In writing and movement, the ratio was almost 1.0:1; teachers and pupils spent the same time in these areas. The pupils, however, spent more of their time in reading, not only in pure 'language' work, but also reading instructions and workcards in mathematics, science, and so on. Pupils spent much less of their time speaking than their teachers did in supervising discussion.

What is clear from Table 4.5, however, is that there was, on the whole, a closer match between teacher and pupil time distribution across the curriculum than there was in the ORACLE classes. Part of this discrepancy must be explained by the larger classes in the ORACLE schools.

4.57 *In search of the integrated day*

It was suggested above that teachers in vertically grouped classes might organize the class so that they could work closely with some children, perhaps grouped by age, in one curriculum area, or topic, where a degree of teacher support and intervention might be needed, leaving other children to work independently in others. This strategy might help to overcome the difficulties of teaching across wide age, ability, and motivation ranges. The teacher observations were therefore analysed to find out how often the teacher's attention moved about from one curriculum area to another, as children needed help with their different tasks in an integrated organization. On the other hand, it could be that the teachers maintained short bursts of interaction, focusing on one curriculum area for a short period, perhaps dealing with a group of pupils working on the same task. We found that three-quarters of all the rounds of teacher observation showed the same curriculum area for over half the observations, and three-fifths had the same 'medium' (writing, reading, drawing, etc). Each round of teacher observation lasted only a minute and a half, however, and there were six rounds at intervals through each session, and so the observations were combined into complete sessions. We found that the same subject area was the focus of teacher attention for over half the time in half of the sessions, while focus on the same medium was slightly less. There tended to be more indications of integration, or of teachers managing several areas at once in the infant classes than in the junior classes, and this was particularly true for reception classes.

Overall, however, the results suggest strongly that the teachers concentrated their efforts within a narrow curricular range during any session, even when, as a check, music and PE lessons, which typically involved the whole class, were excluded from the sample.

The same medium was supervised at least 90 per cent of the time in 14 per cent of the junior lessons and 7 per cent of the infant lessons, while for subject area the corresponding figures were 24 per cent and 7 per cent for juniors and infants respectively.

Further study of the distribution of teacher focus suggested that a common pattern was for the teachers to spend approximately half an hour concentrating on one area, before switching to another area or to less focused supervision. What is more, further analysis indicated that the variation in teacher focus was greater for different lessons taught by the same teachers, than between different teachers.

These observational data may be interpreted in two ways: first, that the teachers supervised two areas of the curriculum at the most, perhaps leaving children to work on their own in others, or, second, that the integrated day is a much less common pattern in the small schools than it was in the ORACLE schools of the late 1970s. The latter interpretation is supported by the research on the teachers' plans for the parts of the day that were not observed. Although this information must be treated with caution as it gives only a broad, verbally reported view, it suggests that for about three-quarters of the time almost all the pupils in any class were engaged on the same curriculum area. Some areas, such as music, religious education, and social and moral eduation, were taught almost exclusively as whole class lessons with all the children doing exactly the same activity. In other areas, such as mathematics, science, language, and some PE, the whole class would work within the same curricular area but on different tasks. For example, when mathematics was recorded on the day sheets, for two-thirds of the time the whole class engaged in the subject. Only 15 per cent of this time involved the same task for all the children and the remainder consisted of individual or group tasks. In one-third of the day records mathematics took place alongside other subject areas.

It would seem then, that the PRISMS teachers coped with the variation in their classes by differentiating tasks within one subject area, rather than trying to manage a number of different areas simultaneously. This form of timetabling accounts, in part, for the teacher-pupil supervision ratios reported above.

The conclusions drawn from this section are supported by the observations in the ILEA study (Mortimore *et al.* 1988), where 75 per cent of all observations consisted of single-subject lessons. They found that mathematics and language were most frequently taught separately, whereas history, geography, and science activities were more frequently integrated. Compared with the ORACLE observations, this, too, suggests a decline in the use of the integrated day. Furthermore, Mortimore *et al.* found that by limiting the number of subjects supervised in any one session, teachers were able to cut down the levels of distraction and needed to engage in fewer routine management tasks. The resulting higher levels of 'time on task' were positively associated with pupil performance.

4.6 Summary and conclusions

This chapter has described the classroom behaviour of the teachers and pupils in the small schools and the major conclusions will be summarized here.

We looked first at the pupils' classroom life. Most of the PRISMS pupils were in small classes where they maintained high levels of task work, particularly when the teacher was the main 'resource'. This was frequently the case in topic work, including aspects of history, geography, science, and environmental studies. In highly individualized tasks, such as drawing, however, the children often worked for long periods without any teacher intervention, and these areas were associated with the highest levels of distraction, although these were still relatively low. The children worked individually for most of the time, but worked harder when collaborating with other children on a task. When they talked to each other, it was usually about their work. All in all, the conclusion was drawn that classrooms in small schools were relatively tranquil places to work. The PRISMS teachers also seemed to be busier than their colleagues in large schools. They spent more of their time interacting with the children, mostly on an individual basis, but gave relatively more attention to groups and the class as a whole than either the ORACLE teachers or the ILEA teachers in more recent studies.

Different patterns of teacher behaviour seemed to be associated with different curriculum areas. In science, for example, teachers asked more task questions, and spent more time giving information, usually to the whole class, than in any other curriculum area. The teachers tended to focus on one curriculum area at a time, and it was unusual for more than three areas to be covered in a session.

Apart from the greater incidence of class teaching, the PRISMS teachers' behaviour was similar to the behaviour of teachers in large schools. Some differences between the PRISMS and ORACLE observations, such as teachers spending less time marking and housekeeping, and pupils getting more individual attention have been found, and may be explained in part by the smaller PRISMS class sizes.

Both Chapters Three and Four have therefore confirmed the view that teachers in small schools work in very similar ways to their colleagues in larger schools. This further evidence that teachers in small schools do the same things as their primary colleagues will be reassuring to some who, in the past, have worried about the limited specialist expertise available, particularly at junior level. To others, however, the extent of these similarities may come as a disappointment. Small schools, after all, enjoy considerable advantages, particularly in relation to class size. One might have hoped to see these advantages more clearly demonstrated in the observation data. We shall return to this issue in the final chapter where the question of special training for teachers in small schools will be considered.

Chapter five

Small and large schools: some comparisons

Helen Patrick and Linda Hargreaves

5.1 Introduction

The work undertaken in the PRISMS project was designed from the outset to be a study of small schools in their own right, not a comparison of small schools and large schools. Much of the debate about small schools, however, revolves round the issue of comparison, implicit or explicit, with larger schools, and in the course of the project we, too, were drawn to consider the comparative implications of our work.

Throughout this book we have compared our findings on small schools with the findings of other studies of primary schools, and we have concluded that in many respects the similarities greatly outweigh the differences. Yet small schools do differ from their larger neighbours, simply because they are small. In this chapter we now wish to draw together the threads of our discussion on the nature of small schools and to look at some issues in more detail. In particular, we want to look at the issue of standards in small schools and to report on some observational data which we collected in a sample of larger schools.

5.2 Defining the small school

The first issue to be considered is one of definition. How small is a small school?

As we explained in Chapter One, our working definition was fewer than 100 pupils or four full-time equivalent teachers. Our definition was based on the spread of schools of different sizes in the authorities taking part in the study, and was considerably different from other definitions which we might have used. The definition suggested to us by the DES when we began our research was less than one teacher per year group, and the definition used by Mortimore *et al.* (1988) was that middle- to small-sized schools had a junior roll of around 160 or fewer pupils. In some of the local authorities in our study such definitions would have encompassed virtually all the schools. Many of our schools did not meet the criterion recommended in the Plowden Report (1967) and in the White Paper, *Better Schools* (DES 1985a), of a minimum of three teachers. In other words, most of the PRISMS schools, which ranged from 16 pupils to 132 and averaged 55 pupils, really were very small.

One result of being so small was that classes in PRISMS schools were also comparatively small. Class size in the PRISMS schools ranged from nine to thirty-three, with an average of around twenty. By comparison, in the ORACLE study the average class size was nearly thirty (Galton *et al.* 1980). Since the ORACLE study took place during the 1970s, class sizes in primary schools have been falling, and when Mortimore *et al.* (1988) conducted their study in ILEA in the 1980s, they found an average class size of twenty-five. In *Better Schools* the average primary school class size in 1984 was given as 24.7, very similar to the ILEA figure. We were working on the PRISMS study between 1983 and 1985, so our average figure of around twenty was considerably smaller than was usual in primary classrooms at the time.

The second result of being a small primary school was the need for vertical grouping. Ridgway and Lawton (1968), among others, were influential in the 1960s in encouraging schools to adopt the system of family, or vertical, grouping which occurred in small village schools and which was considered an ideal intellectual and social learning vehicle. Other commentators, including Her Majesty's Inspectors, however, have pointed out the perceived disadvantages of vertical grouping. Whether or not it is educationally desirable for children to learn and socialize in mixed-age rather than single-age groups, even in larger schools intakes of children do not come in class-sized groups, and mixed-age classes are becoming increasingly common (Mortimore *et al.* 1988). In most of the PRISMS schools vertical grouping was inevitable. Here too, however, there was a problem of definition which we had to face in the PRISMS project. What constitutes a mixed-age class?

In previous studies (HMI 1978; Lee 1984) definitions of vertical grouping were based on the notion that classes contained two or more age levels. A fourth year junior level, for example, would consist of pupils whose eleventh birthday fell at any time in the twelve months beginning on the first day of the school year. Lee (1984) defined a vertically-grouped class as one where there were 'relatively equal numbers of children from at least two age levels'. 'Relatively equal' was taken to mean that not less than a third of a class came from any age level. HMI (1978), on the other hand, appear to have included any class where the age range covered two or more levels, irrespective of the number of pupils in any level.

In small schools, however, the fluctuations in the numbers of pupils entering school, not only in September but at other times in the year, are such that the definitions used by Lee and HMI are not entirely satisfactory. The main drawback which vertically-grouped classes are thought to have is that the width of the age range makes it difficult to teach effectively, and it was this characteristic, namely, the width of the age range, which we decided to use as the basis of our definition of vertical grouping rather than the number of age levels as defined by Lee and HMI. We found in some of our small schools that the teachers split two age levels so that, for example, the older half of the second year juniors were combined with the younger half of the third year juniors, to give a class whose birthdays fell within one chronological year. The associated top junior class would include the top half of the third years, giving an overall age span of eighteen months or so. We would argue that the intention behind such arrangements was to create classes which were as nearly homogeneous as possible with respect to age. Yet the definitions used by Lee and HMI would categorize both the examples just described as vertically-grouped classes containing two age levels.

There were also classes in the study where a small minority of pupils of one age level were combined with a majority of pupils from another age level. For example, having regard to the number of pupils in a class, the teachers might decide to promote a few children whom they considered mature and able enough to cope with the demands of the class above. Lee argues that such classes should be regarded as single-age ones since teachers tended to treat them as such and that 'reactions to vertical grouping were most apparent when teachers were clearly confronted with a class containing two or more age groups' (Lee 1984). HMI, on the other hand, would define such classes as vertically grouped. How vertical grouping is defined, therefore, is problematic.

We decided to circumvent these difficulties by using a different definition of vertical grouping. Rather than using age levels as traditionally defined, for example, second year juniors, we used chronological age as the basis of our definition. Thus a class in which the pupils' birthdays all fell within a period of twelve months was categorized under our definition as a single-age class. Similarly, a class where the birthdays spanned more than twelve months but less than twenty-four months was a two-year vertically grouped class according to our definition. We were not concerned about where the periods of twelve months fell in relation to the school year. What concerned us was the degree to which there was a spread of age within a class, since it seemed to us that it was the spread of age which concerned the teachers, rather than the number of age levels as such.

This method also enabled us to classify vertically grouped classes consisting of a mixture of infant and junior pupils as either infant or junior classes when looking at curriculum differences. In such cases an infant class was one where the mean class age was less than seven while in junior classes it was greater than seven years.

Using age span as the basis of our definition of vertical grouping gave us more single-age classes in our sample than we would have had if we had used a more traditional definition. Even so, the number of single-age classes was only 15 per cent of the total sample and this disproportion made it difficult to investigate the effect of vertical grouping since this was also interrelated with other factors such as age and class size which had to be taken into account in our analysis. Nevertheless, we would offer this definition as a possible alternative to those commonly used when the effects of vertical grouping are under consideration.

In the questionnaire survey, however, it was not possible to adopt this definition because it depended on knowing the birth dates of all the pupils in a class. Although we had this information for the PRISMS schools, we did not have it for the larger schools which were included in the survey. We therefore used the simpler HMI definition, asking teachers to tell us which year groups were represented in their classes. Since all we wanted to do was to check the proposition that the smaller PRISMS schools would be more likely to have mixed-age classes, the HMI definition was sufficient. As we expected, the survey confirmed that small schools were considerably more likely than a random sample of schools to have vertically grouped classes. Approximately 90 per cent of the PRISMS teachers who responded had more than one year group in their class, compared with under half of the non-PRISMS teachers.

On the basis of these definitions, then, we were able to establish that the PRISMS schools were small by any definition, that they had smaller than average classes, and that most of the classes were vertically grouped.

5.3 Are small schools different?

We saw in Chapter One that the assumption is often made that the size of a school has a significant effect on its educational viability in terms of the range of experiences and opportunities which it can offer and the educational outcomes which its pupils enjoy. Yet in the succeeding chapters in which we describe the PRISMS study, we report finding comparatively few features which clearly distinguished between small schools and larger ones.

First we considered the teachers in small schools. They were indistinguishable from primary teachers generally in terms of their qualifications and experience. The main difference was that there were fewer of them. They were only too aware that this laid them open to charges of professional isolation and inability to provide as great a range of curricular experience for their pupils as they could do if they were part of a larger team. They did not deny that there were difficulties, but many of them believed that through working on their own professional development and using their opportunities they could ensure that their pupils were not disadvantaged. From the teachers' perspective, then, there was no reason to believe that the size of a school was necessarily related to its educational viability.

Next we looked at the curriculum in small schools. Our observation schedule was designed to enable us to make a more detailed study of the day-to-day working of the primary curriculum than has usually been possible in studies of this scale. We recorded not only the main content areas but also some of the detail of these areas, along with the skills and processes in which the pupils were engaged and the resources, including the teacher and their classmates, which they used. When we compared our findings with those of other studies such as ORACLE (Galton *et al.* 1980), the work of Barker Lunn (1982, 1984), and the ILEA studies (Mortimore *et al.* 1988, Tizard *et al.* 1988), we concluded that the work going on in classrooms in small primary schools looked much like the work going on in classrooms in large primary schools.

When we looked at the relationship between school size and the curriculum within the PRISMS sample, admittedly comparing small schools with even smaller schools, we found no strong associations. Similarly, when we looked at class size, although we did have a wide range of sizes, it was not clearly related to the nature of the curriculum, and only a small amount of variation in the curriculum was associated with the degree of vertical grouping. There was some evidence that the curriculum experience of an individual child was associated with the average age of his or her class, suggesting that teachers were 'teaching to the middle' to some extent, a danger which was recognized by the teachers even if they were not always able to avoid it. The difficulty of matching the task to the age and ability of the pupil, however, as the detailed study by Bennett *et al.* (1984) has shown, is a problem experienced by primary teachers generally, though it may be exacerbated by high levels of vertical grouping.

We then looked at the behaviour of pupils and teachers in small schools. Here we did find evidence of differences between small and large schools, though only to a limited extent. We found that there was less interaction between pupils in small schools but that more of that interaction was task related. Overall, in small schools we found that pupils spent more time on task and less in distracted behaviour than was the case in the larger schools in the ORACLE study. These differences seemed to be related to the higher levels of interaction between pupils and teachers which were made possible by the comparatively small classes in the PRISMS schools. This view was supported within the PRISMS data which enabled us to compare classrooms with a range of nine to thirty-three pupils, though the variations in behaviour were not great. Pupil-teacher interaction was also associated with the degree of vertical grouping. The wider the age range in the class, the more likely the teacher was to interact with individuals and groups of pupils, while in classes with a narrow age range the teacher was likely to interact more often with the class as a whole.

Overall we found little to distinguish small schools from their larger counterparts. To some extent teachers and pupils behaved differently in small classes and in vertically grouped classes, but the variations were small. On the measures we used, the similarities between small and large schools were much greater than the differences. In answer to the question 'Are small schools different?' we have to conclude that, in general, they are not. Factors such as a pupil's age were much more influential in determining his or her curriculum and behaviour in school than anything related to the size of the school as such. This conclusion was borne out by the data reported in the following section.

5.4 Curriculum and behaviour in large and small schools

Although it was not part of the main thrust of the PRISMS project, we were able to devote a limited amount of time and resources to collecting data in large schools which were directly comparable with data we collected in the small schools. Only a small study was possible and only tentative conclusions can be drawn from it, but on the whole they support our view that school size as such is only a minor determinant of curriculum and behaviour and that other factors are of more significance.

The data described here were collected in nine large and fourteen small schools in two local education authorities. The data on the small schools in the two authorities came from the main PRISMS study and the data on the large schools were collected in the following school year, 1984 – 5.

All the small schools in the two local authorities had fewer than 100 pupils, while all the large schools had over 200 pupils. There was therefore a substantial difference in the sizes of the schools in the two groups. All, except one of the small schools, were all-through primary schools. In the small schools we observed all the classes, but in the large schools a sample of three classes per school was taken. These classes covered the whole primary age range and each class was observed five times. As we expected, there were more vertically grouped classes in the small schools than in the large schools.

We analysed the results of this small comparative study along three dimensions, by school size, by local authority, and by the age of the pupils. Of the three, school size proved to have the fewest associations overall with behaviour and curriculum.

We found some support for the finding of the main PRISMS study that there was more interaction between pupils in larger schools than in small schools. One variable, listening to other pupils talking about routine matters, was recorded consistently more frequently in the large schools, but there were no other consistent differences between large and small schools with regard to pupil behaviour.

Nor was the picture very different when we looked at our findings on the curriculum. As we described earlier, we had over a hundred items on our curriculum observation schedule. On only eleven of these were there consistent differences between the large and small schools, and all eleven items were more often observed in large than in small schools. The items were: sets (SETS), meaning (MEANNG), instructions (INSTR), routine (ROUTIN), reorganize (REORGN), map (MAP), learn (LEARN), apparatus (APARAT), music (MUSIC), religious education (RELIG), and symbol (SYMBOL). Explanations of these labels are given in Appendix 1. They comprise a rather disparate list and suggest no obvious explanation as to why they should be more common in large schools except that organizational categories like instructions and routine might be thought to be required more often in large schools. In any case, some of the differences were not great and they were found on only a small number of items from a long schedule.

We looked in more detail at this issue, however, because where there were differences between large and small schools, they took the form of items being more often observed in large schools. Overall, there were no corresponding items which were observed consistently more often in small schools. We therefore compared the number of categories required on average to code a curriculum activity on our schedule. As we saw earlier, in the PRISMS study as a whole, the number was very close to 6. In the nine large schools where we observed the curriculum, it was 6.6. The difference suggests that in the large schools the pupils' activities were slightly more complex as recorded on our schedule. But this was a small difference and it was smaller than the difference between the two LEAs, where an average of 6.2 categories were used to describe the curriculum in the large schools in one authority and an average of 7 were used in the other.

We then looked further at differences between LEAs. On twelve of our measures of behaviour we found consistent differences between local authorities.

Interestingly, these differences accorded with the different reputations of the two authorities, the one for its comparatively progressive primary education and the other for its more traditional or formal approach. In the latter, LEA 1, higher levels of on-task work, particularly quiet work, and less distraction of different kinds on the part of the pupils were associated with more teacher attention, particularly in the form of whole class teaching, and with less individualization than in LEA 4. There was also more time spent on routine activity in LEA 4. In terms of teacher and pupil behaviour, it seemed that different traditions within the two local authorities were of more significance than school size.

This was also apparent in our findings on the curriculum. There were many more differences between LEAs than there were between large and small schools. In LEA 1 we observed more poetry, science, and religious education, more discussion, listening and acting out, more work on aspects of mathematics, more learning, for example, of tables, and more mapping from one medium to another, for example, reading aloud. In LEA 4 we observed more history and art, more drawing, writing, creative work, more copying, play, and more use of published materials. Again these findings fit to some extent with the more 'traditional' reputation of LEA 1 and the more 'progressive' approach encouraged in LEA 4. It also seemed that LEA 1's drive to increase the amount of science teaching was taking effect.

Next we looked at differences between younger and older pupils. On only two items on the behaviour section of our schedule were there consistent differences between infants and juniors. Infants were more likely than juniors to receive individual attention from the teacher and to spend time waiting for the teacher. The picture was different, however, when it came to the curriculum. As we have already seen, age was an important determinant of curriculum and in the data under consideration here it was of more significance than either school size or LEA. In over a quarter of the items on the curriculum schedule there were consistent differences between infants and juniors in the directions we would expect given our findings from the main PRISMS study. Junior pupils had more complex work in mathematics and language, were more likely to do work which could be recognizably classified by subject headings such as history, geography, and science and spent more time reading and using reference books and text books. Infants, in comparison, spent more time on play, drama, acting out, observation, physical activities, using apparatus, and making models.

It is difficult to draw definitive conclusions from the small sample used in our comparative study. Overall the differences between large and small schools were not great and were outweighed by other factors such as the local authority in which the school was situated and the age of the pupils in determining the nature of the curriculum. Like our findings from the main study, it gave us no evidence of substantial differences between large and small schools.

5.5 Pupil performance in the small school: basic skills

As we described in Chapter One, the findings of previous studies have been inconclusive about comparative standards of academic achievement in small and large schools. Our central concern in the PRISMS study was describing the curriculum in small schools, but we felt it was appropriate to make some measure of pupil achievement at junior level, first, so that we could see how it related to our observation of the curriculum, and second, to provide further comparative background information about the schools in our study.

We adopted two approaches, one traditional and the other innovative, to the issue of pupil assessment. First, in the traditional manner of pupil assessment, short standardized tests of basic mathematics and language skills were used to provide an initial screening of the ability range in the sample, and, after a second administration late in the school year, to provide a measure of progress on the tests. Second, a mini-project entitled the Prismaston File was devised to provide scope for pupils to demonstrate their independent study skills. We therefore had two kinds of measures of pupil achievement, the one standardized and norm-referenced to provide data for comparisons with the ORACLE study, and the other giving pupils opportunities to demonstrate what they could do on a wider range of activities without the imposition of the requirements of standardized testing. We will describe our findings from each of them in turn.

The standardized tests used were a modified form of the Richmond Tests of Basic Skills (France and Fraser 1975) which were in turn a form of the IOWA Tests of Basic Skills adapted for use in English schools. These tests were used in the ORACLE study to assess progress in mathematics and English. The use of the same tests in the present study enabled us to compare the PRISMS schools with the ORACLE schools, allowing, of course, for the passage of time between the conduct of the two studies. The shortened versions of the language and mathematics tests were administered under normal test conditions for the first time in late September 1983 and for the second time in late May and early June 1984.

In the reduced versions of the Richmond Tests which we used in the PRISMS project, pupils answered items on punctuation, usage, spelling, and vocabulary in the language test, and on concepts and problems in the mathematics test. The Richmond Tests are designed so that the items become more difficult as the pupil works through the tests. On the basis of the tests' standardization, older pupils are expected to perform better than younger pupils. Consequently, pupils who retake the tests after a period of time are expected to improve their performance on the second occasion.

In all these respects the PRISMS pupils performed on the whole as the tests predicted they should. Overall, the older children performed better than the younger ones, and the pupils' performance was better on the second administration than on the first.

We then used these measures of pupils' performance in different ways. First of all we compared the results with those obtained in the ORACLE study several years earlier. Table 5.1 shows the mean percentage of correct items obtained by 8-, 9- and 10-year-olds in each subtest in the PRISMS and ORACLE studies. The original ORACLE tests contained a few extra items at the more difficult end of the scale, which gave the ORACLE children the opportunity to obtain higher scores than the PRISMS children, though on more difficult items. The PRISMS scores have been divided by the number of items in the ORACLE subtests.

Table 5.1 Comparison of percentage of correct items in both ORACLE and PRISMS pre-test administration (broken down by subtest and age)

Subtest	Number of items		PRISMS (%)			ORACLE (%)		
	PRISMS	ORACLE	8+	9+	10+	8+	9+	10+
Punctuation	6	8	21	27	33	18	26	25
Usage	6	6	37	47	58	27	38	40
Spelling	9	9	35	45	56	26	43	48
Vocabulary	9	13	31	41	48	33	47	51
Mathematical concepts	11	18	32	38	45	28	41	51
Mathematical problems	9	12	36	44	52	30	46	53

Note: PRISMS scores are divided by the number of items in the ORACLE subtests.

Brief inspection of the table reveals some justification for the claim that pupils in the small schools performed better on the test of language skills than those of a corresponding age from the original ORACLE sample. In mathematics the two groups were more evenly matched. In the test of mathematical concepts, the young PRISMS children did better than their ORACLE counterparts, but this advantage was lost for the older age groups. In the test of mathematical problem-solving, however, the youngest PRISMS group again performed better whilst the older children were almost equal.

It must be remembered that these comparisons refer to groups of pupils who were separated by a distance in time of seven years. The ORACLE tests were administered in September 1976 whereas the PRISMS tests were administered in September 1983. During this time there was considerable pressure on primary schools to increase the amount of testing in mathematics and English. This pattern was already noticeable during the final two years of the ORACLE study and was confirmed by the work of Barker Lunn (1984). Pressures, particularly those resulting from the setting up of the Assessment of Performance Unit, led a number of local authorities to set up 'blanket testing' schemes, and the growth of the accountability movement in recent years has had a similar effect. Thus, in the changed climate, it may be that if the ORACLE schools had been retested in the 1980s the scores on the various subtests would have risen. The issue regarding the equivalence of standards must therefore remain an open one.

From the limited evidence presented here, however, we can say that chidren who took the tests in the sample of small schools appeared to perform no worse and, in some respects, better than an equivalent group of pupils who took substantially the same tests in larger surburban schools some seven years earlier. On this basis, therefore, we had no evidence to suggest that school size as such had an effect on pupil performance.

The comparison just described was based on the first administration of the tests in the PRISMS study but, because the tests were administered for a second time towards the end of the school year, we were able to calculate a measure of progress which we used to make comparisons within and between the PRISMS schools themselves. The way in which we calculated progress is described in Galton and Simon (1980). The measure, known as the residual-change score, avoids the problems of regression to the mean and is independent of initial achievement. We used this measure to look at how progress was related to the curriculum and the pupils' behaviour, in other words, to see if pupils were more likely to make progress in some circumstances than in others.

The relationship between progress and behaviour and curriculum were not straightforward, however, because, as we have already seen, all three were also related to age. As pupils grew older, they made progress, but their curriculum and behaviour also changed over time. Progress on the Richmond Tests might be due to growing older rather than to the nature of the activities in which pupils engaged between the two administrations of the test. We therefore had to look for relationships between progress and behaviour which were independent of age.

The results of this work were difficult to interpret. After looking at behaviour and at curriculum categories in language and mathematics, the areas covered by the tests, we found that variations in pupil progress were only marginally related to variations in behaviour and curriculum. Progress in language was positively correlated with the behaviour category LISTen PUPil TASK and progress in mathematics was positively correlated with TEAM GROUP. This suggests that pupils were more likely to make progress if they had opportunities to work with each other rather than spending all their time working on their own, but it should be noted that the relationship was very small and did not hold for any of the other measures of collaborative work. We found no significant relationships between progress in language and the curriculum categories associated with language. In mathematics, however, five of the curriculum categories were related to progress. Work on mathematical relationships such as number bonds, on form – ANGLES, SYMMETry, and SHAPE, and on data representation – MATRIX, NeTWORKs and GRAPHS, was positively associated with progress. Pupils who, according to our observation, spent more time on such activities tended to make more progress in mathematics over the year. There were also two negative correlations. Pupils who spent more time than average on observational activities (OBSERV) and on using WORKCarDs and SCHEMEs, tended to make less progress than would be expected. Again, however, these results need to be treated with caution. The relationships were small and many other mathematics curriculum categories showed no definite relationship with progress.

These results provided no recipes for ensuring pupil progress. Looked at from another perspective, however, they were reassuring, because they suggested that when it came to basic skills, most teachers in small schools were providing their pupils with a curriculum diet which, at the very least, ensured reasonable levels of progress. There were no major variations to suggest either spectacular successes or failures in the teaching of language and mathematics. To have found greater variations than we did would have meant substantial numbers of teachers were departing from established norms of primary practice. Neither our own findings nor those of other researchers and commentators suggested this was likely to be the case. Teachers in small schools, like teachers in primary schools generally, as Alexander (1984) commented, undertook 'a great deal of routine teaching of the basic skills of numeracy and literacy', which was 'usually competent'.

5.6 Attainment: class size and vertical grouping

This conclusion was confirmed when we looked at how pupil progress was related to factors which, characteristically, distinguished between small schools and their larger neighbours. As we have already seen, the size of the PRISMS schools as such was not related to pupil performance since the results for the PRISMS schools were comparable to those from the ORACLE schools. But we also looked at how pupil progress was related to class size and vertical grouping.

Much of the research evidence on class size conflicts with the intuitive judgements of teachers in that children from larger classes have tended to obtain better scores on achievement tests than those from smaller classes. Burstall (1979), in a review of the literature on this issue, suggests that this paradox may arise from the failure of researchers to ask the right questions. One problem, for example, is finding classes sufficiently different in size for meaningful comparisons to be made. Another is that tests of basic skills are measuring only one aspect of classroom life. It might be that the advantages of small classes are to be found elsewhere. It is also difficult to disentangle class size effects from other factors, such as the teachers' experience and style, which can affect pupil performance.

In the ORACLE study, differences in progress due to teaching could not be attributed to class size because, on average, a class size of about thirty pupils was uniform across all the six teaching styles identified in the study. The features associated with more and less successful teaching styles, however, such as amount of feedback and use of challenging discussion, would seem to be easier to promote in small classes. Class sizes ranged from twenty-five to thirty-eight in the ORACLE study and it appeared that the teachers of larger classes worked harder to maintain interaction rates equivalent to the rates observed in the smaller classes. One possible explanation for this is that no specific attention is given to developing strategies specifically for teaching smaller classes because these so rarely occur. Using the levels of interaction achieved by the more successful teachers, it was estimated that where less than average progress was made class size would need to be reduced to below twenty before similar rates of interaction could be achieved.

This argument is supported by the meta-analysis of seventy-seven different studies carried out by Glass (1976, 1982). He concluded, on the basis of the studies examined, that class size would need to drop to around fifteen before any effect on pupil achievement could be discerned.

In the PRISMS study the class sizes ranged from nine to thirty-three, but even with this range we found only very low correlations between progress and class size. As Burstall (1979) suggests, this may have been because of the interaction of other factors such as the age of the class, and because our tests were measuring only a limited part of all that might be defined as pupil progress. But it may also have been, as we have already suggested, because the experience of pupils in smaller classes differed little from the experience of pupils in larger classes. If there were few clear differences between the curriculum and the behaviour of the teachers and pupils in classes of different sizes, we would not expect to find clear differences in pupil progress. As in the ORACLE study, we might conclude that the advantages that could accrue from smaller classes were not being exploited to the full.

We then went on to look at the relationship between attainment and vertical grouping. Given that pupils were apparently not gaining significantly in terms of progress on basic tests from the smaller classes in small schools, how were they affected by the necessity for vertical grouping in small schools? Here again our work did not yield simple answers.

The ORACLE study found no differences in progress on mathematics or language when single-age and vertically-grouped classes were compared. The HMI (DES 1978) report on primary schools, however, found that pupils in single-age classes of 9-year-olds and 11-year-olds did better in the NFER tests used than did those in mixed-age classes.

In the PRISMS study there were too few single-age junior classes to compare vertical grouping with horizontal grouping. Instead, we compared classes containing two year-groups with classes containing three or more year-groups. We found the same trend as that reported by HMI, but the differences between the two types of classes were so small as not to be statistically significant. There is therefore no substantial support in our findings for HMI's conclusions, but, of course, we were unable to compare single-age classes with vertically grouped ones.

5.7 Small schools: study skills

On the evidence from the standardized tests, we had no reason to conclude that pupils in small schools were losing out in comparison with their peers in larger schools. Neither was there any evidence, however, that they were benefiting from features such as small classes. But standardized tests are of limited value in measuring pupil performance. For this reason we also used the Prismaston File with the aim of charting pupil performance on a wider range of activities unhampered by the requirements of standardized testing.

The Prismaston File (PF) was devised especially for use in the PRISMS study by one of the authors (Hargreaves). The PF took the form of a small project in which pupils had to act as secret agents providing information about an imaginary town, Prismaston, to a group of friendly aliens from the planet Prismos. The children had to perform a variety of tasks, including map work, using reference books, drawing, different kinds of measuring, constructing a bar chart and a Venn diagram, comprehension, and interpreting a time-line. Pupils worked on the Prismaston File towards the end of the 1984 summer term.

The aim of the PF was to assess as broad a range of curriculum activities as possible. It seemed appropriate that the children should work under normal classroom conditions rather than within the limitations normally associated with tests. The PF was designed so that as far as possible teachers could fit it into their usual classroom routines and the children were allowed to use equipment and to consult their

117

friends, their teacher, and any useful reference books, including a short one provided with the PF. Like the tests the PF was intended for use with junior pupils and two levels were designed, one for first year juniors and one for third year juniors. In practice, in vertically grouped classes, many pupils from other age ranges also worked on the project where their teachers thought it appropriate.

The use of ordinary classroom conditions allowed all the uncontrolled variation that test conditions are designed to keep to a minimum, and made it difficult to make generalizations from the results. In order to minimize and control variation, the content of the PF and the tasks set were the same for all the pupils. The choice of content and tasks was dictated partly by the categories on our observation schedule, because we wanted to try to match our observations with pupil performance. We also wanted to be as fair as possible to the pupils and to avoid setting them a series of disjointed tasks. A local study based on the imaginary small town or village called Prismaston made it possible to meet these conditions. We also asked the pupils to keep records of the help they received. The secret agent format of the project helped motivate the chidren, reduced copying by emphasizing secrecy, and justified the need to record the use of resources by means of secret codes.

To simplify the processing of the results, most of the items in the PF took the form of multiple choice questions, but the children had to undertake a variety of tasks to arrive at their answers as well as doing some tasks which had to be answered in other formats such as diagrams. Figure 5.1 gives further details of the PF designed for upper juniors.

Figure 5.1: The Prismaston File for upper juniors

INTRODUCTION	Teacher-led session to introduce class to the story, with instructions and examples to practise.
FIGURES	Map with grid, scale, and compass, roads, buildings labelled; pictures of houses; histogram and Venn diagram on transport use.
ALPHABETS	Practice in using 'secret agent' codes.
HOUSES AND SKY-VIEWS	Location of sites using addresses, compass directions, and aerial diagrams.
TERRITORIES	Shape and relative area of ground plots.
THE TOWN PLAN	Map symbols.
PRISMASTON COUNCIL MEETING	Practical mathematics involving measuring and use of units of area, perimeter, volume; proportions; calendar.

THE MAP	Grid references; decimals.
TRANSPORT	Interpretation of histogram and Venn diagram.
YOUR TRANSPORT SURVEY	Children asked to collect information from ten children on their transport to school and draw histogram of findings.
THE TRANSPORT DISCUSSION	Advanced comprehension involving recognition of arguments supporting and protesting against certain forms of transport.
CASTLES	Comprehension of passage and illustrations in reference book.
HISTORY IN PRISMASTON	Interpretation of time-line in reference book.

The PF was trialled in the spring of 1984 to test its suitability. It was sent to the PRISMS schools in the summer term and over 90 per cent of them took part in it. This was an encouraging response given the other demands on teacher and pupil time in the summer term. Although a few teachers had justified criticisms of the project, many others remarked on the way in which the ideas in it had sparked off activities in other areas of class work. Tables 5.2 and 5.3 show the overall results and the results for each age group on the PF.

Table 5.2 Prismaston File score distribution

Version	Number of items	Mean score	Standard deviation	Maximum score	Minimum score
Lower junior	55	36.5	8.56	53	13
Upper junior	48	29.6	7.51	48	10

Table 5.3 Prismaston File mean scores for each age group

Version	7+	8+	9+	10+	11+
Lower junior	34.7	35.2	37.7	–	–
Number of pupils	10	159	238	–	–
Upper junior	–	–	24.3	29.0	32.4
Number of pupils	–	–	29	234	279

In the lower junior version there were fifty-five items and, although nobody obtained the maximum score, the overall distribution of scores was skewed towards the upper end. In the upper junior version the maximum score was achieved, though overall pupils' scores tended to cluster more closely round the mean. As might be expected, the older children on average scored better on the PF at each level than the younger children. Many of the items in the PF at both levels were answered correctly because, in contrast to test conditions, the children were provided with the information they needed, and what was being tested was their ability to select and use that information.

Because the PF asked the children to record all the sources of help they had used, including reference materials, apparatus, friends, and teachers, we were able to see how far they had in practice used the help available to them. The design of the PF was based on the assumption that for some items it was likely that pupils would need to consult a reference book or use a piece of equipment, and we therefore calculated the maximum number of items on which pupils might reasonably need to use such resources. Allowing for the small number of over-enthusiastic children who recorded a source of help for every item, it emerged that most children had sought help of various kinds within the expected levels, except that their use of apparatus such as rulers was less than we expected.

We then looked at the relationship between different kinds of help and the pupils' overall scores. Interestingly, seeking help from the teacher was not clearly associated with higher scores. Over half of the pupils did not record seeking any teacher help and had the same mean scores as those who did have teacher help. The use of charts, reference books, and apparatus was positively associated with pupils' scores on the PF while help from friends benefited lower juniors but not upper juniors.

The results on the PF suggest that in ordinary classroom conditions children in small schools could successfully tackle a range of tasks and on the whole were able to use resources where appropriate.

As with the basic tests, we looked at how far performance on the PF was associated with the behaviour and curriculum which we had observed in the PRISMS schools, and with factors such as class size and vertical grouping. Again, however, no clear-cut picture emerged of the factors associated with high scores. Unlike the findings of Mortimore *et al*. (1988), our results did not demonstrate that levels of performance on the PF were consistently associated with particular features of classroom life as we observed them. There was some evidence that children in the smallest classes, under twenty pupils, performed better on comprehension and that children in classes with a wide age range performed better on reading for reference, but otherwise no consistent significant associations were found.

But the PF was testing pupils' ability to cope with a range of tasks of the kind commonly included in the primary school curriculum and, as we suggested in the case of the test data, pupils' experience of classroom life would have had to vary considerably before it had a significant and consistent effect on their ability to tackle such tasks. Although we had plenty of evidence that teachers varied in their approach and in the examples and resources which they used, there was a high level of commonality in the curriculum, and this held in classes of different sizes and with different degrees of vertical grouping. The PF was designed to reflect that commonality and the results suggest that it was successful in doing so.

In the course of our analysis of our measures of pupil performance in small schools, one of the factors which did have consistent associations with performance was, as would be expected, age. The initial test results, the measure of progress, and the Prismaston File scores were all associated with age. In addition, the initial ability of the pupils, as measured in the tests, particularly the language test, correlated with the measure of progress, and both sets of test results were strongly associated with performance on the PF. Interestingly, although individually girls and boys did not perform significantly differently, more progress as measured by the tests was made in classes where there was a greater proportion of girl pupils, but scores on the PF were better in classes where the boys outnumbered the girls.

These findings suggest that factors such as the age of the pupils, the ratio of boys to girls in a class, and the abilities of the pupils are stronger determinants of pupil progress and performance than features such as class size and vertical grouping which characteristically distinguish small schools from larger ones. Our study did not provide any evidence for suggesting that children who were educated in small schools performed consistently and significantly differently from children in larger schools. This conclusion is consistent with our findings about the curriculum and the teachers in small schools. Small primary schools are first and foremost primary schools. The factors which distinguish them from their larger neighbours, namely their small numbers of pupils, their small classes, and their need for vertical grouping, do not significantly override the characteristics which they share with all primary schools.

5.8 Conclusion

We set out on this project in the expectation that we would find something special about small schools. The teachers told us there *was* something special about small schools – the atmosphere, the friendliness, the relationships. We did not attempt to measure such intangible qualities, and we may be criticized for failing to do so, but when it came to more tangible features of small schools, we failed to find much to distinguish them from primary schools generally. We felt that our study gave us more insight into primary schools than it did into small schools, and consequently we believe our results will be of interest to all primary teachers, not only to those who work in small schools.

Chapter six

Small schools: the observers' studies

Brian Aldridge, Maurice Galton, Rosemary Grant, Cherry Harrison, and David Lea

6.1 Introduction: *Maurice Galton*

Like the ORACLE study, the PRISMS project employed a group of
teachers to undertake the systematic observation in schools. We were
fortunate that the nine participating local authorities were all prepared to
second a teacher for a year to work on the project. In the case of
PRISMS, however, the observers also played a part in developing the
schedule which was used to identify aspects of the primary curriculum
in small schools.

The experience of moving out of the classroom and becoming a
researcher, particularly in the case of systematic observation, where the
observer must behave like 'a fly on the wall' and remain aloof from the
classroom activity, can be a traumatic experience, initially, for the
teacher. In the ORACLE study the teachers, at first, thought they were
being given the most difficult classes because of what they observed.
This disjunction arises because of what is termed the 'actor-observer
causal attribution effect'. Attribution theory predicts that we will
usually offer explanations for the imperfections in any situation in terms
of factors over which we have little control (Weiner 1986). Thus the
teacher (the actor) sees the children's ability or background as the cause
of many classroom problems. Other teachers may blame the poor
environment such as lack of resources. The observer, on the other hand,
tends to attribute the causes of such problems to the teacher's ineffective
use of certain strategies. The situation is a particularly intriguing one
when, as in the case of PRISMS, the observers were all teachers and
their previous explanations for their own primary practice were very
similar to those offered to them in their new role as observers, by the
PRISMS teachers.

On balance, therefore, it is of considerable interest to hear what our
observers had to say about the aspects of practice they observed. Here in
this chapter, four such accounts of practice in small schools are
presented. Cherry Harrison chose to look at the variations in teaching

time that existed within the local authority schools where she worked as an advisory teacher (Harrison 1986). The monitoring of school time is becoming increasingly important as a result of the National Curriculum proposals and Harrison's study clearly shows the need to reduce the disparities in time allocations between different schools. Even greater disparities were discussed in Chapter Three in respect of London infant schools (Tizard *et al.* 1988),

Following on from this, David Lea discusses the use of workcards or schemes, particularly in mathematics teaching. PRISMS teachers, like those observed by both Mortimore *et al.* (1988) and Tizard *et al.* (1988) used workcards extensively. In the two London-based studies over 95 per cent of teachers used schemes to teach mathematics. Few teachers departed from their chosen scheme and as a consequence there was less emphasis on practical aspects of mathematics teaching than might have been expected. The same patterns were also observed in the PRISMS study.

Lea argues that the extensive use of such schemes arises because teachers have been 'pressurised' into a belief that the only way to teach mathematics is to individualize the work so that in any one session the teacher, in effect, teaches 30 different lessons. Elsewhere, Brian Simon has also argued against this approach, claiming that this emphasis on the individual needs of each child has made it impossible to fashion an effective theory of pedagogy 'since if each child is unique and each requires a specific pedagogical approach appropriate to him or her and to no other, the construction of an all-embracing pedagogy or of general principles of teaching becomes an impossibility' (Simon 1981b, p. 141).

Lea, like Simon, sees the need to establish a set of general pedagogic principles within which teachers do the best they can to meet the individual needs of particular children. He calls on those responsible for 'in-service provision' to base their training on what is feasible rather than on what is ideal.

In the third section of the chapter, Brian Aldridge looks at the dilemmas facing the teaching head who is a feature of most small schools. He found that there were clear indications that distraction levels tended to be higher in headteachers' classrooms than in those of the other teachers in the school. Aldridge, however, questions whether this is a necessary consequence of the fact that the head is also the school manager as well as a class teacher. He argues that, in many cases, headteachers appear to solicit rather than delegate responsibility, even when the tasks involved are of the most trivial kind.

Finally, Rosemary Grant attempts to analyse the 'thought' which lies behind the teachers' actions. Her analysis supports the observation data regarding class composition in that ability rather than age constitutes the deciding factor for selecting tasks and grouping pupils. Her main conclusion, however, is that, in their thinking, primary teachers in small schools appear to differ little from their colleagues in larger schools. This finding is not, of course, dissimilar to those made in earlier chapters where comparisons of teachers' background and behaviour were made.

6.2 School time in the primary school: *Cherry Harrison*

Traditionally English children attend school from 9 a.m. to 4 p.m., with the younger children leaving at 3.30 p.m.. The legislation regarding school hours is in the Statutory Instruments, 1981, No. 1086, Part III, which says:

on every day on which a school, other than a nursery school, meets there shall be provided:

(a) in classes mainly for pupils under the age of 8 years, other than nursery classes, at least 3 hours of secular instruction, and
(b) in classes for pupils of above that age, at least 4 hours secular instruction.

Within these regulations, it is for the headteacher of each school to set the official school times. During the PRISMS project the opportunity arose to investigate the organization of school time in sixty-eight small schools in nine local education authorities. The nine large schools referred to in Chapter Five were also included. In addition, a more detailed investigation into macro-aspects of school time and the rationale behind its organization was carried out in one LEA (referred to as LEA 1).

6.21 Opening and closing times

All seventy-seven schools in the study had a single opening time. Most officially opened their doors to the children at 9 a.m., but the earliest opening time was 8.45 a.m. and the latest was 9.15 a.m.. All five large schools in LEA 1 opened at 9 a.m. as did six of the ten small schools. Of the others, one opened at 8.45 a.m. and one at 8.50 a.m., with the remaining two opening at 9.15 a.m. The reason for these differing times was in all cases directly or indirectly the timetabling of buses or taxis.

School closing times were more complicated. Only about half of the schools had a single closing time, while the others organized different times for their infant and junior children. Several primary headteachers wanted one single leaving time for all the children to help parents, but a shorter working day for the infant children, so they organized longer breaks during the school day for them.

School closing times ranged from 3 p.m. to 4 p.m., with 3.30 p.m.

being most common for junior pupils and 3.15 p.m. and 3.30 p.m. both being fairly common for infants. In the five large schools in LEA 1 all the infants left at 3.15 p.m. or 3.20 p.m., but the junior leaving times ranged from 3.15 p.m. to 4 p.m. In the ten small schools in this LEA both infant and junior leaving times ranged from 3 p.m. or 3.05 p.m. to 3.45 p.m., but the infants tended to leave earlier than the juniors.

6.22 Time at school

As the schools which opened early were not necessarily those which closed early, Time at School was calculated. In the small schools there was a difference of 50 minutes between groups of both infant and junior children. One group of infants had only 5 hours 55 minutes of Time at School a day, while in the same county another group had 6 hours 45 minutes. One group of juniors had exactly 6 hours, another similar group 6 hours 50 minutes. In the large schools there was only 20 minutes variation in Time at School for the infant groups but 45 minutes for the junior groups. There were definite clusters in both large and small schools at 6 hours 15 minutes and 6 hours 30 minutes, but five groups of infants and twelve groups of juniors spent longer than six hours 30 minutes at school each day. One large school required junior children to be at school for 7 hours.

6.23 Non-contact time

Time at School was then divided into timetabled contact time with teachers and non-contact time. The breaks in the day between sessions and mid-session were investigated. Some children had double the amount of time for lunch as others, ranging from 45 minutes to 1 hour 30 minutes. Mid-session breaks also varied. Most schools had two a day, but fifteen schools limited the afternoon playtime to infant pupils only. One small school gave just the juniors a break, but in this school the infants left 30 minutes before the junior children at the end of the day. Total mid-session break time varied between 15 and 45 minutes.

When these times were added to lunch times, the total non-contact time difference was large. There was a variation of 1 hour 15 minutes among the small schools. The junior children in one school, for example, had 45 minutes for lunch and one mid-morning break of 15 minutes, with the infants having an extra 15 minutes at lunch time. By comparison, two schools in another authority allowed all their primary children 1 hour 30 minutes for lunch, a morning playtime of 30 minutes and an afternoon playtime of 15 minutes, a total of 2 hours 15 minutes. There was much less variation among the large schools, with a difference of only 30 minutes for the infant groups and 40 minutes for the junior groups. Most schools clustered at either 1 hour 30 minutes or 1 hour 45 minutes for breaks during the day.

6.24 Time in class

Non-contact time was removed from Time at School to leave Time in Class, that is, the time in school with a teacher. Again there were substantial differences. One group of infants had as little as 4 hours and another as much as 5 hours 5 minutes. For juniors the time ranged from 4 hours 15 minutes to 5 hours 15 minutes. Most infants had either 4 hours 30 minutes or 4 hours 45 minutes, and most juniors between 4 hours 45 minutes and 5 hours, but some infants, including 4-year-olds, had 50 minutes longer in class than some junior children.

Overall, infant children in small schools tended to receive more Time in Class than those in large schools and junior children in small schools tended to receive less Time in Class than those in large schools. Also, large schools tended to be more uniform in both Time at School and Time in Class. It may be that in larger schools the demands of time-tabling and the ease of making comparisons with neighbouring schools had made teachers more aware of the issues of time allocation and had thus led to greater uniformity among larger schools. But this is speculation.

What is clear, however, is that there were wide differences between schools in the length of the school day and in how the time within the day was allocated. The next step was to make a more detailed investigation of the use of time in the schools in LEA 1.

6.25 The use of time in schools in LEA 1

In fifteen schools in LEA 1 it was possible to look in more detail at the use of Time in Class. It was observed that Time in Class, the actual amount of time available for teaching, was eroded by Settling Time, that is, time spent in transit, settling down, and waiting. There was a clear difference between Settling Time in small and large schools. The twenty-three small school classes showed loss of Time in Class on only 61.3 per cent of recorded occasions, while in the fifteen large school classes it was 86.9 per cent. Settling Time was often 5 minutes and sometimes 15 minutes at the beginning of a session or half session. There could be four of these losses of Time in Class in a day.

When Settling Time was removed from Time in Class it left Teaching Time. This was the actual time recorded during the PRISMS observational periods. For the purpose of this individual study Teaching Time was broken down into Time on Task, Routine, Wait for Teacher, and Distraction. Time in Class was used as the basis for calculating the size of each of these categories because it was an official time. It should be stressed, however, that the resulting final calculated times for Time on Task were further eroded by Settling Time.

When Time on Task was calculated it was clear that non-task categories substantially diminished Time in Class, and also that this varied greatly between classes. Time on Task, in the small school infant classes, ranged between 3 hours 40 minutes and 4 hours 35 minutes, and, in the large school infant classes between 3 hours 15 minutes and 4 hours 15 minutes. Of the five large school infant classes with exactly the same Time in Class, one spent just 15 minutes on Routine, Wait for Teacher, and Distraction, but two spent 75 minutes on these activities. In the small school infant classes there was a range between 25 minutes and 75 minutes of non-task time.

Time on Task in the small school junior classes ranged between 3 hours 55 minutes and 4 hours 35 minutes, and in the large school junior classes between 3 hours 45 minutes and 4 hours 25 minutes. The junior classes in all fifteen schools had roughly the same Time in Class but again their Time on Task varied greatly, with one class losing only 20 minutes on non-task matters while another spent 75 minutes on such activities. Interestingly, the class with the longest Time at School had the shortest Time on Task. Overall, Time on Task was only partly influenced by basic school times, and seemed to be more dependent on the individual class teacher.

6.26 Conclusion

The basic organization of a school determines how much Time in Class a child has in a school day. Within the limits of this organization, the amount of Time on Task a child has is under the control of the class teacher.

There were very large differences in Time in Class between schools for both infant and junior children, particularly in the small schools, where there was a difference of 1 hour 5 minutes for the younger children and 1 hour for the older ones. In effect some children were in class for as much time in four days as others were in five days; an extraordinary and substantial difference between schools and groups of children, given that Time in Class was time spent with a teacher. Some children, therefore, had one-fifth less time than others in which to be taught. In addition, for some children, particularly those in large schools, the time available in which to be taught was further eroded by Settling Time, Routine, Waiting for Teacher, and Distraction.

It is clear that, whatever the size of their school, some children had much less time than others allocated and available for their learning. This represents a substantial inequality of opportunity, which is particularly disturbing in the light of American evidence that time spent correlates positively with progress (Denham and Lieberman 1980). For children in schools of all sizes, this is an issue worthy of further investigation.

6.3 The use of published mathematics schemes in small primary schools: *David Lea*

One problem facing small schools is that with few staff it is very difficult to cover all curricular areas adequately. Problems arise both in ensuring sufficient expertise and in having the time to develop schemes of work throughout the school. By considering the teaching of mathematics it is possible to look at how experts in one area of learning have suggested it should be taught, and to see if the advice given is realistic for teachers in general and for those in small schools in particular.

The 1967 Plowden Report made recommendations about primary education in general and also gave specific advice on mathematics teaching. The report sought to move teachers away from what were seen as drill methods and mechanical arithmetic exercises from textbooks. Instead teachers were encouraged to devise their own schemes of work and to derive the mathematics taught from the interests and personal experiences of the children, encouraging them to make their own discoveries about concepts and relationships. The emphasis was on developing understanding, widening the curriculum from the 'basics', applying mathematics to real situations, and adopting a more practical approach. In addition, a child-centred philosophy advocated a concentration on each child as an individual, rather than as one element in a class. All this was seen to preclude any use of commercial schemes, even if they tried to encompass the new thinking.

It was recognized that a high level of mathematical expertise would be required to adopt this approach, but it was believed that an intensive programme of in-service training (INSET) would overcome the problems, and the Nuffield Mathematics Project produced a variety of books and guides to help teachers. Despite such INSET programmes and many publications, however, various surveys since, such as *Primary Education in England* (DES 1978), *Education 5 to 9* (DES 1982), and *9 to 13 Middle Schools* (DES 1983), have made criticisms of schools which include overemphasis on arithmetic skills, failure to relate mathematics to the children's interests and experiences, and failure to apply the subject across the curriculum or to life outside school.

6.31 Use of published schemes in the PRISMS study

Similarly, the advice with regard to the use of published schemes seems to have been rejected. In the PRISMS sample of sixty-eight small schools from nine LEAs it was found that, almost without exception, some use was made of published materials. Observers' reports showed that 83 per cent of the classes took the majority of their mathematics work from commercial schemes, rising to 93 per cent if only junior classes were considered. Seventy-five per cent of all junior classes studied used only one scheme for most of their work. In another study of twenty-two schools of all sizes which I conducted, 97 per cent of all classes used one scheme for the majority of their mathematics work (Lea 1986).

Thus teachers generally seem to have rejected the advice to throw away the published textbooks and workcards, and it could be argued that the problems identified by the surveys are related to over-reliance on them. Why have teachers taken this course? I believe it is because most primary teachers have neither the expertise nor the time to develop a scheme of work which covers the wider curriculum advocated, particularly at junior level. A PRISMS survey, in schools of all sizes, of over 500 teachers, found fewer than 1 in 12 had studied mathematics as their main subject, and in my own survey of 100 teachers this fell to 1 in 20 with 16 having no qualification in mathematics at all (not even 'O' level).

However, while the teaching of mathematics with few or no textbooks has been rejected, that is not to say that teachers have ignored all the advice given. In response to a questionnaire, and to interviews conducted in twenty-two schools, teachers generally supported the aims of Plowden, such as the need for a wider curriculum, more under-standing, more practical work, more relevant mathematics, and the need to make mathematics enjoyable. And the only way they could see of implementing these aims was to employ modern commercial mathematics schemes which emphasized these features and provided the expertise which the teachers lacked. Schemes were also invaluable in saving the teachers' time making all their own materials and allowing more time to make special materials for the needs of particular children.

Using a published scheme also allowed teachers to attempt to follow another of the Plowden recommendations: to adopt a child-centred approach, focusing on individuals rather than the class. Unfortunately this has often resulted in each child simply working through the scheme at her or his own pace. This causes class management problems as each child can receive individual attention for only a couple of minutes, which can result in long queues and a lack of time for meaningful discussion of the mathematics involved. This may explain the findings of the surveys quoted above. Teachers in a constant state of crisis management find it difficult to adapt a scheme to individual needs and interests or to develop the mathematics beyond the scheme. Thus understanding, the fundamental goal, does not develop due to organizational difficulties. More recent reports have recognized the problems of certain interpretations of the Plowden Report. The Cockcroft Report (1982), *Mathematics Counts* and *Mathematics from 5 to 16* (DES 1985b) changed the emphasis from the teaching of individuals to a more balanced approach, urging teachers to use a combination of individual, group, and class teaching, and a variety of styles.

6.32 In-service and the PRISMS teachers

So how might today's INSET develop, given the relative lack of expertise among primary teachers? Teachers in my own study commented that they felt previous INSET efforts failed because they were presented in a vacuum. The courses did not relate to what the teachers were actually doing. There were many exciting ideas but teachers could not transfer these to their own classroom or their own school, and felt unable to fit them into any structure which provided progression and continuity throughout a child's education. Thus the great fund of enthusiasm was not translated into long-term teaching practice.

Perhaps, then, we should start from where we are now, with a large majority of teachers using published schemes for most of their work. Where a staff are using a scheme INSET might concentrate on analysing the rationale of that scheme, its strengths and shortcomings, so that the scheme can be used with discrimination as *Mathematics Counts* (for example para. 313) advocates. Teachers might discuss the scheme with a view to amending it. This would be necessary in any case to meet the requirements of the National Curriculum. By relating advice to familiar materials teachers would gain confidence and could begin to consider strategies such as developing mathematics throughout the curriculum. This would surely be preferable to undermining their confidence by telling them they are wrong to use published schemes at all.

It is also important that teachers should consider how to organize their teaching so that children have sufficient discussion time with the teacher and with other children. Evidence from the PRISMS study and from the ILEA junior study (Mortimore *et al*. 1988) suggests that talking to each other and to the teacher about the work in hand can help promote pupil progress. Exclusive use of individual teaching must give way to group, and perhaps class, teaching on occasions, though it must be acknowledged and accepted that this may result in a less exact match of the work to each pupil. This presents particular problems to teachers in small schools because they have children from a wider age and probably ability range which makes the formation of appropriate groups more difficult. However, it is vital that groups are formed whenever possible so that every aspect of mathematics does not have to be taught individually to every single child. So as not to undermine confidence it should be more widely acknowledged by experts who proffer advice that teaching in today's classes of around thirty must inevitably be about making compromises. Teachers would feel less threatened and criticized and more willing to 'have a go' if the ideal methods often prescribed were something to aim for, rather than being presented as the level at which all should be working all the time.

INSET, which brought together teachers from different schools who were using the same scheme, and which was centred on how that scheme might be used and developed, would be of particular benefit to teachers in small schools. It would enable teachers from small schools to work with a greater range of colleagues than is usually possible on an issue of common interest to teachers whatever the size of their school. This could help to reduce the sense of isolation often felt by teachers in small schools as well as to develop their teaching of mathematics based on their existing practice and materials.

With the advent of the National Curriculum these forms of INSET will become even more necessary. Publishers will inevitably attempt to translate the guidelines issued nationally into commercial schemes, and the danger that teachers will be 'led by the scheme' will be much greater if the scheme has the status of following the National Curriculum. Also, as the National Curriculum becomes law, with statements of attainment and tests for specific ages, some teachers might be tempted to push children through a scheme to reach the targets mechanically without due regard to the development of understanding. Others might over-consolidate work to 'ensure' good test scores when more challenging work could be attempted. It is essential, therefore, that INSET concentrates on helping the teacher develop the understanding of each child, which may mean departing significantly from the scheme, or, ultimately, given sufficient expertise and time, on devising schemes to meet the needs of particular children.

6.4 Role conflict in small primary schools – the head as teacher and manager: *Brian Aldridge*

In the course of recording classroom activity for the PRISMS project, it was observed that headteachers seemed to be called upon to fulfil two distinct but interlocking roles – the role of the head and the role of the teacher. It appeared, for example, that both headteachers and their pupils accepted that frequent visits from the school secretary as well as from

other people, were a normal part of the school day in the heads' classrooms. The head's managerial and administrative role thus seemed to
be, potentially at least, in conflict with the head's teaching role. At the
same time there was evidence from the PRISMS data that there were
higher levels of pupil distraction, as defined by the project, in headteachers' classes. A small study was therefore undertaken to investigate
what kind of relationship, if any, might exist between these two sets of
findings or observations.

It seemed likely that it was something about the varied nature of the
head's role which required heads to undertake a range of tasks normally
outside the framework of the classroom teacher's work which was
resulting in more distraction from work on the part of their pupils. If this
was the case, the problem was how to detect the specific factors responsible for the higher levels of distraction. It was thought, too, that if a
relationship existed between the head's role and the pupils' levels of
distraction, the head might feel the pressures of role conflict, that is,
conflict between the demands of teaching and the demands of
management.

The feasibility of some form of record of tasks undertaken by
headteachers was considered. The hypothesis postulated that a diary of
events occurring within the working day of the headteacher would
enable the researcher to construct a picture that described in some detail
the tasks that made up the structure of any period of time. Further, if
information could be gathered concerning the nature of interruptions to
these tasks, this would be useful in delineating the extent to which strain
between the roles of head and teacher was exhibited. The researcher was
aware that the tasks of teachers in small schools were, as they stood,
onerous enough without this particular study adding an extra burden in
the form of keeping a prolonged diary of events. Some form of diary was
therefore necessary to enable staff to record their working day in such a
way as to keep the task to a bare minimum while still generating useful
information. To this end a diary card (Figure 6.1) requiring only six ticks
for completion was designed for use by all teachers concerned. These
cards enabled the researcher to process the data so as to allow the
construction of tables to determine the range and frequency of tasks, and
the nature of any interruptions to these tasks.

There were six distinct types of information required. These were the
'task' at the time, the 'interrupting' factor, the 'time' of interruption, the
'duration' of the interruption, whether the task was 'postponed or
cancelled' and whether or not the teacher thought the interruption 'valid
or invalid'. Teachers were asked to fill in these cards over two one-week
periods. This meant that each teacher had records for ten working days,
and it was hoped that a picture of interruption and distraction could be
built up.

133

Figure 6.1 Interruption diary card

DAY		SCHOOL				
TASK		INTERRUPT		TIME	DURATION	
Teaching		Sec/Ancl		8–9		
Admin		Teacher		9–10		
Duty		Pupil		10–11	1 min	
Prep		Parent		11–12	1–2	
Marking		LEA - tel		12–1	2–5	
Parent		LEA - visit		1–2	5–10	
LEA		Routine		2–3	10–15	
Other		Other		3–4	15–30	
				4–5	1 hour	
TASK POSTPONED				INTERRUPT. VALID		
TASK CANCELLED				INTERRUPT. INVALID		

6.41 Levels of distraction in headteachers' classes

In order to set the detailed information collected in one authority into a wider context, simple counts of pupil distraction were taken from the data collected in the other authorities participating in the PRISMS project. In the wider sample it was found that as many as 80 per cent of heads' classes experienced higher levels of distraction, regardless of the age of the pupils concerned. In the authority under study a similar pattern was found. Heads' classes had, on average, levels of distraction twice those of their colleagues' classes, a finding which was statistically significant. There also seemed to be a 'knock on' effect in operation, in that deputies' classes were more like heads' classes than like those of their other colleagues. These findings warranted a closer look at the data collected through the diary cards.

Tests of significance were used on all the types of data collected, but these showed only one category to be of significance. The single factor that was found to have any real importance was the relationship between the number of interruptions experienced in a working day and the levels of distraction exhibited by the pupils of that particular teacher. When applied to teachers this correlation was of the order of 0.27. When the total distraction levels and the number of interruptions for heads were computed, however, the relationship was 0.58. For schools as whole entities the relationship was 0.782. It therefore seemed clear that class distraction levels were in some way connected to the number of interruptions during the school day. It seemed that the more interruptions there were, the more levels of distraction rose within those classes. It was interesting to speculate if the corollary would hold, namely that cutting down on interruptions would keep down levels of distraction. It was open to question, however, if it was possible to cut down on interruptions in a small school.

Armed with the findings of this part of the study, the researcher then conducted interviews in the authority under study. When the heads and teachers were asked whether these figures surprised them, there was a mixed reaction. Some had no perception that the two factors were connected, while others took it for granted that if the teacher's attention was elsewhere distraction was bound to be a consequence.

6.42 *The management functions of the headteacher in the small school*

A further question of interest was whether headteachers in particular tried to discourage interruptions. It seemed that in some cases they positively encouraged intrusions into their classroom work. Some heads felt that interruptions could be beneficial in small schools in that they could provide a wider audience for children as a form of positive reinforcement. Thus, for example, a teacher might use an interruption to say 'Go and show Mrs Smith that lovely piece of work', or, 'Children, stop and see the trolley that Michael has made for his model'.

But what of other interruptions? Why should the secretary ask the headteacher if a plumber could inspect a heater? Is it strictly necessary for the head to be informed when the dinner numbers are incorrect? During discussions with the headteachers some indication of their view of their role emerged. Because teaching heads spent most of their time teaching, they sometimes felt that their role was little different from what it was before they became heads. Their main energies had to be devoted to their pupils and their classroom rather than to management of the school from the head's office – if, indeed, there was a head's office. To some extent, the distinctive features which identified the head in a larger school were denied to heads of small schools. As one head said, 'I don't feel like a real headteacher'.

Given such feelings, it might be speculated that heads of small schools seek strategies for making themselves and others around them aware that the head does have a distinctive role. One such strategy may be that heads encourage the mixing of their two main roles, so that their position as head is reinforced even while they are teaching. There is little doubt that there are difficulties inherent in the role of the teaching head, but it may be that heads allow the difficulties to be exaggerated as a means of signalling that they have a role as heads as well as a role as teachers. In other words, while heads may be the victims of their position, they may also be victimizing themselves in so far as they do not take steps to keep their management role separate from their teaching role.

If there is force in this argument, the headteacher as interruptee is only one side, as it were, of a possible equation of role impingement. The question may be posed: if the headteacher invites interruption from members of staff, is the head signalling to other teachers that they are dependent upon the headteacher for validation? If this is so, such a situation would threaten the autonomy of other members of staff. In other words, efforts to define the managerial role of the head could inhibit the professional development of the staff.

The issue of headteacher role conflict is not unique to small schools. In a larger school, however, the headteacher usually has the choice of keeping different aspects of the role separate to some extent from each other. Unless the absence of a colleague precludes it, the head of a larger school can choose to cope with one job at a time: a task can be returned to, a letter can be left when a parent arrives, or a phone call made later. Children requiring attention in the classroom cannot be postponed. The head of a small school has less choice than colleagues in larger schools, though evidence from the study reported here suggests that it may be that some heads of small schools do not choose to exercise the degree of choice which they do possess.

6.5 Classroom characteristics, teaching, and learning – a first attempt to understand teachers' thinking: *Rosemary Grant*

What does it mean to be a teacher in a small school? Are the particular circumstances in which the teacher finds him/herself likely to affect the way he/she practises in the classroom? Are the learning experiences of children in small schools radically different from those of their peers elsewhere? What are the factors and concerns that underpin a teacher's thinking and how influential are they on his/her day-to-day practices? These were the kind of questions that interested me and which – in a small way – I had the opportunity to explore through my work as a PRISMS researcher. The enquiry which is reported here is only part of the work of the whole project. It is primarily based on an in-depth enquiry into the classroom practices of a few teachers in one authority. As such it can be considered as no more than an exploratory exercise, though I have attempted to compare my findings with those obtained from a larger sample of schools by other means.

During the period of research I regularly observed the activities of teachers and children in twelve classrooms in five small schools, all of which happened to be church-aided. The classrooms shared a number of characteristics. They were of small to average class size (between eleven and twenty-six children on roll), comprised children from more than one school year group, and included at least some children of junior school age. Part-way through the project, I interviewed the teachers, asking questions about their espoused philosophies, their preferred styles of classroom management, and the importance of their particular school and class context in influencing their thinking. The majority of the teachers – nine out of the twelve – favoured an individual, rather than a group or class, approach to instruction, particularly in the basic skills areas of English, reading, and mathematics. The remaining three adopted a mixed method of organization, incorporating some class and group instruction alongside individual work, and occasional opportunities for co-operative group work. The high incidence of individual work was the most striking feature of the study. In mathematics, for example, the nine teachers favouring individualization were recorded as spending 94 per cent of their time instructing pupils individually. The point of interest was whether these teachers related their individualized practices in 'the three Rs' to the special features of the small school classrooms, or if these were regarded as 'typical' primary school practices. As a way of checking whether the findings of the small study had wider applicability, a questionnaire was developed and administered to a larger group of junior school teachers from a sample of schools stratified by size. In all, 133 teachers from thirty schools returned questionnaires, making a response rate of 67 per cent. From these data, comparisons could be drawn and findings reported a little more confidently.

Two features of the small school classes – class size and class composition – could have influenced these teachers' practices. First I will consider the importance of class size. The classes ranged from average to below average in size. Two had fewer than twenty children and as such were representative of only 14 per cent of all classes in this geographical region (DES 1979b). The rest fell between twenty-one and twenty-six and were thus in the most typical class size band of twenty to thirty pupils, albeit in the lower half. Given the management demands of individualized tuition, it could be argued that smaller classes might predispose teachers towards this type of instruction. Though the teachers were mindful of the added pressures of working individually with larger classes, this did not seem to be a key factor in their decision to individualize. Most described it as their regular way of working which did not hinge on differences in class size from year to year. Only one teacher indicated that she adapted her teaching method to take account of the number of children on roll. Data from the questionnaire survey supported this finding. Individualized instruction in English, reading, and mathematics was common practice in many primary classrooms and the link between levels of individualization and class size appeared to be weak. Whilst it was found that the teachers of the smallest classes (less than twenty children) were the most likely to instruct individually, these classes were few in number and it is possible that they were 'different' in other significant ways, for example, having a high proportion of less able children. Teachers who favoured an individual approach were also asked to rank factors which had influenced their thinking. Class size did not appear to be critical. It was ranked sixth out of nine possible factors. It may be one factor which teachers take into account, and perhaps carries most weight for teachers of the smallest classes, though interestingly this was not the case in the observational study. The teacher of the smallest class – eleven children – said that she had never got to grips with a wholly individualized approach and preferred to organize her class on a group or a class basis.

6.51 The influence of class composition

In respect of age, all the classes were vertically, rather than horizontally, grouped. Typically children from two year groups, such as top infants and first year juniors, or third and fourth year juniors, were taught together. In one exceptional case, all the junior aged children were in one class. In two of the classes, the composition changed in the course of the year. Five-year-olds starting school in the second and third term had a knock-on effect as other groups of children had to move to accommodate them. Previous research (Bouri and Barker Lunn 1969) has indicated that mixed-age grouping related to higher levels of individualized classroom instruction. Teachers in this study reported here acknowledged its influence on their practices. In particular, they expressed a reluctance to class teach as one consequence of it. The teacher of the class with the widest age span expressed this view most strongly:

> If you have a spread, the sort of spread we are coping with, we all find it hard to give what I would call a class lesson because while you're talking to the J1s, the J4s think you're being babyish and while you're talking to the J4s, you lose J1s.

Not only were children in the classes of different ages and at varying stages of maturation, they also differed in terms of ability. Teachers were quick to point out that age, maturation, and ability did not necessarily correspond. A 7-year-old, for instance, could be physically more mature than a 9-year-old, emotionally less secure than her 7-year-old peers, and of so-called 'average ability' for her age. Faced with a wider range of possible differences than the teacher in a chronologically grouped class, the teachers identified 'ability' as the key factor of concern. One said:

> Well, put it this way, they don't see themselves as being third or
> fourth years. They just see themselves as being in my class.
> They've been in mixed-age bands all the way through school.

And another teacher added:

> The ability range is uppermost in my mind, particularly in language
> and mathematics because I have children who are very capable
> across the age range. I don't say, 'Well the 9-year-olds will do
> this.' If I find a 9-year-old who is able to tackle harder work, I put
> him on to it.

A number of comments like this suggest that the teachers may be
operating from internally constructed norms which are not made
explicit, but which provide rough and ready guides as to the appro-
priateness of tasks for children at different ages and different stages of
intellectual development. Whether these are adequate constructs to
work from is questionable. Some research (Southgate *et al.* 1981;
Harlen 1982; Bennett *et al.* 1984) suggests that teachers' judgements are
often frail and result in children being given work which is 'too hard' or
'too easy'. There is also some indication that this may be more of a
problem for teachers of classes which are of mixed age as well as mixed
ability (Bouri and Barker Lunn 1969; DES 1978).

The questionnaire survey found that the influence of mixed-ability
classes on teachers' decision-making is not confined to teachers in small
schools. The teachers in the survey who reported a high level of
individualized instruction ranked, 'the need to cater for mixed-ability
classes' as the major determinant of their practices. This suggests that,
in this respect, the teachers in the small school study were very much
like their colleagues elsewhere, and that their organizational methods
were a reflection of typical primary practice, rather than a response to
the distinctive features of the small school classroom. Both studies
suggest that the prevailing orthodoxy in primary schools was towards
individualized tuition. In one of the five schools studied closely, the
headteacher demanded that work in all areas of the curriculum be
managed individually as an expression of her commitment to the
Plowden ideology of child-centredness. In others where there was
greater teacher autonomy, teachers themselves spoke of their allegiance
to individualization as a way of acknowledging the uniqueness of each
child. As one teacher said, 'No two children are alike, are they?' In
cases where teachers expressed some ambivalence towards the adoption
of a wholly individual approach and tried to encourage some small
group work or occasional class teaching, the commercial schemes were
used to provide a framework and ensure continuity in language and
mathematics. These also acted as a constraint. The School Mathematics

Project (SMP) box contained only one set of graded cards and where pupils tracked through books at their own pace it was difficult to orchestrate any correspondence between pupils. Though they couldn't always elaborate upon their reasons, some teachers believed categorically that individualized tuition was more effective than other methods. One teacher said, 'I think it is better a lot of the time'. Correspondingly, teachers responding to the questionnaire survey rated their 'strong belief in its effectiveness' as the second most important reason (following 'the need to cater for mixed-ability classes') for practising in this way.

6.52 Qualitative differences in teachers' practices

I have suggested, then, that the organizational practices of the junior teachers in the small school study were very like those of their colleagues in larger schools, But what of qualitative differences? Was the nature of the individual work the same?

I asked teachers in both samples to tell me what they meant by individual work. Both defined it in similar terms as work which is (a) fitted to the different ability levels of pupils which allows them to work at their own pace; and (b) an organizational method mostly used in the promotion of basic skills – reading, writing, and number work. Only a few teachers in the questionnaire survey mentioned other criteria, such as work which accommodates or builds on children's interests or preferred ways of working. In practice, the individual work observed in the nine classrooms was grounded almost entirely in basic schemes of work, mathematics books or kits, spelling workshops, creative writing cards, and so on. Some individual topic work was observed but this mostly involved children in copying diagrams, pictures, and written information from books. Although some teachers said that negotiated work formed part of their regular practices, this was not observed beyond the level of bargaining over the order of tasks or the amount of work to be completed. Individualized practices seemed to amount to children tracking through prescribed texts at their own pace. As an experienced teacher, the practices I observed in these small school classrooms were very similar to those I have encountered elsewhere. This may be because the schools in this particular LEA do not, on the whole, identify themselves strongly as 'small schools' with a unique identity. They are city schools which have become small as a result of falling rolls, rather than schools which serve sparsely populated rural areas. The issue of 'small schools' has not consequently been high on the LEA's agenda. No federations of small schools, for instance, have been formed. In-service work focusing on the different ways of managing mixed-age, mixed-ability classes may be necessary to give teachers the confidence to change well-tried ways of working. Rather, the enquiries I undertook confirmed the conservative picture of primary practices described by other commentators (Galton *et al.* 1980; Barker Lunn 1984), and the message given out by the teachers seemed to be a contradictory one. On the one hand they were expressing a view of learning as an individual process shaped as much by the learner as the teacher. On the other, they were operating a management system which was almost entirely teacher directed and which seemed to take little account of differences in the way that children might learn.

Chapter seven

Parents, governors, and the local authority in one small school

Maurice Galton

The events described in this chapter did not form part of the PRISMS project. Indeed, at the time that the PRISMS research was carried out, the 1988 legislation shifting the balance of power away from local authorities towards parents and governing bodies had not been proposed. The decision to include the chapter, however, is not only because it offers insights into the relationship between the local authority, the parents, and the governors of one small school. Its inclusion also provides an account of the way in which the number of pupils in a small school gradually slips to a critical level where the local authority may begin to think seriously about closure.

In the first chapter we looked at the closure issue by reviewing a number of case studies of particular groups of schools. The most recent of these, that of Bell and Sigsworth (1987), described in some detail the efforts of a small school in Norfolk to avoid extinction. All these studies, however, begin at a point when closure has become a serious possibility. According to Bell and Sigsworth, this critical stage was reached, in most cases, when the number of pupils on the roll fell to between twenty-five and thirty, depending on the particular local authority. It is rare, however, to find cases which describe how schools moved to this critical position. Readers of such accounts are, therefore, left to assume that these falling rolls arise mainly from demographic change as the families of earlier generations grow up and housing costs escalate so that the next generation, with younger families, can no longer afford to move into the village environment.

7.1 Background to the study

The school where the events described below took place had suffered from demographic changes but, at the time of this study, with two full-time teachers and a roll of thirty-four pupils, it was still viable according to the LEA policy. The school, to maintain its anonymity, will be called Carhill C.E. Primary School. Carhill was built in the early

1970s with three 'base' areas each of which could accommodate upwards of thirty pupils. It therefore fitted the Plowden formula that a viable school should consist of three teachers and around 100 pupils. The base areas were linked by a central hall which also served as a gymnasium. There was a library and 'quiet' room and a kitchen. Within a six-mile radius there were a further five primary schools, three of which had inferior accommodation.

The following events occurred during the period September 1985 to July 1988 when the author was one of the two parent governors of Carhill school. The account, therefore, is highly subjective since the author played a central role in the events to be described. It was not possible, in the circumstances, to employ some form of triangulation procedure to compare and contrast differences in the perceptions of the participants.

The situation is very similar in this respect to the one described by David Jenkins (1987) when analysing the differences of opinion which arose between his team of evaluators, the Rowntree Trust, and the Northern Ireland Department of Education (the joint sponsors), concerning the publication of the School's Cultural Studies Project report. The Northern Ireland Government was opposed to widespread publication of the project report. They were, therefore, reluctant to comment on anything that Jenkins wrote relating to this attempted embargo. This present case study deals with the relationships between the school governors, the parents, and the local authority, when the latter, together with key individuals, were concerned to maintain a 'low profile'. Similar difficulties of triangulation therefore apply. In the event it has only been possible to adopt standard journalist practices, using privately acquired information only when it had been confirmed by two independent sources, in addition to published documents, such as minutes and correspondence between the various parties.

7.2 The first year (September 1985 – August 1986): three letters

The author was elected a parent governor in September 1985. At that time there were two full-time teachers. A part-time teacher relieved the head on two mornings a week to enable her to carry out administration. There was a part-time secretary, a young helper on day release from the local Further Education College, and a dinner lady who was also employed as an auxiliary for the equivalent of two days per week. Parents covered activities such as music, dance, sewing, and cooking, but the school policy did not allow parents to hear children read. At this time a local youth awaiting call-up to the Navy took the children for football. There were thirty-four pupils on the roll. In what follows all the names of every participant have been changed to preserve, as far as possible, anonymity.

The headteacher, Mrs Dubray, had spent the previous year teaching in a nearby middle school. The assistant teacher, Mrs Paxton, who lived in the village, took over as acting head during her absence and had instituted a number of changes including team teaching. Mrs Dubray lived in a neighbouring village, but as she did not drive, relied on others for transport. This arrangement regularly brought the head to school close to the statutory opening time of 8.50 a.m. and sometimes later. During the headteacher's secondment, Mrs Paxton took to coming in at around 8.30 a.m. as would be the norm for most headteachers, but reverted to an 8.50 a.m. start once Mrs Dubray returned.

The arrangement for the head to spend the year in a middle school was made hurriedly towards the end of the 1984 school year. The governors then had been angered because of lack of consultation by the LEA. There had also been criticisms of the headteacher's behaviour. In particular, it was claimed, by some parents that she showed excessive favouritism towards certain children and was unduly off-hand towards others, and there had been moves by the governing body to see if she could be replaced. One rumour circulating the village, when the news of her leave of absence became public, suggested that it was the Local Authority's way of dealing with these criticisms and that she would not return to the school at the end of the year.

In the summer of 1985, therefore, when it was confirmed that Mrs Dubray was to return to the school, there was considerable agitation among some parents. Acting for this group, one of the parents went to see the Assistant Director of Education with responsibility for the primary phase and subsequently they exchanged the following letters:

Mr R.P. Woodstock,
Assistant Director of Primary Schools,   20th May 1985

Dear Mr Woodstock,

Carhill Church of England Primary School
Parents and governors at Carhill school were interested to hear about my meeting with you on April 16th. We are grateful for your assurances that you will visit Carhill school at the beginning of next term to deal with the problems I discussed with you.

We should like to know also that you will send a Junior School Adviser to Carhill at regular intervals and that you will encourage the continuation of the team teaching methods which have been started this year.

As parents, we are concerned that there should be equality in treatment of children and ample consultation with other staff and parents. We shall then be able to give our full backing to the school and its Head.

Yours sincerely,

Delia Fielding

Dear Mrs Fielding,   23rd May 1985

Thank you for your letter of 20th May regarding Carhill Primary School.

I confirm that I shall visit the school early next term and I have written to Mrs Dubray to tell her of my discussion with you and of my forthcoming visit.

I shall certainly raise with her the points about visits from a Primary Adviser and team teaching which you mentioned in your letter.

Yours sincerely,

R. P. Woodstock.

It is clear that the matters raised by this parent were the same as reported to this author earlier in that year when he was asked by several parents to write to the Director concerning Mrs Dubray's return and the problems at the school. The following letter was received in reply:

Dear Mr Galton,   14th February 1985

Thank you for your letter of 30th January about education at Carhill Primary School. I note with concern the points you make about Mrs Dubray's timekeeping, her inconsistent treatment of children and parental alarm in the village. The same matters were raised at a recent governors' meeting which was attended by my colleague Richard Woodstock, who has briefed me fully ... At the present time, there is a strong possibility that Mrs Dubray will return to Carhill. The next step, therefore, will be for Richard Woodstock to meet Mrs Dubray and to talk through with her the issues raised by the governors. At the same time he will explore with her any alternative career opportunities. If Mrs Dubray does return to Carhill, she will need as much help and support as possible and I shall ensure that this is given through the advisory service. The important thing is that I and my colleagues are aware of the problems at Carhill and will do our best to resolve them. In this sense the concern expressed by governors and parents and the remarks you have made in your letter will be helpful to us.

Yours sincerely,

Director of Education

My election as one of two parent governors in September 1985 was the result of my acting as 'adviser' to the parents in the village who were concerned at Mrs Dubray's return. In that first year the school's governors, in addition to the two parent representatives, consisted of two representatives nominated by the County Council. One, who was the district councillor for the area, was chairman. There were two representatives from the parish council and two from the parochial church council. One of these was the vicar, who had newly arrived in the parish. In that first year much time was taken up with attempts to obtain from Mrs Dubray a statement of the curriculum structure at Carhill. This demand arose from the complaints by parents about the considerable amount of time given over to dance and physical education activities. The school went swimming each week, hiring a coach to the nearby town, some 11 miles away. This trip took most of the morning and resulted in only twenty minutes' swimming for the children. In addition, one afternoon was given over to football and there was also a dance session each week, of indeterminate length. Most governors, however, were hesitant about becoming involved in curriculum matters, expressing the view that 'it should be left to the teachers'. The minutes of 2nd June 1986 recorded that:

> Professor Galton enquired about the curriculum balance. He pointed out that this was the third meeting and there had still been no details given of the curriculum structure at Carhill.

> The head teacher pointed out that the Education Authority had still not produced a full Code of Practice for the structuring of the curriculum . . . The head teacher did not see the reasoning in curriculum assessment without the directive on the subject from County Hall.

The Local Authority's code of practice, referred to in Mrs Dubray's reply, was not concerned with the whole curriculum but with a policy statement on Equal Opportunities, including multi-cultural education.

7.3 The second year (September 1986 – July 1987)

In the following year, 1986–7, some progress was made on curriculum matters. The concern of parents shifted to the infant class taken by Mrs Paxton, although criticisms of Mrs Dubray did not totally abate. During the previous term, in an effort to increase numbers, Mrs Dubray had allowed children aged 4 to join the infant class. In spite of the obvious problems which the admission of these children raised, the part-time help was still used in the junior class where there were fewer pupils. The chairman of the governors was now the new vicar and he suggested a more conciliatory style in the hope that Mrs Dubray might become co-operative over such matters as team teaching and the allocation of greater curriculum time to subjects such as science, history, and environmental studies. As part of this plan, a seconded teacher, working for a higher degree in the university, came into the school with the author and carried out a project on the abandoned railway network during the summer term.

7.4 The third year (September 1987 – July 1988): the story of five meetings

Matters remained essentially unchanged during the autumn term of the third year. There was a change in the composition of the governing body, where a Parish Council representative was replaced by a younger woman with children at the school. What happened on the last day of term was subsequently reported in the newspaper *Today*, under the headline 'Head Plays Strip With Her Pupils'. According to the newspaper report on 18 April:

The Headmistress of a village school was caught playing strip poker with pupils aged only nine. At one stage, Mrs Dubray took off her underskirt and waved it about her head shouting 'Whoo-pee', according to one girl. When dinnerlady, Mavis Sandown, discovered the end-of-term game, 54-year-old Mrs Dubray told her 'I will play with them if I want to'. Pupils said the Headmistress reprimanded them when she discovered the classroom prank and then joined in. One boy stripped down to just his underpants. Mrs Sandown, who has withdrawn her daughter from the primary school, claimed she caught the pupils playing the same game a year ago. She said: 'One of the girls had no knickers on. The other children were shouting 'She's got them off!' When I went to the Head, she just said 'Oh dear, I told them not to go that far'.

Somewhat surprisingly, reactions in the village to reports of the incident were muted. Most parents, because their children had not ce Galton

mentioned it or seemed unconcerned, appeared not to take too serious a view, although there were a number of adverse reactions. What the incident did, however, was to act as a catalyst in bringing together all the long-standing grievances against the headteacher, including her emphasis on the non-academic elements in the curriculum, her time-keeping, and the alleged inconsistencies in her treatment of pupils. Those with children in the infant class became more concerned at what might happen in the following year when their children transferred to the juniors. These parents felt their children were already behind due to the introduction of 4-year-olds into the infant class. These concerned parents, mostly living on the private housing estate in the village, therefore held an informal meeting to decide what to do. News of this meeting, when it emerged, was regarded with some suspicion by those who lived outside the village, particularly the parents in the neighbouring hamlet some three miles away whose children also attended the school. There were accusations that the Carhill parents were intent on a 'witch-hunt'. The parents therefore decided to hold a second 'open' meeting and invited the governors to attend.

Apart from the author, no governor attended this meeting and no parent from the neighbouring hamlet came. The chairman of the governors declined to attend after taking advice from the local authority. Privately, most governors assumed that the meeting would be acrimonious and 'out for Mrs Dubray's blood'. In the event, the meeting was a very constructive one. Although some parents wanted the head's immediate dismissal, the majority, many of whom, at this stage, were undecided about the future of the headteacher, accepted that the local authority needed time to investigate the issues and to ensure that Mrs Dubray had a fair hearing. Most parents at the meeting wanted not action, but a meeting with the governors and the Local Authority so that they could be assured that those with responsibility for running the school were aware of their concern. Part of the reason for this desire for a face to face meeting arose out of the events which had preceded the earlier exchange of letters in 1985 quoted above. At that time the Director of Education had given assurances that he and his colleagues were 'aware of the problems at Carhill and will do our best to resolve them'. Since then, however, little appeared to have happened and those parents who worked in the school were able to confirm that they had seen little of the promised Junior School adviser. After the alleged strip poker incident, these parents had written to the Director of Education, expressing their concern about the school and had received similar assurances to the ones which were given two years earlier. It was this feeling that they might be 'fobbed off again' which led to the express desire for a 'face to face' meeting.

The meeting agreed to send the following letter to the chairman of the governors:

Dear Rev. Carter,   18th January 1988

At a meeting last night of parents of children attending Carhill Church of England School, at which 22 pupils were represented by 25 parents, I was asked to write to you as chairman of the school governors to request a meeting of parents, governors and teachers, together with a senior representative from County Hall to discuss various issues raised by parents in recent correspondence with the Director of Education. In particular, we seek clarification and reassurance on the following:

Curriculum and teaching standards

Victimisation

Timekeeping

In his replies to parents' letters, the Director of Education promised to undertake advice and support over the coming months. We would like this explained in more detail.

A number of parents are on the verge of removing their children from the school and we would therefore suggest that the meeting is called urgently i.e. within the next ten days. Meanwhile, we recommend that the supply teacher is retained. It was decided at the meeting to suspend the withdrawal of children on Mondays while the supply teacher is at the school.

It should be noted that not all parents attending the meeting were critical of the school, but all were extremely concerned about the welfare of their children.

A copy of this letter is being sent to the Director of Education.

I look forward to your reply in due course.

Yours sincerely,

Geoffrey Simpson.

The letter (3rd paragraph) refers to a threat made at the first meeting by some parents to withdraw their children from the school unless the local authority agreed to act. The 'open' meeting, however, persuaded

149

these parents to withdraw their threat and to give the local authority time to resolve the situation.

The chairman of the governors replied to this letter on January 19th as follows:

Dear Geoffrey,

Thank you for your letter of 18th January concerning the parents' meeting last Sunday.

I have spoken to the Director's office and we have agreed to call a special governors' meeting on Monday 25th January to receive the Director's proposals for dealing with the situation. These proposals are already in the final stage of preparation. Any steps regarding curriculum review should be promptly discussed with governors and staff before general comment and discussion are invited. The two parent governors will naturally be present. The meeting will then decide what further steps might appropriately be taken.

I appreciate the parents' concern and request for immediate action and hope that they will accept the correctness of the procedure proposed and feel reassured that their case is being dealt with as expeditiously as the quite complex situation permits.

A copy of this reply will be sent to the Director of Education.

Yours sincerely,

Sydney Carter.

This reply caused some anger. Even the less severe critics were upset at what they saw as a lack of consultation, as the following letter addressed to the author as parent governor indicates:

Dear Professor Galton,

I understand that the governing body of Carhill school has refused to hold a meeting between parents and governors on the grounds that there can be no meeting without the presence of Mrs Dubray.

I believe that a meeting should be held so that all shades of opinion can be openly discussed. I feel quite disappointed by the unwillingness of the governing body to listen to the views of parents.

Yours sincerely,

Mrs Tina Ascot.

The governors' meeting on 25 January was attended by an Assistant Director of Education and an Assistant Education Officer. The meeting opened with a statement from the two officers indicating that the authority proposed to conduct a thorough curriculum review, that Mrs Dubray, accompanied by a 'friend', had been interviewed, had admitted that the alleged incident had taken place, and had given an undertaking that it would not be repeated. Subsequently Mrs Dubray was taken ill and her doctor signed her unfit for work. Mrs Dubray was therefore informed by letter of the need to meet the Director of Education and make any additional comments on the parents' letters after reflection. She was advised of the likelihood of disciplinary action and informed that she should not return to the school until she had met with the Director of Education.

The minute then continues:

> The Assistant Director asked that the governors endorse these proposals in view of the urgency of the situation to allow diagnostic testing to begin at the earliest opportunity. The results would be made known to the headteacher and governors. It was resolved that the governors agreed to support measures and inform the parents of the action they intended to take. It was agreed to write to all parents following a resolution which was carried by 4 votes with none against and 3 abstentions.

> The chairman agreed on behalf of the governing body to reply to the letter written on behalf of a large group of parents. The letter would refer to the previous chairman's letter, clarify the governors' wish to meet parents at an appropriate time, but state that in all fairness, Mrs Dubray should be invited to attend once she returned to full health and following her meeting with the Director of Education. Wording of such a letter was discussed at considerable length. The governors agreed that Mrs Dubray's friend should be given an opportunity to comment on the draft before it was sent. They agreed that the final draft could be sent to the chairman without further circulation in draft to the governors.

Much of the ensuing dispute hangs on what the minute described as discussions at 'considerable length'. In addition to the chairman, the two other governors to abstain were the parent governor from the nearby hamlet and the Labour-appointed representative from the County Council. Neither was in favour of writing to the parents. Both during the previous two years had been most steadfast supporters of Mrs Dubray and had rigorously opposed any attempt to discuss curriculum matters. Of the four governors who voted in favour of the letter, all lived in Carhill and had experienced considerable pressure from parents. They

Maurice Galton

consisted of the author, the district councillor, the new representative
from the parish council with children in the school, and the other church
representative who previously had been the chairman of governors
when the original discussions referred to in the Director's letter of 14
February 1985 had taken place.

Subsequently there was considerable disagreement about what the
meeting finally decided and the minute does not help to resolve this. The
four governors who voted to send the letter all wished it to give some
indication that Mrs Dubray would not be returning to the school for a
considerable period. Parents were known to be visiting the neighbouring
five schools with a view to transferring their children. It was considered
vital to prevent this by giving an assurance that the supply teacher would
remain for the present term. It was accepted that the letter should be
shown to Mrs Dubray's 'friend' but this was to agree a suitable wording
and not to give the 'friend' the power of veto.

Four days later parents received the following letter from the
chairman of the governors:

Dear Parents,   28th January 1988

Following my letter of 15th January, the governors thought that you
would welcome some further information about the situation at the
school. As you will know, Mrs Dubray is unwell and not at school.
While she is away, Mrs Paxton will continue to act as headteacher
and Mrs Evans will stay at school [Mrs Evans was the supply
teacher]. Once Mrs Dubray's doctor says she is well enough to return
to school, the Director of Education will see her in order to follow up
investigations I referred to in my previous letter.

Following more recent approaches from parents, I met with the
Director of Education and told him of specific concerns. As a result
of this meeting, I decided to convene a special governors' meeting to
discuss the way in which the local education authority proposed to
review the school's curriculum. This meeting has now taken place
and there were long and detailed discussions concerning the action
that the local education authority had taken and is proposing to take
over the next two terms.

At this meeting, the governors requested the local authority as a
matter of urgency to provide full support and advice for the staff of
the school including the programme of diagnostic testing in literacy
and numeracy. The outcome of these tests will then form the basis of
further work in the school in discussion with the governors and
parents. In view of the urgency of this work, it is anticipated that it
should begin immediately.

I shall write to you again should there be any further information to communicate. In the meanwhile, if you would like to discuss this letter with me I shall be pleased to speak to you.

Yours sincerely,

Sydney Carter.

That letter was received five days after the governors' meeting. In the nature of such things, most of what had been decided at the governors' meeting was public knowledge on the same evening as the meeting had taken place. Parents had been generally reassured by the reports that action was being taken and that it was unlikely that any decision about Mrs Dubray's possible return could be taken until the summer term at the earliest. But whatever interpretation, with hindsight, might be put upon the chairman's letter, the result was to convince some parents that Mrs Dubray's return was imminent.

The very sentence which had been taken out from the penultimate draft paragraph of the letter had, after informing parents about the programme of testing and review, gone on to state that it was anticipated that this process would take at least a term and that when these results were available they would be discussed with Mrs Dubray prior to a decision being made about the timing of a return to school. It was felt by those governors who voted for this section to be included that it gave a 'strong hint' that Mrs Dubray's return to school could not take place for some time.

Given that this paragraph of the letter was omitted, the effect of the letter was immediate. On the following day, two of the parents broke ranks and withdrew their children from the school. The outcry among the rest of the group was fierce and passionate and mostly directed against the chairman. Explanations for his perceived betrayal ranged from a scurrilous rumour that he was having an affair with the headteacher to complaints that he had strong objections to the dinner lady, Mavis Sandown, who had originally told parents about Mrs Dubray's alleged indiscretion. He was alleged to have called Mrs Sandown 'a troublemaker' who had withdrawn her child from the school to exacerbate the already strained situation.

It was at this point, and in response to these various pressures, that the author, before departing abroad, wrote to the spokesperson of the parents' group, Geoffrey Simpson. The vital sentence in the letter stated:

I have no longer confidence in the chairman to find a satisfactory solution to your problem. His actions are not, I believe, malicious, but are politically naive. In the circumstances, I now think that the

only way forward is to take your case direct to the local authority
and to exert as much pressure as possible.

The letter was in the nature of a holding operation until a meeting
could be held to decide future action. It also strove to reduce the wave
of antagonism felt by some of the parents involved towards the chairman
and to prevent any further withdrawal of pupils. As a private communication it might have done this job admirably, but a member of the
parents group duplicated copies and sent it to every parent in the school.

The very day after the letter had been circulated, the school was
invaded by journalists from the local paper. The journalists seemed
remarkably well-informed and rang key parents to ask if they could
interview children to hear a full account of what had taken place on the
last day of the Christmas term. In response to the author's letter, the
chairman called an emergency meeting of the governors for 9 February.
The meeting was called for an evening when neither the parent governor
concerned nor the other strong supporter of the parents, the councillor,
could be present. Argument centred around the interpretation of the
letter. Against the view that the chairman's letter could now be
interpreted 'that Mrs Dubray's return was imminent', the chairman:

> explained that the letter had been agreed apart from a few minor
> alterations in the interests of grammatical correctness.

The minutes reveal that the local authority representative then:

> explained that he had advised the chairman to remove the clause
> concerned (the one dealing with Mrs Dubray's return). He had felt
> it advisable to read the letter to Mrs Dubray's 'friend'. The 'friend'
> did not have power of veto but he had reacted to part of the letter
> and it was the Assistant Director's view that its inclusion could lay
> the governors open to grievance. If Mrs Dubray had forced the
> issue, the governors would have had to suspend her and the Deputy
> Director's advice was that the governors did not have grounds to
> suspend Mrs Dubray.

There followed a brief comment about the author's letter. One
governor reported that a parent had asked him to say that she objected to
the letter and thought the comments about the chairman of the governors
were uncalled for. Discussion then took place about the curriculum
review and the testing. The Assistant Education Officer explained that
the reason for the delay in starting was because of the need to consult
with the NFER. The meeting then agreed without voting to endorse the
current action and not to hold a meeting with the parents.

The meeting then went on to discuss the chairman's letter to parents
dated 28 January. The chairman argued that the first paragraph was an

attempt to suggest obliquely that Mrs Dubray would not return for some time. However, the assistant teacher, Mrs Paxton, and another governor both confirmed that there had been strong rumours that Mrs Dubray's sick note had ended and that she would return to school. The minute continues:

> governors noted that the rumours were not as a result of the chairman's letter.

The Assistant Director of Education then again stressed that the chairman had acted on his advice. The minute records that:

> he [the Assistant Director] had not felt that the sense of the letter would be altered and he was of the opinion that the inclusion of the omitted words could leave the governors in a formal dispute where grievance procedures would arise because certain assumptions about Mrs Dubray appear to have been made.

Asked about the removal of the three children from the school the minute records that:

> The chairman confirmed that the Education Department's record showed that parents had made their decision before the chairman's letter had been dispatched.

Subsequently this statement proved to be untrue but it may have had an effect on the meeting since the governors were asked to endorse the action of sending the letter on 28 January on their behalf and five governors voted in favour of this proposition with one abstention.

The meeting then went on to discuss the author's letter criticizing the chairman. Among the minutes recorded was the fact that:

> it was felt that things had started to settle down and the letter had stirred everything up. Some parents had been outraged by the letter.

The chairperson explained that his serious concern about the letter was that it completely disregarded the agreed confidentiality of the governors' meeting. It was then proposed by the two governors who had opposed sending the original letter to parents that:

> governors register their distaste for the letter of 3rd February 1988 and its breach of confidentiality of the governors' meeting as agreed by the governors, and this was carried with one abstention.

The governors accepted the advice of the local authority representative that they could not hold a meeting with parents until Mrs Dubray had returned to work. They therefore agreed to defer their annual meeting for parents until the summer term and to delay their ordinary spring term governors' meeting until March. Meanwhile, they asked the acting headteacher to arrange a parents' evening on 14 March at which the LEA representative would be present. This would give parents an opportunity to discuss, on an individual basis, any concerns they had about their children.

In spite of the stress placed upon confidentiality details of the governors' meeting were widely known by next day. From the perspective of some parents, the construction to be put upon these events was unmistakable. First, the meeting had been so organized that the two most prominent governors supporting their right to be heard had been excluded and second, the governors had yet again, under the direction of the local authority, decided to defer a full meeting with parents where the various issues could be fully aired. The offer to hold a parents' evening was seen by some as a device by the local authority to 'divide and rule'.

No formal indication was given to parents that the annual meeting, due to be held on 21 March, had been cancelled. It was argued at the Extraordinary Governors Meeting that, since the parents had not yet received official notice of a March meeting, there was no reason they should be told that it had been cancelled. Some parents, however, decided that they would attend the parents' evening as a group in order to put their case. This provoked the following letter, dated 11 March, to all governors from the chairman:

Dear Colleague,

It has been brought to my notice that a suggestion has been made that parents should stay behind after next Monday's meeting in order to divert the intended purpose of the evening into a more open meeting.

I appreciate the wish to hold an open meeting and I support its principle but have no reason to recommend altering the early decision of the governors that such a meeting could most usefully be held when there was something substantial to put before parents as a result of the work of the advisory and support services. A great deal of time and careful thought has been put into this work which is reaching a stage where a report could be prepared for consideration by governors and subsequent presentation to parents.

The parents' evening next Monday was intended to provide an opportunity for the parents to discuss their own children and to raise any general concerns individually. Although there will be limited time for private discussion with teachers, personnel from the LEA and governors will be more flexibly available. The opportunity should therefore be sufficient for all concerns to be expressed. These can be discussed at our governors meeting on 21st March.

At the meeting, I suggest that we should fix a date at the beginning of next term for holding a meeting with parents, governors and representatives of the LEA. I should like this date to be communicated to parents by the end of this term.

It seems clear that the decision of parents to pressurize governors in this way had an effect as, for the first time, a commitment was given to hold a full open meeting with parents. The previous reasoning, namely that a meeting could not be held without the presence of Mrs Dubray, had now been abandoned.

The parents' evening proved relatively uneventful. Few governors, other than the chairman, were subjected to hostile questioning. Something of the anxieties of parents can be seen from one unsigned letter which was sent to the author with a request that the contents be communicated to the governors at their next meeting. It began:

1) Parents are *still* concerned. This was proved by (a) the usual ten minutes not being sufficient. After eight parents the teacher was running 50 minutes late and (b) parents were prepared to wait an hour and a half to see the four people from County Hall.

2) Parents still wish to know (a) if Mrs Dubray will return, (b) the teacher for next term and (c) the plans for the future of the school.

I personally felt it sad that the governors were so obviously divided. As chairman of the governors I should have thought his job was to try to unite his members, not argue with them publicly during a school parents' meeting. His answer to my one question concerning the teacher for next term was not in the tone I would have expected. To speak in the way he did was appalling. I see now why people have little faith in the governing body.

The delayed governors' meeting on 21 March was relatively uneventful. There was general relief that the parents' evening was over and the local authority officers appeared appreciative of the way that parents had put their questions and expressed their concerns. The meeting heard from the mathematics adviser and from the chief educational psychologist concerning the test results. The minute reports the mathematics adviser saying 'the results did not give rise to concerns'. The principal educational psychologist reported that:

whereas both vocabulary and reading were within the expected range, spelling results were disappointing.

According to the minutes, the Assistant Director of Education:

then outlined the future programme which consisted of (1) making the school an 'on target' school which would mean that it received an input from the primary advisers, (2) continuing the cyclic process of curriculum review, (3) having colleagues from various disciplines join the discussion to offer their advice, (4) giving mathematics support for various activities which could be followed such as the practical side of mathematics, (5) offering the support of the literacy support service to help the development of language teaching and (6) providing support to the acting head and her colleague through a weekly meeting to discuss progress.

For a school which was claimed to have average results, this amount of support did seem to some governors present extraordinary, but generally the proposals were welcomed. In response to these concerns the Assistant Director of Education urged that at the parents' meeting:

care must be taken not to give the impression that the LEA is deploying a plethora of resources in response to dire results. The quality of education is not the main issue. The recreation of parental confidence in the school was of prime importance.

It was then agreed that:

the chair take note of any comments of a personal nature but not invite discussion of Mrs Dubray's circumstances because of her absence through illness.

The only other item concerned the question of confidentiality. There were now signs that the parental concerns about the previous meetings had had an effect since minute 3 (bii) reported:

several governors indicated the disquiet which confidential minutes had created among parents. It was agreed that the minutes of this meeting be as open as possible.

Before the annual parents' meeting governors received a long letter from the Assistant Director of Education. According to this letter:

It might be helpful for the chairman to introduce the meeting on 14th April by explaining its purpose. In response to a request from the governing body the LEA has worked extensively with staff and children in the school in a review of the curriculum. Aspects of mathematics and reading have received particular attention. The purpose of the meeting is to share with parents the first results of the review, describe the next steps of the review and give parents an opportunity to comment on these developments.

The letter then goes on to warn governors of the danger of being associated with complaints about an individual teacher which might lead to a possible civil action by the individual concerned and concludes:

> Parents may of course raise questions regarding the return of the Head to the school. I should like to suggest that the LEA representative should be asked to respond to such queries. I appreciate that in practice it is difficult to structure a public meeting in the precise way I have described and it will be important that the governors are seen to act collectively and support the chairman in his conduct of the meeting.

At the opening of the annual parents' meeting on 14 April it was soon clear how the acting chairman, a representative of the Diocesan Education Board, had interpreted the Assistant Director's final paragraph. When one parent attempted to ask why, although the concerns had been expressed in December, this was the first opportunity they had been given to discuss them openly with the governors, the chairman ruled this was not a proper question for the meeting and that its purpose was for parents to hear 'what the LEA had to say'.

The LEA representatives than explained the results for Mrs Dubray's class. On the British vocabulary scale the mean was 104.5, with a standard deviation of 8.48. Only two children achieved more than one standard score above the population mean on this test. For the infants, however, there was a mean of 106.5 and a standard deviation of 15 which suggests that these pupils were much more typical for the population on whom the test was validated. However, the chief educational psychologist in his report stated:

> this gives an average very slightly above the national average in a spread of schools that is of a much more limited range than one would expect to find nationally. This is the kind of result that can occur, however, with a small number of children. It does indicate, however that the vocabulary levels at junior class at Carhill are not significantly different from the national average.

The statistical interpretation of such a result is, of course, open to the opposite interpretation. With a small sample of children random errors should lead to a much wider distribution because of the possibility of 'rogue' results. The fact that junior scores cluster very tightly around the mean could lead to a statistical interpretation that the results are of educational significance. In contrast, the infant results which were not mentioned were more typical of what one would expect with a small sample. The result could be therefore be interpreted as vindicating the parents' anxieties to some extent.

The psychologist went on to argue that the vocabulary test was the best predictor of general achievement. The importance of this judgement is not hard to see when the results for reading and spelling were presented. Two children were identified as having serious problems in reading, of whom only one had previously been referred to the reading support service. In the analysis seven children scored below average on accuracy and three below on comprehension. In the infants, of the nine children tested, five were below average. On the Vernon spelling test, four juniors were more than 18 months behind, another four were between 6 and 18 months behind, another three were within 6 months of the expected result for their age group. Eleven out of fourteen junior children were therefore below average.

The psychologist, however, concluded that, overall, the results for reading were marginally disappointing and that the test results for spelling were also disappointing. The psychologist did have words of comfort for these parents. Having earlier cautioned parents that with such a small sample it was difficult to generalize, he nevertheless concluded:

Of the 28 children tested, 4 give rise for concern and a number of others need to be monitored in at least one aspect of their literacy development. However, the Warnock report on special educational needs which led to the 1981 Education Act, indicates that some 20% of children at any one time are likely to have special educational needs which warrant some additional attention, either from within the school's own resources or from outside. The figures from this testing are consistent with that conclusion.

Results in mathematics gave an overall mean of 97.5 with a range of 81-114. Parents again were not impressed, pointing out that on these scores none of the children would have passed the old 11 plus, nor would any of these children, on the basis of these scores, have been placed in an 'O level' set in a comprehensive school. All governors in response to parents' questions agreed that these results were disappointing.

Much discussion then followed about the level of support which the LEA would now guarantee. Parents were not slow to take the view that the Assistant Director of Education in his letter to governors had been eager to dispel, namely, that if the school was being given all this help, something must have been wrong in the past. Questions were asked about the balance of the curriculum, which were not answered. Parents were critical that the authority had been in the school for a term and could not say how much time was given to activities such as dance, swimming, and games, compared to English and mathematics.

The future of the headteacher, Mrs Dubray, was raised indirectly by only one parent. The general feeling that emerged from this discussion was that whatever had happened in the past was best forgotten, but the school needed a new start. The only source of discord came at the end of the meeting, when the acting chairman closed it abruptly, saying 'I think I must close the meeting now as you have all had a fair chance to raise questions'. There then followed some sharp informal exchanges when it was pointed out that it was a meeting which parents had waited a long time for. The meeting continued in informal groups and by the end there was a general feeling of satisfaction. Most parents seemed pleased that, at last, they had been able to say what they felt and had been listened to.

7.5 A sequel: petition and counter-petition

There the matter might have ended but for the publication in the newspaper of the whole story four days later and two further days of notoriety with the visit of television cameras to the school. It was naturally assumed that someone had leaked the story immediately after the meeting. In fact, the journalist, a freelance, had held the story over since Christmas in the hope that a public meeting might lead to more serious disputes and accusations. When it appeared that there was nothing which could enlarge the existing story, it was sold to whatever national newspaper would take it. The backlash in the shape of the first petition, signed by nine families with, it was claimed, eighteen children in the school was, according to the other parent governor 'the voice of the silent majority at last'. Many who had signed had not attended the open meeting. The petition expressed sympathy for Mrs Dubray:

in the cruel and remorseless programme of character assassination that had been conducted by some members of the village over the past two years, culminating in the grossly exaggerated reaction to an error of judgement last Christmas.

It then continues:

Lastly we were extremely unhappy about the behaviour of a parent governor. Publicly quoted statements have caused outrage within the village in general and constant undeserved criticism of most aspects of school life have served to undermine morale within the school. This is strongly resented. We believe note should be taken of the full spectrum of opinion amongst parents rather than an unrepresentative minority. We have no confidence in a governor who behaves in this fashion.

In reply, the other nine families responded that:

they were surprised that they were not given an opportunity to comment on the petition although they too had children at the school.

161

Maurice Galton

They go to say that:

> had more of those who signed the petition been at the meeting, they
> would have realised the concerns expressed 'dealt with purely
> professional aspects to do with standards, balance of the
> curriculum, timekeeping and favouritism'. There has never been
> any attempt to vilify Mrs Dubray. Indeed, many of us following an
> earlier attempt three years ago to resolve similar parental concerns,
> gave an active support by working voluntarily in the school in the
> hope that they could be solved internally.

And the petition continues:

> We wish to express our absolute confidence in the parent governor
> referred to in the statement. He was the only governor prepared to
> meet and talk with us during the early part of the year. We have
> used his advice and guidance but would stress that in no way have
> we been pressurised into anything which we did not whole-
> heartedly agree with.

In the accompanying letter to the Director of Education these parents
pointed out that had not three families by then left the school, they
would have represented an equal number of children; and there the
matter ended until the formal announcement in October 1988 that Mrs
Dubray had taken early retirement on health grounds.

7.6 The LEA and parents: paternalism or partnership?

The eventual departure of the headteacher in one sense resolved the
situation. Had she returned at least four other parents with six other
children had threatened to remove their children from the school,
bringing the number on roll to well below thirty. More importantly, the
fact that so many parents in Carhill sent their children to other local
schools might have been expected to influence the choice of newcomers
to the village. While with its modern facilities Carhill itself might not
have been at risk of closure, its falling roll might have had implications
for neighbouring schools.

Although, therefore, the issue of closure was never raised by local
authority representatives, there remains the question of the relationship
between the local authority, the parents, and the governors. The events
occurred at a time when the 1986 Education Act had guaranteed parents
greater access to information about the workings of their school. The
local authority concerned had promised to implement a 'new partner-
ship' in response to the Act. Subsequently the 1988 Education Reform
Act has now shifted this balance of power further in favour of parents.
Yet throughout the events described the local authority appeared to

162

adopt a paternalistic attitude towards the parents concerned. Meetings would be held when there was information to be given rather than at the parents' request. Even formal meetings required under the 1986 Act were postponed without any public reasons being given for the delay.

How, then, should one interpret these events? The easiest and simplest explanation would be that the local authority hoped that if they 'did as little as possible' the situation would resolve itself. Three years previously, a similar situation was stabilized once the children of the parents most concerned had transferred to secondary school. In his response to Mrs Fielding's letter of May 1985, Mr Woodstock had promised substantial support for the school, yet, as the minutes record, the promised support appeared to make little difference to the curriculum. During this period, however, there was little substantial public criticism of the school. In the case described in this chapter, since the most vociferous opposition to Mrs Dubray came from parents whose children were in the top half of the junior school, it might be hoped that a similar resolution could be achieved with time. The task of the local authority officers was therefore to play down the extent of the crisis, make promises of action but drag out the consequences as long as possible until the situation gradually resolved itself.

The actual incident of strip poker was therefore treated as 'an error of judgement'. We might speculate on the LEA response had a male headteacher been involved. At the beginning the local authority warned governors of the consequences of even meeting with parents to discuss the issues, arguing that they (the governors) might then be personally liable in any legal proceedings for unfair dismissal.

There was also the prolonged delay before testing. Literacy testing did not begin until March, two months after the promise of an investigation, on the grounds that the NFER had to be consulted. To take this claim seriously we have to believe that within the whole of the local authority's psychological service there was no one capable of choosing appropriate tests for primary school children. As might be expected, most of the governors were easily convinced of the LEA's point of view that no meetings with parents could take place until the authority was ready to supply parents with the 'full' facts. Only after the parents' evening, when it appeared that the opposition was less militant, was the LEA's original recommendation that no 'open' meeting should be held in the absence of Mrs Dubray, withdrawn. Even then the LEA took steps to control the 'agenda' of the meeting as far as possible.

An alternative explanation sees the local authority doing its best to solve a difficult situation, confident that, given time, it could counsel Mrs Dubrary to take early retirement through ill health. The aim was to offer as much support to the school as possible, in the hope that it would satisfy the parents, while doing nothing that might give the impression that the authority wished to remove Mrs Dubray. Those responsible for making a medical judgement about the headteacher's condition would then have no grounds for suspecting that the authority was using Mrs Dubray's ill health as a convenient way of solving a long-standing problem. Hence the Director had no option when writing to parents but to imply that Mrs Dubray would, as a matter of course, return to duty once she regained her health. The psychologist and the mathematics adviser had to put the best possible gloss on the test results so that there could be no suspicion that the authority might be trying to get rid of an ineffective teacher. The tests were delayed in order to allow the temporary replacement teacher to give children as much practice as she could in basic numeracy and literacy. Only the chairman of the governors could be taken into the authority's confidence and he, therefore, had to face the brunt of the criticism in acting exactly as the authority recommended. With these delays it was always likely that some parents would grow impatient and withdraw their children, but this would not continue once a new headteacher was appointed and confidence restored.

In this scenario, however, there seems to have been a number of serious miscalculations and errors of judgement by the LEA. The authority initially wrongly assessed the reactions of parents if a meeting had been held. The majority of parents wanted to hear the facts and have the opportunity to express their concerns about their children. Among these parents was a bank manager, an ex-primary teacher, and a temporarily unemployed housewife with a Master's degree in philosophy. Whatever the final strategy, it would seem important for the LEA to have tried to get such people on their side. More importantly, once the fact had been leaked that Mrs Dubray was seeking early retirement on 'health grounds' parents could not let matters settle. In the words of one: 'we have to provide her with evidence that she has something to be stressful about'.

Whichever view one takes of the LEA's motives, the price of such strategies was a high one. At the beginning of the 1987–8 year there were thirty-six pupils in the school. By the March when testing took place there were thirty-one pupils, and by the autumn term of 1988 the roll had fallen to thirty. Over the period numbers were maintained by admitting 4-year-olds. Since concerns were expressed about the headteacher in 1985, nineteen other children in the village of Carhill had been eligible to attend the school. Of these, just under half were educated privately and might have been expected to have been so in any case. The remaining children were scattered around the five other local schools. Had they attended Carhill, it could have been a three-teacher school instead of two and would not have found itself near the critical size for closure.

There is a third possible explanation for these events. In the light of the massive support finally offered the school, the local authority would appear to have failed to redeem the Director's 1985 promise to parents that the LEA would do all they could to rectify the problems at Carhill. The clue to this failure might be found in an 'off the record' remark made by one of the local authority's officials concerned. 'If we had to get rid of Mrs Dubray on the grounds of incompetence, then you would be asking us to get rid of nearly half the staff teaching in our small schools', he is alleged to have said. It is perhaps this negative attitude to the value of small schools, held by many people within local authorities, that lies at the heart of the earlier neglect of a school such as Carhill. As the data in the previous chapters amply demonstrate, with the right teachers and the positive support of parents, which was readily available, small schools can and do compete well with larger ones. It may well be some time before the confidence of parents in the village of Carhill is restored to a level where this fact is fully recognized.

Chpater eight

The small school: trends and possibilities

Maurice Galton and Helen Patrick

In the preceding chapters attention has been paid to various features associated with curriculum provision in small schools. First the teachers' own opinions were sampled and then succeeding chapters described the observed curriculum and the behaviour of pupils and of teachers. Then, the performance of the pupils on standardized tests and also on a range of other skills associated with independent study were presented. These findings, when considered as a whole, suggest that it is inappropriate to provide a portrait of the small school solely in terms of a 'typical' or average member of the sample. The data generally suggest that the variations from the average are sufficiently large to justify the need for extreme care when attempting to apply the results to particular cases. Nevertheless, these findings are interesting in that they tend to contradict some of the myths associated with the small schools debate.

8.1 Overview of the main findings

In this section we present an overview of the main findings from the PRISMS project along with comparative material from other studies.

The data obtained from the questionnaire survey do not support the view that teachers in small schools differ from their colleagues in larger institutions. Like primary teachers generally, most of those who taught in small schools were women, and over half were aged forty or over. Almost all had a teacher's certificate and had trained to teach within the primary age range. Most had studied arts subjects with English and art being the most popular. On average, teachers in both small and larger schools surveyed had substantial teaching experience in a range of primary schools. Those teaching in small schools had experience of teaching in more schools and of teaching a wider age range of pupils than their colleagues from larger establishments. Teachers from small schools appeared to attend as many in-service and other professional meetings as colleagues in larger schools. They also visited teachers' centres as often and received visits from LEA advisers and inspectors in the same proportion as teachers from large schools. The smaller schools did not appear to attract a certain kind of candidate for a teaching post. The respondents to the survey from the small schools had chosen their posts usually for reasons such as promotion, convenience, and availability rather than because they were in small schools. In most respects, therefore, the teacher in a small school was indistinguishable from her colleagues in larger schools.

There were, however, clear structural constraints within which teachers in small schools had to work. The headteacher was usually responsible for teaching a class as well as for running the school. There was less part-time secretarial and caretaking help. Teachers in small schools, therefore, had to take on a wider range of duties. Their views on the curriculum seemed little different from the picture painted by commentators such as Alexander (1984) of the typical primary school curriculum. Most teachers in the PRISMS survey regarded the 'three Rs' as basic but also wanted their pupils to experience a range of subjects and activities of a physical, academic, aesthetic, and social nature. Half the teachers were confident that they could, by dint of opportunism and hard work, provide this broad curriculum. Whenever possible they did so by forging links within the community and with other schools. Of the remaining half only a small minority, all but one from the same school, felt that they could not match the curriculum provision in larger schools while the remaining 40 per cent or so were uncertain, but aimed to do so. In these respects, therefore, teachers in small schools appeared to differ little from the general population of primary teachers. Thus the prevailing myths, discussed in Chapter One, that teachers in small schools were older, more resistant to change, and unlikely to be interested in new curriculum developments were not sustained from this comparative survey of a sample of teachers in both large and small schools from nine local authorities where the PRISMS research took place.

Turning to the curriculum, the patterns observed here were remarkably similar to those obtained in earlier studies of primary schools. Work in computation and what in the ORACLE study was termed 'correct English', took up the largest proportion of the school day. Science, art, mainly in the form of drawing and painting, social studies, and physical activities received similar amounts of attention as that provided by larger schools according to surveys by Bennett *et al.* (1980) and Bassey (1978). Differences between infant- and junior-aged classes were small, with the obvious exception of the amounts of time devoted to listening to children reading. This finding, relating to the overall balance of the curriculum in infant classes, was also compared with data from the recent project concerning educational achievement in some London infant schools, carried out at the Thomas Coram Institute.

When activities such as playtime, tidying up, and dinner breaks were excluded, 58 per cent of the day remained for various curriculum activities. Of this remaining time 38 per cent was given over to language work and nearly 19 per cent to mathematics (Tizard *et al.* 1988). These figures may be compared with those in Chapter Three where 39 per cent of the time in PRISMS infant classes was given over to language activities and nearly 24 per cent to mathematics. The difference in mathematics time may be a function of the different samples, or it may result from the different ways in which the curriculum categories were defined and coded. At the junior level, however, the range of curriculum subjects studied in the PRISMS classrooms, including science, and the proportion of time directed to each curriculum area followed patterns similar to those described in other studies of junior schools. If balance is to be equated simply with coverage then no case can be made against small schools.

To achieve this wide coverage, however, clearly made considerable demands on the teachers. Thus there was a heavy reliance on worksheets and published materials in some curriculum areas, and on teacher-directed work in others. In science, for example, the children had relatively few opportunities to pursue their own ideas but tended to be taught as a class irrespective of the range of age and ability. In mathematics, in contrast, there was a heavy reliance on published schemes. In Chapter Six, for example, Lea reports that over 90 per cent of all mathematics classes used a set scheme of work. Among the classes studied there was little evidence of creative mathematical work or of problem-solving involving practical measurement. Teachers tended to work through the examples in the book and, with some exceptions, rarely set exercises which related to the children's school or class environment.

Because classes in small schools tended to be smaller than those in larger ones, the pupils interacted more frequently with the teachers. Much of this attention had to do with instruction. This was particularly true of class and group settings where, as a result of this more frequent attention, there were fewer opportunities for distraction. Even where children worked independently of the teacher in small groups, a greater proportion of pupils' conversation concerned the task although, overall, there was less pupil-pupil interaction than in larger schools.

Turning to the patterns of teacher interaction, the main strategies used by teachers to cope with pupils of different ages within the same classroom were analysed. The majority of teachers, during any one session, concentrated their attention on one or two main curriculm areas involving the whole class. In this respect PRISMS teachers appeared very similar to those in London junior schools who were studied by Mortimore *et al.* (1988). Thus, where worksheets were widely used, as in mathematics, the teacher might start a group on a topic, then leave them to do examples while moving to another group in the class to begin some work in English, before then returning to the first group to correct and mark the work. At other times, particularly for science and social studies, teachers might set whole class work. This accounted for the relatively high levels of teacher direction in these curriculum areas since it could be difficult to find a range of independent tasks, related to the same theme or topic, that allowed each child to work at his or her own level. When class teaching was used, it was often accompanied by a considerable amount of teacher direction and demonstration rather than pupil participation.

Small classes did allow the teacher to spend extended times with individual pupils, unlike the earlier ORACLE study where the observers' accounts described most individual interactions as of short duration. Even so, when the teacher in a small school was working in areas such as mathematics, children were generally engaged on individual tasks and the teacher moved rapidly from one to another marking work and giving further instructions. One interesting finding was that, even with fewer pupils in the class, the teacher did not spend proportionately more of her time interacting with individual children than did teachers in the ORACLE study. While, because of the smaller class sizes, the pupils received more individual attention than in ORACLE, the ratio between the two levels of attention corresponded very closely to the ratio of the average class sizes in the two studies. It might have been expected that, with the wide age range which existed in most PRISMS junior classes, teachers would have tried to increase the proportion of individual attention, overall, to cope with the difficulties of matching work to the needs of individual pupils. Instead, many teachers preferred to use more whole class teaching, particularly in topic work.

In a topic on leaves, for example, some of the older children might be engaged in examining sections and measuring the areas of different leaves while the younger ones would be concerned with observing and drawing various specimens. While it was clear from the interviews that many teachers were concerned to ensure that in work of this kind the younger children would progress at some later stage to more detailed and precise observations involving accurate measurement, it would be doubtful, under this pattern of organization, whether these younger pupils would ever apply these advanced skills to extend their knowledge about leaves. Given the teachers' reluctance to engage the pupils on the same topic in the following year lest the children should lose interest, these younger pupils would evenutally learn these advanced skills within a different context.

This practice of choosing tasks on the basis of the teacher's estimate of what a particular child or group of children might achieve within a topic has two important consequences. First, there will be little progression in terms of content unless pupils are given opportunities to develop a range of skills using similar themes or topics rather than practising specific skills in a particular subject context. The latter approach results, as we found in the PRISMS project, in the practice of certain skills being associated with particular content areas – observation in science, measuring in mathematics, creativity in art – rather than being experienced across the curriculum. Second, it is unlikely that pupils will consolidate a skill, since psychologists suggest that for this to happen it is necessary to ensure that pupils should be given opportunities to practise that skill in different subject areas as an aid to transfer (Gage and Berliner 1984). Defined in this way, progression as embodied in skills-based curriculum planning occurred to a limited extent in the PRISMS schools. This is a difficult problem, however, and, as we discussed in Chapter Three, is applicable in the primary curriculum generally and not only in small schools.

None the less, it appears there has been little attempt to develop strategies of classroom organization relevant to these problems which would maximize the advantages of small classes. Teachers in small schools receive little in-service training specifically relating to their special circumstances. They therefore apply the organizational methods they learnt during their induction to the profession and which they had used in larger schools, methods which were largely derived in the aftermath of the Plowden Report to cope with the demise of streamed classrooms and the prevalence of mixed-ability grouping.

Another set of issues which we examined concerned the progress and performance of pupils in small schools. Although the emphasis in the research was on the process rather than the products of the primary curriculum, standardized tests in mathematics and English were administered at the beginning and end of the year. These data strongly support the contention of Nash (1978), and other previous researchers, who have claimed that there was no evidence that children in small schools did less well than those in large schools on the 'bare' measures of attainment. In Chapter Five comparison of the results of the present sample with those of the earlier ORACLE study demonstrated that the PRISMS children performed as well as, and in many cases better than, their ORACLE counterparts. The PRISMS teachers can take great satisfaction from this result although supporters of small schools should be cautious in claiming, as some have done, that small schools are superior. The ORACLE study took place seven years before PRISMS, and in the intervening period considerably more emphasis has been placed on testing in junior schools. Standards have probably risen over the last decade and the superiority of the PRISMS sample over ORACLE is most likely a reflection of this fact. What it is fair to say, however, is that children in small schools do not appear to be under-achieving in these basic curriculum areas.

Attempts were also made to assess achievement on a broader range of skills related to the curriculum processes in areas other than basic mathematics and language. To make the assessment of these 'study-skill' areas less formal and integrate it into normal classroom procedure, a series of activities centring around the visit to an imaginary town by beings from another planet was devised. The Prismaston File required pupils to become 'secret agents' and to help the visiting 'Prismons' to find out about the lives of ordinary Earth children and the place where they lived. There was much evidence from the reports by teachers that the children greatly enjoyed the exercise. This part of the work was in many ways experimental in that it attempted to break new ground in methods of assessment and to relate the subject matter and the skills covered by the questions more closely to the curriculum taught.

There was little evidence from the study that the pupils' achievements on the Prismaston File were strongly affected by their curriculum experiences. While one explanation of these findings might be that, in the development of measures of this kind, there is still much to be done to improve reliability and validity, it is also possible to argue that the low correlations are the result of a uniformity of approach to the teaching of such topics giving rise to a uniformity in the curriculum experiences of the pupils. Again, these results seemed unaffected by class size. Few relationships emerged, indicating that in small classes children did better, even though the general finding of the observation study showed that the children in the smaller classes did receive more help from the teacher. To teachers the advantages of small classes are logically and emotionally indisputable. The research evidence suggests, however, that these advantages are not always realized in practice.

Throughout this summary of the main PRISMS findings comparisons have been made regularly with the earlier ORACLE research. The importance of treating these comparisons with caution was emphasized in the opening chapter. It is always difficult to be sure that differences reported are not artefacts of a general change in practice during the past decade. To remedy this defect, to a limited extent, small-scale case studies of larger schools were undertaken in two of the local authorities with contrasting styles of organization. The results of these comparative studies are described in Chapter Five and the evidence suggests that there are very few systematic differences between small and large schools. As we have seen, because of smaller class sizes, teachers in small schools tended to engage in greater amounts of class teaching. Classroom research, both here and in the United States, has demonstrated a high degree of correlation between individual attention and the need for routine instruction. It is not surprising that there was therefore a greater number of routine interactions in the larger schools. Research also shows that there are higher levels of distraction when teachers engage in one-to-one interactions with pupils. This generally occurs when pupils who are not in the direct line of vision of the teacher stop working and engage in various kinds of off-task activities. Again, therefore, it is to be expected that in small schools, where there was a greater proportion of class teaching, there was less distraction of this kind. One needs to be cautious in interpreting this latter finding, however, because it has also been demonstrated in the earlier ORACLE studies that, while children do pay more attention to the teacher during class activity, they find ways of slowing down the rate of working. The observation schedule used in both studies only recorded whether the pupils were seen to be either on- or off-task. No attempt was made to assess the relative efficiency of this task engagement.

For the curriculum categories there were some items where consistent differences were found between small and large schools. There were indications that large junior classes in schools engaged in a slightly greater number of mathematics 'higher-order' cognitive activities. This was reinforced by the fact that in such schools the average number of categories used to describe a curriculum task was slightly higher than in small schools. However, when the analysis was carried out in relation to differences between local authorities, then, with respect to both behaviour and the curriculum, there was a greater number of significant differences. Furthermore, differences within the sample of both small and large schools were even greater, thus reinforcing the earlier conclusion that it is not possible to judge schools in terms of an average. Among any group of small schools, as with large schools, there was a wide range of practice. Practice in local authorities differs and practice in different schools within the local authority differs irrespective of their size.

This comparative study of large and small schools, although restricted to only two of the nine local authorities participating in the PRISMS research, therefore tends to reinforce the argument developed in the earlier chapters namely, that in presenting the case for or against the small school, it is necessary to evaluate the curriculum of that particular school rather than relying on what has been shown to be typical practice. The average values for the many classroom variables presented in the report, can serve as a standard against which these evaluations can be made, but in most cases the variation of individual scores around this central tendency is such that no reliable conclusions can be drawn concerning the general effect of school size on the range of curriculum opportunities offered at primary level.

8.2 Some implications and conclusions concerning small schools

Thus the data show that if we define breadth of curriculum, at its simplest, as the number of different activities (skills, resources, and so on) associated with a particular type of curriculum content, then there existed within the sample of small schools a wide range of practice. By the same token, although the number of schools sampled was small, there was also a similar range in the larger schools. The magnitude of differences between small and large schools was less than that which existed between the two local authorities, between different age ranges, and more importantly, between schools within a local authority. This suggests that each school should be considered on its merits and that proper evaluation procedures should operate before questions of closure are decided.

In our visits to small schools we came across a range of practice not too dissimilar from the parodies of good and bad schools provided in Chapter One. There were schools, for example, where the teaching was done mostly from worksheets and where there was little involvement by either advisory teachers or by 'expert' parents. In the school described in Chapter Seven, children had yet to study the history of the village although its buildings had been a staging post for Cromwell's army before one of the major battles of the Civil War. The area was surrounded by disused railway workings, but transport had never previously been chosen as a topic of study.

In another case there was a wide variation in the overall time for schooling available to children. In the study of one particular local authority, reported by Harrison in Chapter Six, the difference between starting and finishing times in a sample of small schools came to one whole day a week in the most extreme case, although the reasons for these different starting times were obscure.

Set against these examples were other cases where, it seemed to the observers, children experienced a curriculum which was comparable with the best available primary practice. In such schools teachers usually operated as a team covering for each other's lack of expertise in certain key areas. Links were established with other small schools in the same area so that both resources and expertise could be shared and heads made use of their entrepreneurial skills to improve resources. Parents were actively involved in the teaching but these interventions were carefully planned to ensure that a broad balance across a range of activities was maintained. In-service opportunities were also chosen to provide a coherent pattern of staff development. Arrangements were sometimes made to exchange with schools from neighbouring inner city areas so that pupils in the small rural school could have first-hand experience of schooling in a multi-ethnic climate. In such an atmosphere the children appeared to develop considerable resourcefulness and independence. Such schools may be in a minority, but from the evidence of the Plowden Report (1967), the HMI Survey (DES 1978), and the ORACLE findings (Galton *et al.* 1980) this had also been the case among large schools.

As a result of studies such as ORACLE and PRISMS, there now exist comparative data which can be used to conduct the more formal parts of an evaluation of small schools. On standardized tests it may be difficult to interpret some of these results for the reasons already given, for example, the problem of making comparisons over a period of time and the difficulty of matching intake, but at least one could check whether the average performances of pupils in the small schools were significantly different from those found in the PRISMS sample. Estimates of time on task, the extent of collaborative working between pupils, the division of time between different curriculum areas and the extent to which each part of the curriculum is largely taught by means of worksheets and published texts, can all provide a semi-empirical basis for school evaluation in the manner suggested by Shipman (1979). The PRISMS data provide a useful comparison as part of this exercise, and while there is also a range of qualitative judgements to be made, these quantitative measures do at least establish the starting point for discussion.

In the final analysis, closing small schools is largely a political decision determined in part by the financial arrangements which operate in the particular authority. Our experience suggests that the criteria on which these financial judgements are based are often very general. Few of the local authorities taking part in our study could, for example, produce figures relating to the global sums spent on small schools as distinct from primary schools as a whole without a great deal of difficulty. This particularly applied to aspects of in-service provision. Financial comparisons between large and small primary schools are therefore based largely on capitation, maintenance, and salary costs. But, as research discussed in the first chapter has shown, actual costs vary considerably from school to school, partly because of the entrepreneurial activities of headteachers. When resources are limited they should be shared equally or at least allocated according to a prespecified policy designed to overcome weaknesses within the small school system. One of the important gains to come out of the current moves for teacher appraisal may well be to provide better information about the in-service needs of individual schools.

8.3 Small schools and the National Curriculum

The introduction of the National Curriculum into the primary school is an attempt to provide a structure which will be helpful in planning and monitoring the pupils' coverage of the core and foundation subjects. Such an approach assumes a greater degree of collaborative teaching and curriculum planning and a careful appraisal of the place of specialist help and teaching. It is here that the small primary school would appear to be most vulnerable. While it appears to be true that, at present, the small primary school differs in very few aspects from the larger school, its critics might argue that, as greater use of specialist teaching becomes more widespread than hitherto, then the standards in smaller schools will begin to fall behind those of larger ones.

The National Curriculum will require schools to look most carefully at certain features of their practice, particularly those concerned with continuity and progression. If the class teacher's time is not to be taken up in a continuous round of assessment in the core subjects of language, mathematics, and science, then it will require schools to engage in a more detailed analysis of the nature of tasks which pupils undertake. In particular, tasks must be looked at so that they are capable of yielding assessments in more than one target area. A science task, for example, must also be capable of yielding information about the pupils' capacity to engage in practical mathematical activities. If this kind of planning does not occur then there will be a real danger that some of the other areas of the curriculum, including the creative arts, will be squeezed out of the timetable.

It will also be important for teachers to learn how to monitor time. Recent classroom research, including that carried out in the PRISMS study, has pointed to the large disparities which can exist in the time available for pupils to engage in curriculum tasks throughout the school day. The guidelines recently produced by one LEA distinguished between this productive time and 'evaporated time' which is taken up in lunch breaks and transition times between different activities. Such monitoring is obviously harder to accomplish when a wide range of activities is taking place within the same classroom. It is likely that, in many large schools, staff will seek to minimize such problems by re-examining the arrangements of classes, including grouping by levels of attainment for all or some parts of the work rather than, as at present, by age.

In principle, none of these problems should prove insurmountable to small schools. Indeed, it could be argued that with sufficient guidance small schools will find it easier to plan for progression and continuity since they already operate flexible patterns of organization in their effort to cope with the problems of wide age ranges within any one class. The area of gravest concern must be the capacity of many small schools, as presently organized, to improve the planned experiences for pupils particularly in the area of the science curriculum, and later in the

175

introduction of technology, which at the moment receives even less attention in the primary school than science. Without greater co-operation than hitherto between neighbouring small schools, there seems little way that they can hope to meet these new demands.

8.4 Collaboration and co-operation within small schools

Many local authorities already organize neighbouring small schools into clusters or federations. Most of these, however, are loosely organized and the involvement of a particular school is largely left to the head-teacher and governors. Very often parents and governors are even more jealous than the staff of a school's autonomy, fearing that too close a collaboration with neighbours might encourage the local authority to interpret such co-operation as a wish for full amalgamation. Since 1985, however, as a result of a government initiative involving funds from the Education Support Grant (ESG) programme, fourteen local authorities have been exploring different forms of collaboration in a more systematic manner. Each of the authorities has employed a local evaluator, generally a member of the nearby university department or college of education, whose task it has been to monitor the effectiveness of the programme and to make recommendations for further activity. Currently one of the authors (Galton) is assessing these programmes and these local evaluations.

Many of these programmes share the same objectives. In most cases transport has been purchased for each cluster, usually consisting of between five and eight schools, which allows the transfer of pupils and teachers from one school to another. Most of the programmes have a group co-ordinator, a seconded teacher, who works alongside colleagues in each of the schools and also arranges a programme of in-service. Each cluster or federation is given an additional sum of money to spend on resources. In one local authority, for example, this sum amounts to £1,500 and the resource centre is housed in one of the schools in the cluster. In another authority a resource bus, similar to the rural travelling library service, has been developed.

Most of the evaluation reports produced so far testify to the success of these arrangements. As a result of the additional funding there has been a much wider sharing of facilities and pupils have gained by being able to work in larger peer groups of their own age. These visible effects of co-operation have largely dispelled the original fears of parents and governors, that the local authority had some ulterior motive, linked to possible closures, for advancing the cluster scheme.

But the evaluations also show that much remains to be done. Co-operation has tended to remain at a level of sharing resources and teaching facilities. Curriculum planning still largely remains the province of the individual school. When shared planning does take place it usually operates at headteacher level only and decisions are then handed down to individual teachers within the different schools so that they do not have the sense of 'ownership' which comes from shared decision-making. Several of the evaluation reports give examples of the kinds of INSET activities which have taken place. Most of these INSET days have been used to widen the range of teaching techniques in particular curriculum subjects. For example, there have been sessions dealing with the use of computers or specialized instruction in weaving. There are few courses which have devoted time to consideration of issues of classroom organization and pedagogy with specific reference to the problems of teaching in small schools. Not surprisingly, therefore, the local evaluation reports conclude that four years after the start of these ESG programmes there is little sign of any sizeable shift in practice or in attitudes to children's learning.

Within the context of the demands which will be made by the National Curriculum it is difficult to see how these loose federations can engage in the required level of detailed planning that will enable the constituent schools to satisfy the attainment criteria at the different stages of primary schooling. If each school, its governors, and headteacher, jealously guard their right to make appointments to the staff, on the grounds of what is thought best for the particular school, it will be impossible to develop the necessary expertise within each cluster that will be adequate for the demands of the National Curriculum. At the same time, if local authorities operate local financial management (LFM), adopting the same criteria for both small and large schools, then the former will, on their own, be unable to provide sufficiently well-resourced classrooms to enable teachers to meet these new attainment targets. The implications for small schools, in the era of the National Curriculum, would seem to be that they need to pool resources, including staff expertise, so that as a group they provide the same facilities and personnel as found in suburban schools of greater size.

It is doubtful whether the present informal arrangements can ensure this degree of co-operation. One possible solution is for the local authority to provide an additional teacher, in place of the co-ordinator, which would allow one of the heads in the cluster to be relieved completely of teaching duties and to act as overall manager for all the schools. So that the danger of one school dominating the cluster could be avoided it would be possible to rotate this management role between the different schools on a two- or three-year basis. A similar arrangement already exists in one of the nine ESG-funded local authorities. Cases can also be found in some Scandinavian countries, notably Sweden, although there the arrangement is more formal and the head-teacher is made the permanent head of several small schools. The major function of the non-teaching head would be to plan resource allocation and co-ordinate staffing needs while supervising the arrangements for shared timetabling activities and organizing in-service provision. It might be argued that such suggestions are far too radical, given the traditions of autonomy which exist and the difficulties which some local authorities have had in persuading some schools to pool existing resources other than the extra funds provided by the ESG programme. Local authorities, however, do have bargaining power, in that without greater co-operation between schools within clusters they will be unlikely, at a time of scarce resources, to provide sufficient extra support to enable individual small schools to meet the National Curriculum criteria. Unless small schools are seen to be pro-active in their response to the National Curriculum then pressure for further closures from central government is likely to grow.

8.5 Small schools and the future

Already it is clear from the published schemes that the proposed National Curriculum for primary schools is not simply a demand for teachers to 'return to basics'. The criteria laid down so far include a range of standard assessment tasks which can be classified as 'higher-order cognitive activities', demanding independent thinking and working by pupils. In the United States and in this country, with the publication of the ILEA junior study (Mortimore *et al.* 1988) there has been a tendency to emphasize various forms of what has been described as 'direct instruction', including the use of drills, greater amounts of class teaching, and structured activities with heavy emphasis on academic content. However, research in the United States has also shown that the direct instruction approach, while very suitable for teaching basic skills such as reading, writing, and computation, is far less successful for the very kinds of task which best develop these 'higher-order' thinking skills. According to some recent research by Jennifer Nias (1988) these tasks require teachers to foster a particular kind of relationship with their pupils which is very different from the form of dependency which the direct instruction model deliberately sets out to create. It would seem that small schools with reduced class sizes and a more intimate atmosphere are in an excellent position to create the kind of relationship that is supportive of these kinds of more complex learning. Yet, as the results of the PRISMS study show, teachers in small schools have, to some extent, failed to capitalize on their unique opportunities in this respect.

What can be said, therefore, is that in these respects small schools do not maximize their potential. This seems particularly true in the matter of class size. In the PRISMS sample very few positive effects were found to be associated with decreasing class size. In small classes, the advantage of greater teacher attention was often frustrated by organizational arrangements. While some of these difficulties must relate to the fact that small classes in small schools are also associated with mixed-age and therefore wider ability ranges, it is difficult not to draw the conclusion that the teacher in the small school may need special training to cope with these problems. As our data show, teachers in small schools differed little in background and in training from colleagues from larger institutions. Their practice was very similar to that described in many other studies. There is an urgent need for those involved in in-service training to encourage teachers in the small school to research their own classrooms on issues such as class size and vertical grouping, so that data can be collected which probe beyond the quantitative differences which the PRISMS study has exposed. To summarize, local authorities who intend to maintain their small schools need to address themselves to the problem of evaluation and careful monitoring of resources, and to institute special in-service arrangements to maximize the advantages which small schools enjoy, as well as seeking to overcome their apparent disadvantages.

In the last analysis, small schools, like primary schools in general, do not appear to operate in ways which are consistent with the theories on which their practice is supposedly based. During the twenty years since the publication of the Plowden Report, little has been done to increase teachers' understanding of the ways in which children learn effectively *in a school context*. This is due to the fact that learning has largely been treated as a cognitive activity and its social implications have been neglected. The ideology of 'progressivism' appears at times to be presented in terms of anarchic principles with the main emphasis placed on the individual child's needs and freedom of choice. The teacher's role is reduced to that of facilitator with little say or control over classroom events. Good practice is modelled on descriptions taken from schools in the private sector where freedom to experiment goes far beyond that which could be tolerated in a state primary school. The success claimed for these approaches in private schools has been attributed to the fact that staff adopted a consistent approach to both learning and behaviour problems. Children who stole received the same kinds of treatment as those who refused to attend mathematics classes. Within such a structure children had the advantage of knowing what was expected of them (Hemming 1972).

In state primary schools teachers have never felt free to adopt such strategies (Nias 1986). General policy has been to try to maximize the opportunities for independence in children's learning while retaining firm control over pupils' behaviour. A 'soft' version of the 'don't smile until Christmas' advice to new teachers is still prevalent and in the

ORACLE study teachers talked about being highly directive until the children had learnt 'correct habits of study'. The observations showed that most of these directions were to do with discipline and control.

Recent research has focused on the difficulty that pupils experience when coping with a style of 'progressive practice' based on the principle that 'when pupils are engaged in a cognitive activity they do as they think but when the issue concerns either conduct or behaviour then pupils must do as the teacher says'. The work of Walter Doyle, for example, shows how children continually negotiate with teachers to clarify this ambiguity (Doyle 1979, 1983). In questioning, for example, children are often unsure of the status of the teacher's demands. While being encouraged to speculate they fear that if the answer is inappropriate they will be accused of not paying attention by the teacher because they have given the wrong answer. Faced by such dilemmas most children devise procedures, described by Measor and Woods (1984) as knife-edging strategies, whereby they seek to avoid participation in these exchanges. They also bargain for tasks which carry less 'risk' of failure, behaving well while completing a straightforward worksheet but disrupting the lesson when the work becomes more difficult and challenging (Elliott *et al.* 1981).

Pollard, in his book, *The Social World of the Primary School*, identifies similar examples of pupils' dilemmas (Pollard 1985), and Galton, in a study of collaborative group work, describes instances where children report 'getting done' for their ideas when in fact the cause of the teacher's displeasure was the manner in which they gave their opinions (Galton 1987). Both Pollard and Galton argue that the area of negotiation between teachers and pupils should include classroom rules and behaviour as well as the curriculum. This will enable a structure to develop where pupils are more confident and, as a result, are prepared to take more responsibility for their learning in the manner advised by the Plowden Committee.

Implicit in this view is the notion that some aspects of the classroom relationship are not negotiable, one obvious example being matters concerned with safety. In schools around the country there are many teachers who are struggling to define these boundaries between freedom and licence. In the follow-up ORACLE study, for example, there were classes where children and teachers negotiated about the classroom organization, starting with the teacher's formulation of the problem in terms of a question to the pupils:

> There's one of me and thirty-three of you. Much of my time is spent trying to deal with lots of trivial questions so that I never get time to spend more than a few seconds to talk about work and

about any problems. How can we organize ourselves so that if you want a long time you can have it?

Such negotiations are not easy. Initially they can lead to high levels of stress, particularly in schools with a large staff, where some colleagues may not understand or may be opposed to such ideas. It is, however, a proud boast of many teachers from small schools that one of the advantages they enjoy is ease of communication between colleagues, and the excellent relationships that are developed with a small group of children. Small schools, therefore, have considerable advantages when attempting to innovate along these lines. It may be that the greatest contribution small schools can make over the next decade will be to develop our ideas about classroom practice in ways which replace what John Dewey as long ago as 1928 described as 'the negative aspects of progressivism' by a more coherent theory of teaching and learning for our primary schools.

Appendix I: Curriculum categories of the observation schedule

Each curriculum task was analysed in terms of several characteristics. First, the task CONTENT was recorded, second, the RESOURCES used were noted, and third, the various DEMANDS made upon pupils while they performed the task were coded.

Content was classified either as mathematics, language, or topic (including science, expressive arts, history, and geography). Resources included the use of charts, textbooks, and apparatus. Task demands recorded such information as the STAGE the task had reached, the CRITERION to which the pupils' performance had to conform, and the MEDIUM by which pupils took in information about the task or expressed their results.

The full list of categories together with their meaning is given in Table AI.1. These may be located in the table by means of the following key category numbers:

01 - 17	Mathematics	NUMBER
18 - 26 & 100	Mathematics	PRACTICAL
27 - 32	Mathematics	CONCEPTS
33 - 37	RELATE	(the relation which the pupil has to take into account between the terms being dealt with)
38 - 45	STAGE	(the stage the pupil has reached in the task)
46 - 53 & 110	MEDIUM	(the manner in which pupils take in information for the task or express the result [mathematics number not coded])
54 - 61	ACTION	(the action the pupil takes to convert the information acquired to the required presentation)
62 - 67	CRITERION	(criteria to which the pupils' performance should conform)

68 - 71	GAMES	(includes physical and educational games and activities requiring either competition or co-operation between individuals or teams)
72 - 82	RESOURCES	
83 - 88	EQUIPMENT	
89 - 99	TOPIC	(all content other than mathematics and language)
101-109	LANGUAGE	

Table AI.1 Full list of categories used with brief description of their meaning

No.	Category	Meaning	% of observations Infants	Juniors
01	DIGITS	(the problem has at most one digit in any term)	7.4	2.0
02	DIGITS	(the problem has two digits in some terms)	7.3	7.8
03	DIGITS		0.3	5.4
04	DIGITS		0.00*	1.8
05 to 09	DIGITS		0.04	0.6
10	COUNT	(the problem involves counting)	12.6	7.9
11	PLACEV	(the problem involves place-values)	4.1	9.5
12	ADD	(addition must be performed)	5.3	6.6
13	SUBTR	(subtraction must be performed)	3.2	4.6
14	MULT	(multiplication must be performed)	1.0	5.1
15	DIVIDE	(the problem involves division, fractions, or decimals)	0.3	5.5
16	CARRY	(the problem involves carrying between columns)	1.6	6.6
17	TABLES	(there is explicit use of tables or number-bonds)	0.4	1.9
18	LENGTH	(either sums about lengths, or measuring lengths)	1.9	2.7
19	WEIGH	(either weighing or sums about weight)	0.6	0.8
20	TIME	(either measuring time or sums about time)	1.4	1.7
21	AREA	(either measurement or sums about area)	0.1	0.7
22	VOLUME	(either measuring or sums about volumes)	0.5	0.5
23	ANGLES	(angles are involved in the problem)	0.1	1.0
24	SYMMET	(the problem uses symmetry, e.g. in art)	0.4	0.6
25	SHAPE	(shapes must be recognized or measured)	3.9	3.7
26	MONEY	(recognizing, counting, using, or sums about money)	0.8	2.6
100	TEMP	(temperature)	0.04	0.03
27	SETS	(classification into sets, or unions and intersections)	3.1	1.4
28	SCALE	(ratios of fractions, e.g. on maps)	0.00	0.6

29	LOGIC	(logical puzzles, writing computer programs)	0.04	0.5
30	MATRIX	(using two-dimensional tables of data)	0.1	1.2
31	GRAPHS	(graphs, bar-charts, pie-charts, etc.)	1.1	2.0
32	NTWORK	(networks, e.g. flow-charts, road maps)	0.02	0.2
33	MATCH	(e.g. find the difference between two pictures, find the word whose meaning matches the definition)	7.0	2.7
34	ORDER	(place a series of things in order)	2.1	2.1
35	COMPAR	(compare according to a criterion, e.g. find the strongest adjective or the largest number in a set)	1.9	2.7
36	PREDIC	(make a prediction, e.g. pick the right word in a cloze procedure, estimate numerical result before calculation)	0.4	2.2
37	MEANNG	(meanings of words or concepts, e.g. cloze procedure)	4.3	6.8
39	WAIT	(waiting, e.g. for paint to dry; or task not yet given)	4.0	3.4
40	INSTR	(receiving instructions on how to do task)	5.0	6.4
41	PLAN	(the pupil has to plan in advance of doing the task)	0.2	0.8
42	ROUTIN	(tidying up or getting things out as the given task)	8.9	7.4
43	ASSESS	(assessing own progress on task; or weighing evidence)	0.3	1.3
44	REPORT	(reporting results, either written or verbal)	0.7	2.5
45	FEEDBK	(receiving feedback about performance or ideas)	1.1	2.6
46	READ	(the task involves reading)	16.7	21.6
47	LISTEN	(the task involves listening, to speech, or music)	30.6	29.1
48	OBSERV	(acquiring information by looking, excluding reading)	17.1	13.2
49	WRITE	(presenting results of task by writing)	17.6	22.8
50	VOCAL	(vocal presentation, i.e. talking or singing)	17.4	13.1
51	DRAW	(drawing; this includes paint or crayons)	19.8	15.6
52	ACTOUT	(results embodied in movement, e.g. dance, play music)	10.6	4.8
53	MATERL	(results embodied in material, e.g. clay, LEGO)	13.9	11.8
110	HARDWR	(pupil operates equipment, e.g. computer, tape recorder)	0.04	0.03
54	SELECT	(select an answer or item from several given or known)	15.9	15.2
55	CLASFY	(classify words, concepts, or things by some criteria)	2.2	1.6
56	REORGN	(reorganize given material, e.g. rewrite story in own words)	2.9	4.0
57	CONSTR	(construct from pre-fabricated parts, e.g. SRA cards)	4.0	1.5
58	ANALYS	(analyse information, bring together for conclusions)	0.5	1.9
59	QUESTN	(the pupil must formulate questions)	0.3	0.4

60	ANSWER	(the pupils must answer questions, excluding maths)	5.1	8.2
61	DISCUS	(pupils discuss problem, or extended question-answer session)	6.5	7.8
62	CREATE	(the pupil is required to create for him- or herself)	16.0	16.5
63	MAP	(the pupil is required to transform information from one medium to another, e.g. reading aloud or following instructions to make something)	18.7	18.0
64	COPY	(the pupil is supposed to copy as accurately as possible in the same medium, e.g. handwriting from examples)	19.0	16.6
65	LEARN	(the pupil is required to learn, e.g. spellings)	2.7	2.2
66	TEST	(the pupil is being tested, perhaps informally)	0.2	1.5
67	PLAY	(the absence of other criteria)	7.7	0.9
68	PHYSCL	(P.E., football, etc.)	2.5	2.3
69	EDUCNL	(educational games or puzzles, e.g. crosswords)	1.9	1.3
70	COMPTV	(competition, e.g. chess, spelling competition, football)	1.3	2.1
71	COOPTV	(co-operation, e.g. role-play, football)	3.6	3.2
72	TCHR	(information from the teacher is essential for the task)	25.5	26.2
73	PUPIL	(information from other pupils is essential)	7.9	7.2
74	BRDOHP	(information displayed on board or overhead projector)	4.1	8.4
75	CHART	(information on prepared chart, map, or pictures)	2.3	2.0
76	TEXTBK	(non-fiction reading book)	0.8	4.6
77	REFBK	(reference book, e.g. encyclopaedia, dictionary)	1.7	4.9
78	READBK	(reading book)	6.6	7.7
79	WORKCD	(workcard: includes work-schemes even if in book form)	21.3	22.7
80	PUBLSH	(published resources are being used)	16.8	25.0
81	ENVIRN	(the environment is used as a resource, e.g. draw teacher)	1.5	3.2
82	UNSUPR	(unsupervised task, but behaviour may be supervised)	0.6	1.6
	SCHEME	(PUBLiSHed WORKCarDs)	12.6	18.3
	TPREP	(teacher-prepared materials: BRDOHP CHART, unpublished WORKCarDs)	15.0	14.2
	BOOK	(TEXTBK, REFBK, or READBK)	9.6	17.1
83	TAPE	(pupils or teacher using tape recording made in class)	0.7	1.1
84	RADREC	(radio, or record-player, or equivalent tape recording)	4.0	2.3
85	TVFILM	(television, cine-film, or equivalent videotape)	4.7	3.7
86	CALCUL	(task requires teacher or pupil to use calculator)	0.02	0.7
87	COMPUT	(computer: either lesson about or actual use)	0.4	1.9
88	APARAT	(apparatus e.g. Unifix cubes)	21.3	14.8
	EQUIP	(total equipment)	29.9	23.5

89	HIST	(work with historical elements)	2.1	7.1
90	GEOG	(work with geographical elements)	0.7	3.6
91	BIOLGY	(work with elements of biological study)	3.0	3.5
92	PHYSCS	(work with elements of physical science)	0.4	4.6
93	ENVIRS	(work having aspects of environmental studies)	3.9	4.6
94	ART	(art and craft, including cooking, woodwork)	14.6	15.3
95	DRAMA	(dramatic work: plays, puppet plays)	3.2	2.4
96	MUSIC	(playing, listening, singing, or moving to music)	7.0	5.3
97	RELIG	(religious studies of any kind)	2.6	4.6
98	MOVEMT	(movement: gymnastics, dance)	5.7	3.3
99	SCLMRL	(social and moral education; must go into general concepts)	8.4	4.3
101	LETTER	(work concentrates on letters, e.g. handwriting)	5.4	2.7
102	PARTWD	(work uses partwords, e.g. phonics with letter-pairs)	3.0	1.7
103	WHOLWD	(work concentrates on whole words, e.g. CLOZE)	13.4	11.7
104	SYMBOL	(work uses symbols other than numbers, e.g. map-work)	1.4	2.0
105	SENTNC	(work concentrates on sentences, e.g., creative writing by infants, or cloze sentences – this is WHOLWD also)	11.0	10.4
106	PASSAG	(work with extended passage, e.g. creative writing, reading aloud by juniors, following long instructions)	12.1	23.2
107	POEM	(involves metre or rhyme, e.g. song, story in verse)	2.9	3.6
108	STORY	(the teacher reads or tells a story or poem)	7.0	4.4
109	FOREGN	(foreign language, including ESL)	–	–

Notes * Item observed on less than 0.005% of observations.
– Item not observed in this half sample
Category 38 was used by the observer to record technical matters

Appendix II: Combined curriculum categories of the observation schedule for use in correlation analysis in Chapter Three

NUMBER:	any of COUNT to TABLES
PRMATH (Practical Maths):	LENGTH to ANGLES, MONEY, SYMMET, and SHAPE where these are not associated with ART
MCNCPT (Mathematical Concepts):	SETS to NTWORK
SCIENCe:	BIOLGY, PHYSCS, ENVIRS
SOCIAL (Social Topics):	HISTory, GEOGraphy, RELIGious studies, SoCiaL and MoRaL education
FINe ART:	ART (and craft), DRAMA, MUSIC, MOVEMenT
GAMES (and puzzles and role-play):	PHYSCL to COOPTV
LANGuage:	LETTER to WHOLWD, SENTNC to POEM
HIGHER-order cognitive skills:	PLAN, ASSESS, ANALYS, QUESTN
MIDDLE-order cognitive skills:	ORDER, COMPAR, PREDIC, REPORT, CLASsiFY, REORGaNize, DISCUSs, LEARN, TEST
TCHRR (Teacher as Resource):	INSTRuct, FEEDBacK, TeaCHeR
SCHEME:	PUBLiSHed, WORKCarDs
TPREP (Teacher Prepared Materials):	BRDOHP, CHART, unpublished WORKCarDs
BOOKs:	TEXTBK, REFBK, READBK
EQUIPment:	TAPE recorder to APpARATus

In addition to the fifteen composite categories above, sixteen of the main individual categories were also used.

Appendix III: Pupil and teacher observation records

Table AIII.1: Pupil observation categories

No.	Symbol	Meaning	% observations Infants	Juniors
1. Interaction between pupils				
1	TALK PUP TASK	(At the time of observation, the target pupil is talking to another pupil about the authorized task)	2.8	2.7
2	TALK PUP ROUT	(the target is talking to another pupil about a routine matter, e.g. borrowing a pencil)	1.4	1.2
3	TALK PUP DSTR	(the target is talking about something unconnected with work, e.g. the football teams)	1.7	1.9
4	LIST PUP TASK	(the target is listening to another pupil who is talking about the authorized task)	4.7	4.6
5	LIST PUP ROUT	(the target is listening to another pupil who is talking about a routine matter)	1.2	0.9
6	LIST PUP DSTR	(the target is listening to another who is talking about something unconnected with work)	1.8	1.7
2. Non-conversational behaviour				
1	QUIET TASK	(the target pupil is quietly working)	46.2	50.1
2	QUIET ROUT	(the target is engaged in a routine activity, e.g. sharpening a pencil)	11.7	10.7
3	QUIET DSTR	(the target is distracted from work, e.g. is looking around)	10.6	10.1
4	FOOLS AROUND	(the target is acting so as to distract others, e.g. pulling faces)	0.2	0.1

3 Interaction with teacher

1	TALK TO TCHR	(at the time of observation, the target pupil is talking to the teacher)	3.7	2.0
2	LIST TCHR IND	(the target is getting individual attention from teacher, who is talking at the observation time)	2.6	1.9
3	LIST TCHR GRP	(the target is a member of a group which is being addressed by the teacher)	2.8	3.1
4	LIST TCHR CLS	(the whole class is being addressed by the teacher)	17.2	16.9
5	TCHR PRESENT	(the teacher is close to the target pupil, but is not talking to the target at observation time)	2.6	1.5
6	WAIT FOR TCHR	(the target pupil is waiting for the teacher's attention)	6.6	4.6

4. Location of a pupil

1	OUT OF BASE	(the target is not in the place where he or she is supposed to be working, e.g. has gone to find a book)	14.9	11.6
2	BASE ALONE	(the pupil is sitting alone)	7.2	7.4
3	BASE 2SS	(the pupil is with one other of the same sex)	6.3	12.7
4	BASE 2OS	(the pupil is with one other of opposite sex)	2.3	3.3
5	BASE SSS	(the pupil is with more than one other, in a group all of the same sex)	12.6	19.0
6	BASE SOS	(the pupil is with more than one other, in a group of mixed sex)	42.7	37.7
7	BASE CLASS	(all the class are together, e.g. for story)	27.5	18.7

5. Collaboration

1	TEAM INDIV	(the pupil is working alone)	79.1	81.2
2	TEAM PAIR	(the pupil has to collaborate with one other, e.g. to share a book or to discuss a problem)	3.5	4.2
3	TEAM GROUP	(the pupil has to collaborate with several others)	4.8	5.0
4	TEAM CLASS	(the whole class must co-ordinate their actions, e.g. singing in unison)	10.7	8.0

189

Table AIII.2: Teacher observation categories

Category	Description

A. *Teacher's interaction or activity*

QT	Teacher asks question related to the pupil's task, e.g. 'What do 4 and 7 make?'
QR	Question about routine matter, 'Is the door shut?'
SC	Statement of task content, '4 and 7 make 11'.
SF	Statement of feedback in response to a pupil's work contribution or question, 'Yes, you may paint now'.
SR	Statement abour routine, 'Please close the door'.
ST	Teacher reads or tells a story to pupils
LI	Teacher listens to pupils
WA	Teacher watches pupils
SP	Teacher shows pupils or participates in their activity
MA	Teacher marks pupils' work
RO	Teacher does routine activity, e.g. tidies classroom
OA	Teacher interacts with another adult
OP	Teacher interacts with a pupil from another class
NO	Teacher is not observed, e.g. has left the room

B. *Teacher's audience for interaction*

IND	Teacher interacts with an individual pupil
OIN	Teacher interacts with a different individual from the one on the previous observation
IFG	Teacher talks to one pupil, expecting group to watch/listen
IFC	Teacher talks to one pupil, expecting class to watch/listen
GRP	Teacher interacts with a group of pupils
CLA	Teacher interacts with whole class
GFC	Teacher talks to group, expecting class to watch/listen
OIG	Teacher talks to a different individual for a group
OGR	Teacher talks to a different group from the one on the previous observation

C. *Main medium being used by pupil being supervised*

WRITE	The pupil is writing (but not just figures in maths)
READ	The pupil is reading (quietly or aloud, not just figures)
ORAL	The pupil is engaged in oral work
MAT	The pupil is working with materials (excluding drawing)
MOVE	The pupil is engaged in movement exercises (e.g. mime)

D. *Subject area for task of pupil being supervised*

MATHS	Mathematical work of any kind
LANG	Language work
HUMAN	Humanities, history, geography, religious education
SCIEN	Science, either physical or biological
ARTCR	Art or craft work
MUSIC	Includes singing and music and movement

PLAY   Any kind of play
SOCMR   Social and moral education

E. *Emotional tone of interaction with pupil*

POS   Teacher praises pupil or shows affection
NEG   Teacher criticizes pupil or shows displeasure

F. *Location of teacher*

DESK   Teacher is at own desk or area, e.g. blackboard
MOBL   Teacher is mobile
BASE   Teach is at pupil's base

Bibliography

Alexander, R.J. (1984) *Primary Teaching*, London: Holt, Rinehart & Winston.

APU (Assessment of Performance Unit) (1981) *Science in Schools: Age 11: Report No. 1*, London: HMSO.

APU (Assessment of Performance Unit) (1983) *Science in Schools: Age 11: Report No. 2*, London: HMSO.

Barker, R. and Gump, P.V. (1972) *Big School, Small School: High School Size and Student Behaviour*, Stanford: Stanford University Press.

Barker Lunn, J. (1970) *Streaming in the Primary School*, Slough: National Foundation for Educational Research (NFER).

Barker Lunn, J. (1982) 'Junior Schools and their Organisational Policies', *Educational Research*, 24: 250–61.

Barker Lunn, J. (1984) 'Junior School Teachers: their Methods and Practices', *Educational Research*, 26: 178–88.

Barr, F. (1959) 'Urban and Rural Differences in Ability and Attainment', *Educational Research* 1(2): 49–59.

Bassey, M. (1978) *Nine Hundred Primary School Teachers*, Slough: NFER.

Bell, A. and Sigsworth, A. (1987) *The Small Rural Primary School*, London: Falmer Press.

Bennett, S.N. (1976) *Teaching Styles and Pupil Progress*, London: Open Books.

Bennett, S.N., Andreae, J., Hegarty, P., and Wade, B. (1980) *Open Plan Schools: Teaching, Curriculum and Design*, Slough: NFER.

Bennett, S.N., Desforges, C.W., Cockburn, A., and Wilkinson, B. (1984) *The Quality of Pupil Learning Experiences*, London: Lawrence Erlbaum Associates.

Blyth, W. and Derricott, R. (1977) *The Social Significance of Middle Schools*, London: Batsford.

Boulter, H. and Crispin, A. (1979) 'Rural Disadvantage: The Differential Allocation of Resources to Small Rural Primary Schools', *Durham and Newcastle Research Review* VIII(41): 7–17.

Bouri, J. and Barker Lunn, J. (1969) *Too Small to Stream: A Study of Grouping in Small Junior Schools*, Slough: NFER.

Brophy, J.E. and Good, T.L. (1985) 'Teacher Behaviour and Student Achievement', in M.C. Wittrock (ed.) *Handbook of Research on Teaching*, 3rd edn, New York: Macmillan.

Burstall, C. (1979) 'Time to Mend the Nets: A Commentary on the Outcomes of Class Size Research', *Trends in Education* 3:27–33.

Calderhead, J. (1984) *Teachers' Classroom Decision Making*, London: Holt, Rinehart and Winston.

The Cockcroft Report (1982) *Mathematics Counts*, Report of the Committee of Enquiry into the Teaching of Mathematics in Schools, London: HMSO.

Comber, L. *et al.* (1981) *The Social Effects of Rural Primary School Reorganisation in England*, Final Report, Birmingham: University of Aston.

Croll, P. (1986) *Systematic Classroom Observation*, Lewes: Falmer Press.

Dearden, R. (1976) *Problems in Primary Education*, London: Routledge & Kegan Paul.

Denham, C. and Lieberman, A. (eds) (1980) *Time to Learn*, Department of Health, Education and Welfare, Washington, DC: National Institute of Education.

Department of Education and Science (1977) *Falling Numbers and School Closures*, Circular 5/77, London: HMSO.

Department of Education and Science (1978) *Primary Education in England: A Survey by HM Inspectors of Schools*, London: HMSO.

Department of Education and Science (1979a) *A Framework for the School Curriculum*, London: HMSO.

Department of Education and Science (1979b) *Statistics in Education*, vol. 4, London: HMSO.

Department of Education and Science (1981) *The School Curriculum*, London: HMSO.

Department of Education and Science (1982) *Education 5 to 9: An Illustrative Survey of 80 First Schools in England*, London: HMSO.

Department of Education and Science (1983) *9 – 13 Middle Schools: An Illustrative Survey*, London: HMSO.

Department of Education and Science (1985a) *Better Schools*, Cmnd 9469, London: HMSO.

Department of Education and Science (1985b) *Mathematics from 5 to 16, Curriculum Matters No.3*, London: HMSO.

Dewey, J. (1928) 'Progressive Education and the Science and Education', *Progressive Education* 5:197–204.

Downey, M. and Kelly, A.V. (1986) *Theory and Practice of Education: An Introduction*, London: Harper & Row.

Doyle, W. (1979) 'Classroom Tasks and Student Abilities', in P. Peterson and H.J. Walberg (eds) *Research on Teaching: Concepts, Findings and Implications*, Berkeley: California, McCutchan.

Doyle, W. (1983) 'Academic Work', *Review of Educational Research* 53(2): 159–99.

Edmonds, E.L. and Bessai, F. (1977, 1978) 'The Myth and Reality of Small Schools', *Head Teachers' Review* 9:54–6; 10:2–5.

Eggleston, J.F., Galton, M., and Jones, M.E. (1975) *A Science Teaching Observation Schedule*, London: Schools Council/Macmillan.

Elliott, J. (1976) *Developing Hypotheses about Classrooms from Teacher Practical Constructs*, (mimeo) Cambridge Institute of Education.

Bibliography

Elliott, J. *et al.* (1981) *School Accountability: The SSRC Cambridge Accountability Project*, Oxford: Grant McIntyre.

Finch, D. (1986) *A Study of the Social Environment of Rural Schools*, unpublished M.Ed thesis, University of East Anglia.

Flanders, N.A. (1960) *Teacher Influence on Pupil Attitudes and Achievement*, Final Report, Co-operative Research Programme Project no. 397, Minneapolis: University of Minnesota.

Forsythe, D. (ed) (1983) *The Rural Community and the Small School*, Aberdeen University Press.

France, N. and Fraser, I. (1975) *Richmond Tests of Basic Skills*, London: NFER-Nelson.

Gage, N. and Berliner, D. (1984) *Educational Psychology* (3rd edn) London: Houghton Mifflin.

Galton, M. (1987) 'ORACLE Chronicle: A Decade of Classroom Research', in S. Delamont (ed.), *The Primary School Teacher*, Lewes: Falmer Press.

Galton, M. (1989) *Teaching in the Primary School*, London: David Fulton.

Galton, M. and Simon, B. (eds) (1980) *Progress and Performance in the Primary Classroom*, London: Routledge & Kegan Paul.

Galton, M., Simon, B., and Croll, P. (1980) *Inside the Primary Classroom*, London: Routledge & Kegan Paul.

Gittins Report (1967) *Primary Education in Wales*, London: HMSO.

Glass, G.V. (1976) 'Primary, Secondary and Meta-analysis of Research', *Education Researcher* 5:351–79.

Glass, G.V. (1982) 'Meta-analysis: An Approach to the Synthesis of Research Results', *Journal of Research in Science Teaching* 19(2):98–112.

HMI (1978) *Primary Education in England: A Survey by HM Inspectors of Schools*, London: HMSO.

Hadow Report (1931) *Report of the Consultative Committee on the Primary School*, London: HMSO.

Hagedorn, J. (1986) 'The Close Conspiracy', *Education Guardian*, 18 November.

Harlen, W. (1982) 'Matching' in Richards, C. (ed.) *New Directions in Primary Education*, Lewes: Falmer Press.

Harrison, C. (1986) *The Organisation of Small Schools: Its Effect on Time on Task*, unpublished M.Ed thesis, University of Leicester.

Hemming, R. (1972) *Fifty Years of Freedom, A Study of the Ideas of A.S. Neill*, London: Allen & Unwin.

ILEA [Research and Statistics Branch] (1986) *The Junior School Project (parts A, B, C)*, London: ILEA.

Jackson, S. (1976) 'School Progress and Adjustment in Rural Areas', in M. Chazan, A. Laing, T. Cox, S. Jackson, and G. Lloyd *Deprivation and School Progress*, Oxford: Basil Blackwell.

Jenkins, D. (1987) 'Chocolate Cream Soldiers: Sponsorship, Ethnography and Sectarianism', in R. Murphy and H. Torrance (eds) *Evaluating Education: Issues and Methods*, London, Harper & Row.

Kelly, A.V. (1982) *The Curriculum: Theory and Practice*, 2nd edn. London: Harper & Row.

Kelly, A.V. (1986) *Knowledge and Curriculum Planning*, London: Harper & Row.

Kliebard, H. (1986) *The Struggle for the American Curriculum 1893–1958*, New York: Methuen Inc.

Lawton, D. (1983) *Curriculum Studies and Educational Planning*, London: Hodder & Stoughton.

Lea, D. (1986) *The Use of Published Mathematics Schemes in Primary Schools: Its Effect on Teaching*, unpublished M.Ed thesis, University of Leicester.

Lee, J. (1984) 'Vertical Grouping in the Primary School', *School Organisation*, 4 (2): 133–42.

Measor, L. and Woods, P. (1984) *Changing Schools: Pupil Perspectives on Transfer to a Comprehensive*, Milton Keynes: Open University Press.

Medley, D.M., Quirk, T.J., Schwek, C.G., and Ames, N.P. (1973) 'The Personal Record of School Experience', in E.G. Boyer, A. Simon, and G. Karafin (eds) *Measures of Maturation: An Anthology of Early Childhood Observation Instruments*, vol. II, Philadelphia: Research for Better Schools.

Meyenn, R.J. (1980) 'Peer Networks among Middle School Pupils', in A. Hargreaves and L. Tickle (eds) *Middle Schools: Origins, Ideology and Practice*, London: Harper & Row.

Ministry of Education (1961) *Village Schools*, Building Bulletin 3, HMSO.

Morris, J.M. (1959) *Reading in the Primary School: An Investigation into Standards of Reading and their Association with Primary School Characteristics*, London: Newnes for NFER.

Mortimore, P., Sammons, P., Stoll, L., Lewis, D., and Ecob, R. (1988) *School Matters: The Junior Years*, London: Open Books.

Nash, R. (1977) 'Perceptions of the Village School', *Research Intelligence*, 3 (1): 10–13.

Nash, R. (1978) 'More Evidence in Support of Village Schools', *Where* 139: 189–90.

Nias, J. (1986) *What's it like to be a Teacher? The Subjective Reality of Primary Teaching*, monograph, Cambridge Institute of Education (mimeo).

Nias, J. (1988) 'Informal Education in Action: Teachers' Accounts', in W. Blyth (ed.) *Informal Primary Education Today*, London: Falmer Press.

Plowden Report (1967) *Children and their Primary Schools*, Report of the Central Advisory Council for Education in England, London: HMSO.

Pollard, A. (1985) *The Social World of the Primary School*, London: Holt, Rinehart & Winston.

Richards, C. (1982) 'Primary Education 1974–80', in C. Richards (ed.) *New Directions in Primary Education*, Lewes: Falmer Press.

Richmond, W.K. (1953) *The Rural School: Its Problems and Prospects*, London: Redman.

Ridgway, L. and Lawton, I. (1968) *Family Grouping in the Primary School*, London: Ward Lock Educational.

Rosenshine, B. (1980) 'How Time is Spent in Elementary Classrooms', in C. Denham and A. Lieberman (eds) *Time to Learn*, Department of Health, Education and Welfare, Washington DC: National Institute of Education.

Scarth, J. and Hammersley, M. (1986) 'Questioning ORACLE: An Assessment of ORACLE's Analysis of Teachers' Questions', *Educational Research*, 28(3): 174–84.

Bibliography

Shanks, D. and Welsh, J. (1983) 'Transition to Secondary School', in D. Forsythe (ed.) *The Rural Community and the Small School*, Aberdeen University Press.

Shipman, M. (1979) *In-school Evaluation*, London: Heinemann Educational.

Simon, B. (1981a) 'The Primary School Revolution: Myth or Reality?', in B. Simon and J. Willcocks (eds) *Research and Practice in the Primary Classroom*, London: Routledge & Kegan Paul.

Simon, B. (1981b) 'Why no Pedagogy in England?', in B. Simon and W. Taylor (eds) *Education in the Eighties*, London: Batsford.

Skilbeck, M. (1976) 'Ideologies and Values, Unit 3, Course E203', *Curriculum Design and Development*, Milton Keynes: Open University Press.

Slocombe, I. (1980) 'Making Decisions on Rural Primary Schools: Administrative Constraints and Considerations', in *Educational Disadvantage in Rural Areas*, Centre for Information and Advice on Educational Disadvantage, 113–19.

Southgate, V., Arnold, H., and Johnson, S. (1981) *Extending Beginning Reading*, London: Heinemann (for the Schools Council).

Standing Conference of Rural Community Councils (1978) *The Decline of Rural Services*, SCRCC.

Thomas, N. (1972) 'When Small Schools Die They Die Alone', *Education*, September.

Tizard, B., Blatchford, D., Burke, J., Farquhar, C., and Plewis, I. (1988) *Young Children at School in the Inner City*, Hove and London: Lawrence Erlbaum.

Trew, K. (1977) *Teacher Practices and Classroom Resources*, Northern Ireland Council for Educational Research.

Weiner, B. (1986) *Attributional Theory of Motivation and Emotion*, New York: Springer-Verlag.

Index

31–2, 44–5; sex 27; stereotypes 23–6, 30; teaching experience 27; turnover 28; views, on class size 33, 137, on classroom organization 35–40, 130, 137–40, on community involvement 43, 46, on curriculum 38–43, 130, on in-service 29–30, 42, on links with other schools 47, on progression 39, on resources 41, 42, on schemes 40, 130, on small and large schools 31, 32, 33, 38, 41–3, on vertical grouping 34–6, 37, 39; visits from advisers 30; voluntary help 32

team teaching 144

tests: Richmond 23, 112–14; statistical interpretation of 159

time: allocated 19–20, 76; engaged 20; instructional 19–20; organization of 123–4, 125–9, 173, 175

transfer: to secondary school 16–17, 24; from home to small school 16

vertical grouping 12, 76, 168, 179; and attainment 115, 117; and classroom organization 84, 100–2, 169; and the curriculum 65–7, 108, 169; definitions of 105–6; and Prismaston File 120–1; and pupil-teacher interaction 109, 138; teachers' views on 34–6, 37, 39, 138–9

waiting for teacher 78, 80, 83–4, 86, 127–8